SAINT PAUL

Michael Grant is a highly successful and renowned historian of the ancient world. He has held many academic posts including those of Fellow of Trinity College, Cambridge; Professor of Humanity at Edinburgh University; Vice Chancellor of The Queen's University, Belfast and Vice Chancellor of the University of Khartoum. He is a Doctor of Letters at Dublin and a Doctor of Laws at Belfast. He has also been President of the Classical Association of England, the Virgil Society and the Royal Numismatic Society, and is a Medallist of the American Numismatic Society. He lives and writes in Italy.

A Selection of works by Michael Grant

The Twelve Caesars
The Classical Greeks
The Climax of Rome
The Fall of the Roman Empire
The Roman Emperors
The Rise of the Greeks
The Myths of the Greeks and Romans
The History of Ancient Israel
The Jews in the Roman World
The Roman World
Cleopatra
Cities of Vesuvius

ST PAUL

Michael Grant

PHOENIX
PRESS

5 UPPER SAINT MARTIN'S LANE
LONDON
WC2H 9EA

A PHOENIX PRESS PAPERBACK

First published in Great Britain
by Weidenfeld & Nicolson in 1976
This paperback edition published in 2000
by Phoenix Press,
a division of The Orion Publishing Group Ltd,
Orion House, 5 Upper St Martin's Lane,
London WC2H 9EA

A CIP catalogue record for this book
is available from the British Library.

Printed and bound in Great Britain by
Clays Ltd, St Ives plc

ISBN 1 84212 008 5

Contents

*N.B.: Words and phrases followed by an asterisk
in the Text are explained in the List of
Ancient Writings and Terms at the end of the book.*

Introduction

Paul is one of the most perpetually significant men who have ever lived. Without the spiritual earthquake that he brought about, Christianity would probably never have survived at all. Yet his importance also extends very widely beyond and right outside the religious field. For he has also exercised a gigantic influence, for generation after generation, upon non-religious events and ways of thinking – upon politics and sociology and war and philosophy and that whole intangible area in which the thought-processes of successive epochs become formed.

He has to be considered, therefore, not only as a religious figure of exceptional power, but as one of the outstanding makers of the history of mankind.

Nor has the passage of time diminished his ability to exercise such effects. Many people in our own age still recognize him as the force capable of bringing twentieth-century Christianity back to life. But his potency is not by any means limited to practising Christians. Jews, too, who in the past sometimes felt him to be the great betrayer, have recently written distinguished books reassessing his role. And people who practise no religion whatever, and have no intention of doing so, should find infinite interest in Paul – not least because his view that the world had been launched on a disastrous course, from which nevertheless rescue was possible, is deeply relevant today.

The man whom I have tried to describe in this book is not a figure of myth, but a person. And his own authentic voice can still be heard in his surviving Letters or Epistles, which not only contain numerous autobiographical clues, but are the earliest Christian documents in existence – much older than our written texts of the Gospels – and rank high among the most valuable literature that the world has ever produced.

I believe it a mistake to consider that ancient (or for that matter modern) life and thought falls neatly into two separate, watertight compartments, one of which is secular, reserved for historians, while the other is religious, reserved for clerics. Athens and Rome on the one hand, and Jerusalem on the other, ought to be looked at and studied on the same basis and according to the same historical criteria. It was in this belief that I wrote *The Jews in the Roman World* and *Herod the Great*, and I have here attempted a similar treatment of Paul – who pressingly invites such an endeavour to bring our methods of studying these various cultures together in a single volume, since he was a Jew who wrote in Greek and was a Roman citizen.

There is, of course, one strong practical objection to studying Greek, Roman and Jewish affairs in conjunction: to gain even the most tentative mastery of all the principal evidence for ancient Greece, Rome *and* Jerusalem as well is beyond anyone's powers. An attempt, therefore, to tackle such a many-sided figure as Paul can only be made with great and all too amply justified diffidence. I am not qualified, obviously, to write this book as a theologian would. But what I have tried to do instead is to bring Paul to life as a human being of outstanding and altogether peculiar gifts who has influenced people of widely divergent beliefs and races and epochs, and who merits study and admiration amid the great and rapidly growing emergencies with which we ourselves are struggling today.

I am very grateful to Susan Loden and Olivia Browne of Messrs Weidenfeld and Nicolson, to Kate Shearman of Phoenix Press, to Sally Curtis and Julia Locke, and to my son Antony Grant, for their help.

Michael Grant
Gattaiola, 1976, 1999

I

The Life and Work
and Character of Paul

Paul is said to have been 'a man of small stature, with a bald head and bow legs, who carried himself well. His eyebrows met in the middle, and his nose was rather large and he was full of grace, for at times he seemed a man and at times he had the face of an angel.' That description is owed to a work of the second century AD known as the *Acts of Paul and Thecla*.[1]* The sixth-century Byzantine historian John Malalas added that he had a thick grey beard, light bluish eyes, and a fair and florid complexion; and that he was a man who often smiled.[2] Nicephorus Callistus, in the fourteenth century, noted further that Paul's beard was rather pointed, that his large nose was handsomely curved, and that his body was slight and rather bent.[3] Are these descriptions accurate? The *Acts of Paul and Thecla* are crammed with myths and miracles, and Malalas and Nicephorus are late. But they may go back to reliable traditions, since heads on fourth-century paintings in Roman catacombs, and other relatively early portraits, show his pointed beard and sparsely covered head.[4] Literary accounts like these illustrate a problem which extends far beyond Paul's personal appearance: the problem created by the fragmentary, tenuous character of the evidence available to us in our search for information about his life, work and character. The descriptions just mentioned are merely curiosities. But we do also possess other, much earlier sources which, fortunately, are able – after careful scrutiny – to justify our attempts to reconstruct and estimate the achievement of Paul, not merely as a legendary personage but as a man who played a mighty part in human history. These sources

3

are Greek writings: his own Letters or Epistles and the *Acts of the Apostles*.

The dates of Paul's surviving Letters and the places where he wrote them have been the subject of endless arguments, but the probable results may be summed up as follows. *I Thessalonians* and *II Thessalonians*, both ostensibly addressed to the Christian communities at Thessalonica (Salonica) in Macedonia (although it is conceivable that the recipient of the second letter was Philippi in the same province), were written in *c.* AD 50 at Corinth in Achaea (Greece). *I Corinthians* was sent to Corinth from Ephesus in western Asia Minor between 52 and 55, and *II Corinthians* seems to have been written in Macedonia during the same period. *Galatians*, addressed to the Christians of the Roman province of Galatia in central Asia Minor – probably the southern part of Galatia, which Paul is known to have visited – is placed by some scholars first of all the Letters, in *c.* 49, but is more likely to have been written shortly after *II Corinthians*. *Romans* appears to have been composed at Corinth or Ephesus a few years later. In *Philippians, Colossians, Ephesians,* and *Philemon*, the writer describes himself as a prisoner. Traditionally these Letters are assigned to the period of Paul's imprisonment at Rome (*c.* 61–3), though there are alternative theories assigning them to earlier captivities in other cities. But there is no sufficient reason to abandon the attribution to Rome.

The question of the *development* of Paul's thought is a difficult one, which can only be pursued to a limited extent;[5] the relatively few identifiable instances and trends of evolution will be mentioned in the course of this book. We may refrain from eliminating most of the fairly numerous passages from this or that Epistle which have at one time or another been regarded as subsequent interpolations – by no means always with good reason. But it cannot be denied that *Ephesians*, the great ecumenical Letter, and *Colossians*, which presents Christ as the answer to men's questions about the cosmos, do not read quite like the rest of Paul: they show signs of having been somewhat rewritten and worked up at a later period, though they probably go back to him for their principal themes and are still to a considerable degree Pauline in character. Such rewriting has evidently been the fate, to an even larger extent, of the 'Pastoral Epistles', purporting to be written by Paul to Timothy (two letters) and Titus to give them pastoral advice in their supervision of churches: in their present form these letters seem to be of early second century date.

The Letters of Paul are marvellous works, as the effects they have exerted on some of the world's greatest personalities throughout the ages amply demonstrate. In the words of John Donne, they are 'thunder, and universal thunder, thunder that passes through all the world.' Martin Luther said of *Galatians*: 'I have betrothed myself to it; it is my wife!' Others have felt that *Philippians* give the truest, completest picture of the many-sided Paul. *I Corinthians* provides extraordinary testimony to his indomitable belief in the power of his faith. Of *II Corinthians* (which may comprise what were originally two separate letters) R. P. C. Hanson writes: 'here, broken sharply off, with none of the jagged edges filed down, is a chunk of Paul's life.'[6] *I Thessalonians* is perhaps the earliest surviving evidence for Christianity: and from *II Thessalonians* we can learn of Paul's deepest reflections on man's relationship to God. As for *Romans*, it was the inspiration of Augustine, and the prime origin of the Protestant Reformation. Samuel Taylor Coleridge described this letter as 'the most profound work in existence', and in our own time it has inspired the 'New Reformation' of the Swiss theologian Karl Barth.[7]

A powerful manifesto composed at the height of Paul's missionary activity, *Romans* is the nearest approach among all these Epistles to a general statement of his beliefs. Yet, even so, it is nothing of the kind. For like the rest of his extant writings, it was drawn up for a special occasion, to meet the topical needs and problems and emergencies of an individual church and to attack the views of his critics whom that church happened specifically to harbour. Paul's words, on all occasions, are only random answers to random questions; dynamic, ecstatic and exalted, but by no means systematic or logical. Nevertheless, behind them lay a background of many passionate sermons, debates and discussions, as well as such traditions as were already being handed down in the infant Church, and had been handed down to Paul.[8] The Letters are full of direct evidence for what Paul intensely believed, and for what he did.

The congregations of mostly rather humble people[9] who received these messages from afar off must have been stunned by their torrential, idiosyncratic drive. For Paul was an intellectual of the most imposing calibre, capable of soaring flights that have earned him comparison with Plato.* His restless mind never left any subject until he had pursued it back, in his own peculiar way, to its remotest origins and forward into all its consequences, and had worried it almost to bits. It was a truly extraordinary destiny for the Christian community, originally led by more or less uneducated apostles, to have received suddenly in its midst, at a moment when its life had scarcely begun, a man whose brain-power made him for evermore the patron saint among Christians of active, original, constructive *thought*.

He was also the creator of far the largest part of Christianity's classic forms of expression. Yet this expression, like the cerebral activity that lay behind it, comes to us in a disconcerting shape. For Paul's mind, despite its great strength, remained undisciplined, paying scant attention to the niceties of rational coherence. The Letters are vividly varied and lively, but unrounded, unarranged and muddled, making their points not by any orderly procedure but by a series of hammer-blow contrasts and antitheses. Paul is far too impulsive and enthusiastic to standardize his terms or arrange his material. He is often ambiguous – with results that have reverberated down the centuries. And he commits flagrant self-contradictions, which caused Augustine, among many others, the deepest anxiety.[10]

Besides, Paul, although his culture was Jewish, wrote and dictated his Letters[11] not in Hebrew or the related Aramaic,* which were the national languages of the Jews, but in Greek. Indeed, Greek may even have been the language he spoke at home; certainly he read the Jewish scriptures in their Greek version, the Septuagint.* Nevertheless, Aramaic was probably the language he thought and dreamt in, and he was only imbued with Greek and pagan ways of thinking to a limited and superficial extent.[12] When he attempted to address the Athenians in terms they would understand, quoting Greek poets and using Greek rhetorical style, most of them found the results unconvincing.[13]

Thus although Paul's expression was externally Hellenic, his inward meaning and the structure of his thought remained Jewish.

And indeed, in spite of the cosmopolitanism of this near-eastern world the two ways of thinking had on the whole remained obstinately distinct.In its simplest form the contrast was between Greek polytheism and Jewish monotheism. But it was also emphasized at every point by divergences between the cultures: between Greek literature with its humanistic tone, and the Jewish Bible, the Old Testament, with its resolute determination that everything depends on the will of the deity. And the distinctive nature of this Jewish way of life had persistently survived many centuries of political eclipse.

Nearly a millennium ago, in the tenth century BC, Israel had been a large and powerful state under David and under Solomon. Then it had split into two kingdoms, Israel in the north with its capital at Samaria and Judah in the south, centred upon David's Jerusalem and its Temple created by Solomon. This was the age of the prophets, but their warnings rang out in vain. For in 721 BC Israel was annexed by the greatest of the middle-eastern powers, the Assyrians. Next in 597–586 Judah succumbed to their successors the Babylonians; its capital and Temple were destroyed, and many thousands of its inhabitants were taken off into captivity in Babylonia – the first Dispersion. When the Persians, later in the sixth century, displaced the Babylonians as the principal imperial state of the region, they repatriated a number of Jews, but Palestine remained a mere dependency; and it continued so under the three successive Greek regimes that followed, of Alexander the Great (d. 323), the Egyptian Ptolemies, and the Seleucids based on Syria and Mesopotamia.

The Seleucids, finally, were ejected from Palestine by the Jewish house of the Hasmonaeans (Maccabees), who reconsecrated the Temple in 165–164 BC. But before long they became puppets of Rome, and in due course they were replaced by another such dynasty, founded by that politically very successful puppet Herod the Great (37–4 BC). After his death, the Romans split up his kingdom, leaving his son Archelaus as prince of Judaea, the central area around Jerusalem, while his brothers were allowed princedoms in outlying areas of the Jewish homeland. But in AD 6 the Emperor Augustus removed Archelaus, and Judaea became a Roman province governed by a prefect (later known as procurator*).

Throughout this whole period, ever since the time of Alexander the Great, Greek cultural influences – now prevalent throughout the near and middle east – had impinged in a variety of ways upon Judaism. In the Dispersion – which now comprised millions of Jews – this process was of course particularly evident. As we have seen, men of the Dispersion such as Paul had a Greek version of the Bible available to them; and the works, for example, of the Alexandrian Jew Philo are strongly Hellenized. Yet there was also strong resistance to such Hellenization, especially in the Jewish homeland itself. It is true that a certain amount of Greek thought had filtered into Palestinian Hebrew culture during these centuries of cultural contact. Yet, in the process, it had usually become adapted to the traditions of Judaism, so that, sometimes, in the Jewish writers of the time, it requires considerable effort to detect serious traces of these Greek influences.

In Judaism's Christian offshoot the same history is repeated in a somewhat different form. On the whole, substantial Hellenic influences are harder to find than in Judaism; and this was partly, no doubt, because Jesus himself was brought up in Galilee and was thoroughly Jewish in culture and outlook, so Jewish indeed that his contacts with the Gentile world were only slight. Thus in the early days of the church there was no Christian Philo. The writer of the so-called Gospel according to St John, it is true, had strong Hellenistic affinities: but even he had strong Palestinian roots. And as for the authors of the other Gospels, although they were writing for Christians of Gentile origin, they wrote in Jewish tone; modern theories comparing their story of Jesus to a pagan mythology of dying and rising Gods have misfired, since such legends were quite alien to the background of Judaism. Paul, too, though he came from outside Palestine, was so completely Jewish in education and outlook that if we leave aside a few deliberate efforts such as his address to the Athenians the only Hellenisms apparent in his work were those which reached him indirectly through their infiltrations into contemporary Judaism. And yet he wrote in Greek. His highly idiosyncratic ways of thinking and expressing himself already make the problem of understanding him a daunting one. And his blend of Jewish thought with Greek expression – a forcible bringing together of two alien cultures – merely serve to make it more daunting still. In consequence, it has always been possible to take widely differing views of what he intended to say. These difficulties were already noted in the so-called *Second Letter of Peter*, probably written (not by Peter) soon after AD 100:

Bear in mind that our Lord's patience with us is our salvation; as Paul, our friend and brother, said when he wrote to you with his inspired wisdom. And so he does in all his other Letters, whenever he speaks of this subject, though they contain some obscure passages, which the ignorant and unstable misinterpret to their own ruin, as they do the other scriptures.[14]

But that Epistle, in its eagerness to denounce variant interpretations which it regarded as heretical, was wrong to suppose that it was only 'the ignorant and unstable' who found it hard to interpret Paul's words. On the contrary, men of the highest mental capacity and integrity throughout the ages have stumbled into the thousand pits of ambiguity he involuntarily left for puzzled questioners.

One feels sympathy for those who dined at the house of John Colet,

Dean of St Paul's, early in the sixteenth century. While guests ate, 'a servant would read aloud in a clear, distinct voice a chapter from Paul's Epistles or the *Proverbs of Solomon*'* – and then their host was accustomed to ask them what they believed the significance of the passage in question to be. Even Martin Luther* would have found this an awkward predicament, for he was not always at all sure what Paul really meant, though he 'thirsted ardently to know.' To this day, the Epistles set the same remarkable challenge. But it is a challenge that has to be met. For its reward is the comprehension of this man who has influenced his fellow beings so uniquely.

The Letters of Paul, despite all their enigmas, are by far our most reliable source of information about his life and personality and ways of thinking. Yet so occasional, fragmentary, and often spontaneous and excitable is their nature that they clearly do not add up to a story of his career; nor were they ever intended to serve any such purpose. This was, however, up to a point the aim of another work, the *Acts of the Apostles*; or, that is to say, of the second half of the *Acts*. The first half of the work deals with the very earliest history of the Church, after the death of Jesus and prior to the conversion of Paul, but the second half describes selected scenes from Paul's missionary journeys up to the time of his arrival in Rome, near the end of his life. According to an ancient tradition the author of the book was Luke the physician,[15] who accompanied Paul on some of his travels and was also believed to be the author of one of the Gospels, of which *Acts* is presented as the sequel.[16] Some plausibility is given to this view by the so-called 'we-passages' in *Acts*, which, by the use of the first personal plural, seem to indicate participation by the writer in the events he is describing. Nevertheless, on the question of the authorship of the book, it still remains advisable, after all the arguments on both sides have been considered, to suspend judgment.[17] What must be accepted, however, is the opinion recently put forward by Günther Bornkamm, as by others before him, that *Acts* is far inferior to Paul's Letters as a source of evidence for his actions and thoughts – and indeed as a historical source at all.[18]

But, to do the author of *Acts* justice, that is not in the least what he was intending to provide. His aim, which he pursued with an impressive blend of emotional sincerity and literary skill, was entirely different. He was not so much trying to record exactly what had happened as to present an adjusted, idealized, general picture of what the early Church had been like; and he was doing so when no less than twenty eventful years had passed since the time of Paul's death. After all that had happened during those two decades, the major preoccupations of Christians had altered considerably. There had been a terrible Jewish rebellion against Rome, the First Jewish Revolt* or First Roman War (AD 66–73). Thereafter, as we shall see further in the last chapter of this book, it seemed imperative to Christian writers to dissociate the non-Jewish, Gentile Christians – whom their work represents and applauds – from the disgraced Jews and scarcely less discredited Jewish Christians. This was one of the main purposes of *Acts*. And it was imperative also to show that the Romans and Christians had always, traditionally, got on pretty well with one another – so that it was reasonable, the writer of *Acts* implied, for the Romans to continue to manifest tolerance to the Christians of his own day. Furthermore, he wanted to present, in retrospect, those early days of the Christian community as times of roseate unity – which they had quite evidently not been at all. The driving power of the Holy Spirit, before which the Church could not fail to expand: that was what this author wanted to display. He was primarily writing to show the deeds of God, not those of man. As the divine plan begins to unfold, the air fills with wonders and legends.

True, ingenious use is often made of local colour and atmosphere; for example, in the towns of Asia Minor and Macedonia. But there are also manifest factual errors and exaggerations,[19] and the method is so highly selective as to record only a fraction of the hardships which Paul himself reports (see the quotation on pp. 25f., n. 75). Besides, the speeches recounted in *Acts*, like those of the classical literary tradition of Greece and Rome, could not possibly have been copied down by any bystander at the time and are for the most part inventions.

A notable example of the method employed in *Acts* is displayed by the account of Paul's final journey from Judaea to Rome. The passage contains brilliant and plausible narratives, including an engrossing account of shipwreck at Melita (Malta).

For days on end there was no sign of either sun or stars, a great storm was raging, and our last hopes of coming through alive began to fade . . .

The fourteenth night came and we were still drifting in the Sea of Adria. In the middle of the night the sailors felt that land was getting nearer. They sounded and found twenty fathoms. Sounding again after a short interval they found fifteen fathoms; and fearing that we might be cast ashore on a rugged coast they dropped four anchors from the stern and prayed for daylight to come. The sailors tried to abandon ship; they had already lowered the ship's boat, pretending that they were going to lay out anchors from the bows, when Paul said to the centurion and the soldiers, 'Unless these men stay on board you can none of you come off safely.' So the soldiers cut the ropes of the boat and let her drop away.

Shortly after daybreak Paul urged them all to take some food. 'For the last fourteen days,' he said, 'you have lived in suspense and gone hungry; you have eaten nothing whatever. So I beg you to have something to eat; your lives depend on it. Remember, not a hair of your heads will be lost.' With these words, he took bread, gave thanks to God in front of them all, broke it, and began eating. Then they all plucked up courage, and took food themselves. There were on board two hundred and seventy-six of us in all. When they had eaten as much as they wanted they lightened the ship by dumping the grain in the sea.

When day broke they could not recognize the land, but they noticed a bay with a sandy beach, on which they planned, if possible, to run the ship ashore. So they slipped the anchors and let them go; at the same time they loosened the lashings of the steering paddles, set the foresail to the wind, and let her drive to the beach. But they found themselves caught between cross-currents and ran the ship aground, so that the bow stuck fast and remained immovable, while the stern was being pounded to pieces by the breakers. The soldiers thought they had better kill the prisoners for fear that any should swim away and escape; but the centurion wanted to bring Paul safely through and prevented them from carrying out their plan. He gave orders that those who could swim should jump overboard first and get to land; the rest were to follow, some on planks, some on parts of the ship. And thus it was that all came safely to land.

Once we had made our way to safety we identified the island as Malta. The rough islanders treated us with uncommon kindness: because it was cold and had started to rain, they lit a bonfire and made us all welcome. Paul had got together an armful of sticks and put them on the fire, when a viper, driven out by the heat, fastened on his hand. The islanders, seeing the snake hanging on to his hand, said to one another, 'the man must be a murderer; he may have escaped from the sea, but divine justice has not let him live.' Paul, however, shook off the snake into the fire and was none the worse. They still expected that any moment he would swell up or drop down dead, but after waiting a long time without seeing anything extraordinary happen to him, they changed their minds and now said, 'He is a god . . .'[20]

It is an engaging and brilliantly told story, and in its main lines it may be true. But miracles abound, and the endeavour to show Paul's wisdom and leadership as superior to the qualities of human kind is patent and didactic: a sad complement to the book's failure to do justice at all to his actual opinions and teachings and controversies as revealed by his Letters. For despite all its skilful narration, *Acts* is not in their intellectual class at all. In comparison with the Letters' vivid flashes of brilliant insight combined with real historical events, *Acts* is a composition which often seems closer to Greek romantic novels and travellers' tales, or to fictionalized works celebrating ancient religious heroes. For example, there is a collection known as the *Acts of the Pagan Martyrs** with which, though superior, it has something in common.[21]

The Acts of the Apostles, then, is a secondary source for Paul, not primary as it is often believed; and when it deviates from what we are told in the Letters, as it quite often does, it is the Letters that we generally have to believe. Yet *Acts* remains indispensable all the same. For however emphatically it may select its scenes from Paul's career on the basis of edification rather than history, nevertheless, when the appropriate allowances and subtractions have been made, there is still a great deal of history to be extracted from its pages. The author of *Acts*, with imperfect sources at his disposal,[22] was the first man to realize that there was such a thing as Church history to be written. And in its chosen, romantic way, the work is a superb success. It needs approaching by the historian with the utmost caution; but any student of Paul can only ignore any part of it at his peril.

The Letters and *Acts*, then, give us almost all the evidence about Paul's career that we possess. Viewed as collections of historical evidence, as we have seen, they present difficulties. Yet these difficulties are not fatal. The eighteenth-century German writer and critic Gotthold Lessing found it hard to see how the certainty required for faith could be related to the mere probabilities of historical research. Yet in considering Paul as a personage in history, although this divergence between the two sorts of approach has to be constantly borne in mind, it need not overawe us too completely. For the Letters and *Acts*, despite all the problems they present, *are* sufficient to enable us to build up a good deal of information about the life of Paul.

It can be reconstructed from them, with some caution, but also with some measure of confidence, approximately in the following terms.

He was probably born at about the same time as Jesus. He was a Jew of the Dispersion, that is to say, a member of one of the Jewish communities outside Judaea or Palestine. These communities were both numerous and extensive. How extensive cannot be said for certain, but out of a total of not far short of eight million Jews in the world (they

number fourteen million today) there may have been six
million in the Roman Empire (the rest being mostly in Babylo.
other parts of the eastern kingdom of Parthia). This total of about six
or seven million Jewish subjects of Rome included not only perhaps
something like two and a half million in the Judaean homeland, but a
million in Egypt, and nearly another million in Syria, in addition to
sizeable communities in Asia Minor and as far afield as Rome itself.[23]
These figures, though conjectural, are enough to suggest the importance
of the Jewish Dispersion to which Paul belonged. He came from the
'free' (that is to say self-governing and privileged) Greek city of Tarsus
in Cilicia, a region of south-eastern Asia Minor which was part of the
Roman province of Syria-Cilicia. Paul claimed descent from the Jewish
tribe of Benjamin and belonged to a family of strict Pharisees.[24]* *Acts*
even suggests that he studied at Jerusalem under the principal Pharisee
of the day, Gamaliel I, though a passage in his own Letters suggests that
he had not yet visited Jerusalem at this period at all – 'I remained
unknown by sight [or personally] to Christ's congregation in Judaea'[25] –
and it is more probable that he spent his youth at his native Tarsus, as a
Jew of the Dispersion.

His father was a Jewish merchant there, engaged in the weaving of
cloth for tents, carpets and shoes from the goat's hair which was named
cilicium after the country; and the merchant's son learnt the same craft
in his turn,[26] and presumably practised it from his youth onwards. The
family was evidently prosperous, and Paul, although sometimes prepared to accept financial contributions from local communities,[27] always
remained very proud of not accepting funds from them, and of not even
living on the proceeds of his preaching. For he had two resources to fall
back on, his own capital and the work of his hands; since, in accordance
with Jewish precepts,[28] he was always prepared to work at his trade,
wherever he went.[29]

Tarsus was also a centre of advanced Hellenic culture, and that was
why Paul was so familiar with Greek and wrote his Letters in that
language. Greek cities like Tarsus had their own citizen bodies, of which
a small number of resident Jews were members according to their individual rank and means; though for the most part Jews in these Hellenic
townships had to be content with the special, considerable, privileges
which the Roman imperial government accorded to their own quasi-
autonomous communities. So Paul and his relatives, like most other
Jews of Tarsus, possessed local Jewish privileges but were not enrolled

in the Greek citizen-body of the place. Nevertheless, they enjoyed a more unusual distinction. For they were one of the families, found in inconsiderable quantities at such towns (and rarer still among their Jewish inhabitants), which had been granted Roman citizenship.* It had perhaps been acquired by Paul's father, either as a reward for services rendered to the Romans or because he was a freed slave or prisoner of war. When he had a son, he gave him the Jewish name of Saul. But this was on occasion replaced by a Roman equivalent, Paul – probably chosen because it was the Latin name which most closely resembled Saul.[30]

Thus Paul possessed the remarkable multiple qualification of belonging to three different worlds, Jewish, Greek and Roman; and he proved able to make excellent use of this threefold status.

Above all, Paul was a Jew, and a very active one. Soon after the Crucifixion (?*c*. AD 30), he began to object strongly, perhaps as a member of an extreme ultra-pious group, to Jesus' Jewish disciples, who believed that their leader had been the Messiah the Jews failed to see in him. Some years later one of these disciples, Stephen, met his death at the hands of indignant Jews in Jerusalem. That Paul was present when he died and held the coats of his killers, as *Acts* reported,[31] is unlikely, because, as he suggests (p. 110), apparently he had not yet visited Jerusalem. Nevertheless, he took an active part, he tells us, in the sanctions the Jewish authorities pursued against these dissidents, in accordance with the coercive powers which the Romans delegated to the Jews' Council (Sanhedrin*) at Jerusalem, and its smaller counterparts at other cities. Which of these councils entrusted Paul with his punitive missions we cannot say; since he had not been to Jerusalem his immediate instructions may well have come from the Council in Tarsus itself (or maybe from the greater city of Syrian Antioch) – though the Sanhedrin at Jerusalem may have been the ultimate source of the order (p. 105). Presumably what Paul had to do was to exercise upon his deviants the force of his eloquence, supported by such sanctions as the council's writ could impose – for instance expulsion from the synagogues. In any case it was on some such disciplinary mission, shortly after Stephen's death, that Paul departed, perhaps from Tarsus or Antioch, for Damascus. This was an important 'free' Greek city which was loosely attached, like Tarsus, to the Roman province of Syria-Cilicia, and contained a Jewish community of appreciable size. It was the devotees of Jesus among their number whom Paul had been commissioned to bring to order.

Instead, on the road to Damascus, Paul claims that a blinding vision of Jesus descended upon him.[32] The vision overpowered him and felled him to the ground, and when he recovered he had utterly changed his attitude to Jesus and his followers and was a fanatical member of the group which before long would be described as Christians.[33]

Paul had never, it seems, known Jesus personally. The light came to him out of his own psychological wrestlings, which will be reconstructed from his Letters in the course of this book. Once converted he entered Damascus to meet and join the Christian community, but was compelled by the local administration to leave. At this juncture the city had been ceded or leased by the Romans to one of their dependent or 'client' kings, Aretas IV of Arabia (Nabataea), and either his representative or the local Jews, or both, had Paul evicted.[34] He then travelled round other parts of Arabia, doing we know not what but presumably proclaiming his conversion, and in that distant area he remained for three years.

During the period that followed, the youthful Jewish movement which accepted the Messiahship of Jesus assumed a variety of divergent forms, thus mirroring contemporary Judaism itself. In particular a split developed between those Christians wishing to restrict the new faith to the people who, like Jesus himself and his disciples, were Jews, and those displaying eagerness to convert the Gentiles,* that is to say the Greeks who populated the eastern provinces of the Roman Empire.

The former school of thought was sponsored by the leaders of the community at Jerusalem, where Jesus had died. The best-known personalities of these Jewish Christians were Peter, who had been a close personal associate of Jesus, and James the Just, who was Jesus' brother. James had not joined the cause of Jesus during his lifetime, but adhered to it after the Crucifixion, and before long superseded Peter as its head. However, it was Peter, for the time being at least, who directed the fairly extensive missionary movement which this recently established Christian community was already directing towards its fellow Jews in Judaea and in neighbouring lands. Paul on the other hand came to assume the leadership of a mission to the Gentiles of his own Dispersion. This was something substantially new, since, even if there were Gentile converts to Christianity before, they had not amounted to more than a few isolated individuals.

15

Paul himself attributed God's demand for a Gentile mission to the moment of his conversion; but *Acts* ascribed his own determination to undertake it to two later occasions. What he did for nearly a decade after his conversion remains a mystery which neither his Letters nor *Acts* effectively clarify. But after his retirement to Arabia came to an end, he spent ten years as a missionary in Syria and in his native country Cilicia – primarily to Jewish converts who, it was hoped, would form the principal human source of supply to the Christian community, in the Dispersion as in Judaea itself. But it was perhaps during this period, at the Syrian capital of Antioch (Antakya) which became his base of operations for a year, that Paul and others of like mind formulated the idea of seeking out Gentile converts, initially as supplements and appendages to the Jewish body of the faithful.

Then, in *c*. 45, Paul and Barnabas, who for the time being shared his activities and views,[35] set out on a missionary tour in Syria, Cyprus and Asia Minor – the First Journey of Paul, lasting several years. It seems probable that they had the cautious backing of James the Just and Peter in Jerusalem, and that the travellers were to speak in Jewish synagogues, probably on the understanding that they might also as far as possible convert suitable individual Gentiles as well. Yet matters did not turn out that way. For the Jews of the Dispersion, unable to accept Jesus as the Messiah, proved shocked and recalcitrant, so that Paul and Barnabas turned more and more to the Gentiles instead. But the question whether such Gentiles ought to be expected to undergo circumcision (as many of them were unprepared to do) raised difficult problems at Jerusalem. These dilemmas are symbolized in *Acts* by an account of a Jerusalem Council convened to discuss the matter. No such single dramatic meeting may ever have been held (chapter V, section 2). But discussion and tension were evidently vigorous.

Before long, however, Paul was away on another great journey, covering huge areas of Asia Minor, Macedonia and Achaea (Greece). This second journey continued for three years and included an encounter with the Roman governor (proconsul*) of Achaea, Gallio, whom we know from pagan sources to have held office in *c*. 52.[36] His provincial capital was Corinth, where Paul spent eighteen months or more. Next he returned to Antioch, and then, presumably in spring 53, left for his third missionary journey. This may have lasted for five years, of which about three were spent at Ephesus, the great Greek city on the Aegean coast of Asia Minor.[37]

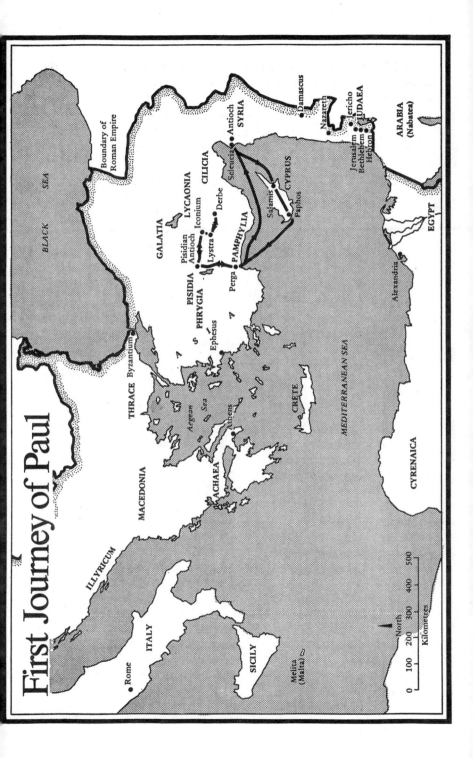

First Journey of Paul

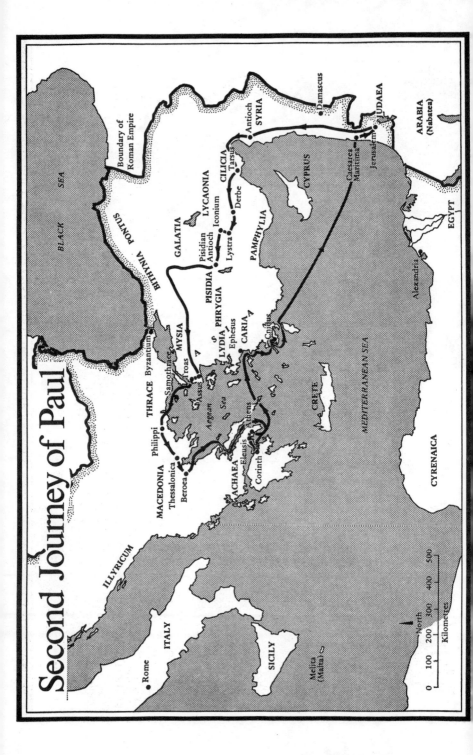

Second Journey of Paul

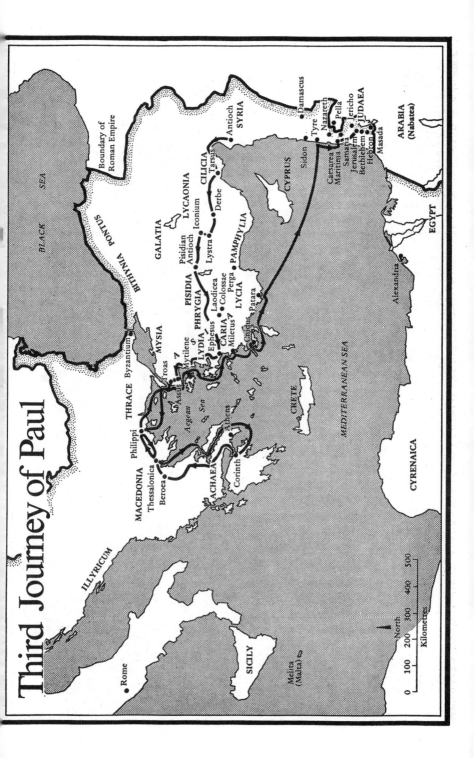

Third Journey of Paul

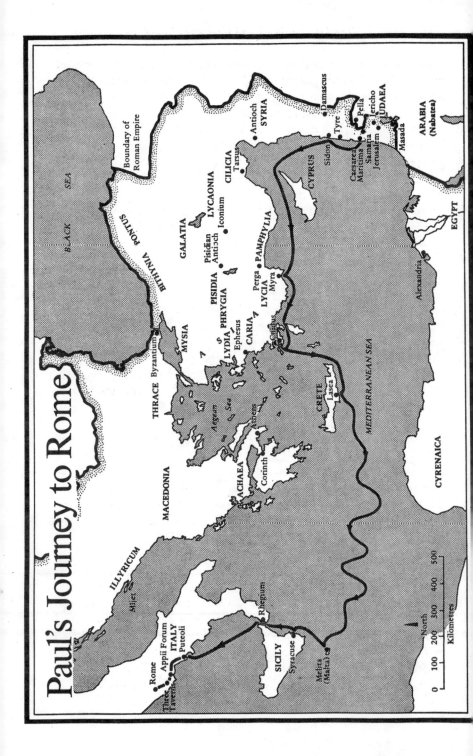

Paul's Journey to Rome

BLACK SEA

Boundary of
Roman Empire

BITHYNIA
PONTUS
THRACE
Byzantium
MYSIA
GALATIA
LYCAONIA
Iconium
PISIDIA
Pisidian
Antioch
PHRYGIA
LYDIA
Ephesus
CARIA
Perga
Myra
LYCIA
PAMPHYLIA
CILICIA
Tarsus
Antioch
SYRIA
Damascus
CYPRUS
Sidon
Tyre
Pella
Caesarea
Maritima
Samaria
Jericho
Jerusalem
JUDAEA
Masada
ARABIA
(Nabatea)
EGYPT
Alexandria

MACEDONIA
ILLYRICUM
Aegean
Sea
ACHAEA
Athens
Corinth
CRETE
Lasea
MEDITERRANEAN SEA
CYRENAICA

Milet

Rome
Appii Forum
ITALY
Puteoli
Three
Taverns
Rhegium
SICILY
Syracuse
Melita
(Malta)

North

Kilometres
0   100   200   300   400   500

On returning to Jerusalem in 58 (his third visit there to be recorded by the Letters, his fifth according to *Acts*) he was detained by the Roman authorities in order to save his life from the angry Jews, who were nevertheless undeterred from bringing official accusations against him. These charges were heard by the governor (procurator*) of Judaea, Antonius Felix, at his capital Caesarea Maritima (Sdot Yam). But no verdict was pronounced, and for two years Paul was in prison at that city. In 60 a new governor, Porcius Festus, again deferred a decision, and when Paul, in his capacity of Roman citizen, appealed that his case should be transferred to the Emperor's court at Rome, the request was granted.[38] His journey to the imperial capital, recounted with many dramatic details by *Acts*, was broken by a stay of three winter months at Melita (Malta), after the shipwreck that *Acts* so vigorously describes.

At Rome Paul spent two years. He seems to have been at first under informal house arrest, and thereafter in prison (the report that he left for a time to go to Spain is dubious). The Romans put him on trial, but whether there was one trial or two is unclear. In the end, however, it seems that Nero's court condemned him to death and he was executed. This was possibly part of the Emperor's action in AD 64, attested by the Roman historian Tacitus, against the Christian community as scapegoats for the Great Fire of Rome; but Paul's death may have taken place later.

Paul's surviving Letters, written at various periods of his life, were follow-ups to his teaching and preaching, and as such they give us a good idea of what this must have been like. 'I cannot help myself,' he told the Corinthians, 'it would be misery for me not to preach.'[39] 'Proclaim the message,' urged *II Timothy*, 'press it home on all occasions, convenient or inconvenient; use argument, reproof and appeal'[40] – and whether or not Paul wrote this Letter himself, that is just what he had done, over a huge geographical area. Somehow or other, he mustered up the enormous courage and endurance needed to perform almost incredible feats of missionary travelling. In Asia Minor alone if we add up the mileage of Paul's three journeys we arrive at the following figures: the first journey from Attaleia to Derbe and back, 625 miles; the second journey from Tarsus to Troas, 875 miles; the third journey, from Tarsus to Ephesus, 710 miles.[41] I myself have covered part, *only* part, of this territory with benefit of mechanical transport. How Paul traversed it all, as well as vast regions in other lands, without any such aid, often in the crushing heat of summer and equally savage cold of winter, one can only marvel.

And everywhere he went he taught and preached. It was a slavery, he said, not a source of personal satisfaction. He felt he had to do it. The task was all the harder because he knew he created an impression of personal ineffectiveness which hindered his ability to be persuasive.

I am so feeble (you say) when I am face to face with you, so brave when I am away ... 'His Letters,' so it is said, 'are weighty and powerful; but when he appears he has no presence, and as a speaker he is beneath contempt'.[42]

In consequence, he admitted,

I came before you, weak, nervous and shaking with fear.[43]

And yet he was capable of extreme and rigorous firmness. 'Have I in any way come short of those superlative apostles? I think not. I may be no speaker, but knowledge I have'[44] – and his instructions *must be obeyed*.[45] Paul's Letters display a startling mixture of conciliatory friendliness and harsh, bitter, inexorable bullying. On the one hand, he had a genius for friendship and depended longingly upon affection and appreciation. Yet if once his motives were questioned, he would object with ferocity.[46] Although constantly urging his correspondents to practise sensitive tactfulness and in dealing with the principles of others, and no less frequently asserting that this was precisely the method he practised himself,[47] he nevertheless indulged in violent, stubborn outbursts, devoid of any consideration or sense of humour.[48] And yet as we shall see at the end of this book, all his passionate arguments, all his resounding eloquence, did not gain him during his lifetime the adherents he had hoped for. He seems to have been an exciting person with a talent for upsetting people, but he was not, apparently, winning or attractive.

His character was torn apart by inner conflicts. One of the strangest of them was a clash between genuine modesty and overwhelming self-confidence. It was a conflict of which he was only too well aware, since his surviving Letters use the word 'boast' nearly sixty times, with a host of explanatory comments and justifications.[49] He realized that he 'had not yet reached perfection',[50] and in the spirit of Jewish insistence on the divine goodness and omnipotence[51] he insisted that whatever he may have achieved stood not to his own credit but to God's.[52] Nevertheless, since his life was 'the life which Christ lived in him,'[53] he unhesitatingly claimed full equality with the prophets of old and with the apostles who had known Jesus personally. Indeed, after his death he hoped for early, individual translation to the presence of Jesus himself in heaven.[54] And meanwhile he bore no resemblance whatever to Paul the docile follower of other men's leads whom we find described in *Acts*. On the contrary, his Letters reveal a man who is extremely touchy about not wanting to work where others have laboured. On another's foundations he disdains to build.[55]

Paul is the very opposite of a tranquil, serene personality. Always pursuing, always pursued, he is the victim of violent, manic-depressive alternations of moods. And he feels a terrible discord between his actions, as they were, and what he would have liked them to be.

> I do not even acknowledge my own actions as mine, for what I do is not what I want to do, but what I detest . . . though the will to do good is there, the deed is not . . . Miserable creature that I am![56]

Some have denied that this passage is strictly autobiographical, preferring to see in it a general dramatization of the human predicament.[57] But it is difficult not to detect an echo of his own psychological experience. When the German philosopher Nietzsche called him a tormented, morbid crank, repellent both to himself and others, he was perhaps speaking too strongly. But Paul was tormented all the same – tormented by a constant feeling that he did not accomplish what he wanted to and that he fell agonizingly short of perfection.

One trouble was that he suffered on occasion from what he describes as a *skolops*, a 'thorn' (or mass of thorns) in the flesh – a disability of which he three times asked God to relieve him, without success.[58] Some have believed that this is a metaphorical term, meaning 'a painful wound to his pride'. But certain of the Fathers of the Church* and many subsequent writers on asceticism thought it referred to sexual temptation, and they may have been right. A great modern Pauline scholar, Arthur Darby Nock, although unwilling to commit himself on the meaning of the particular phrase in question, has lent his authority to this interpretation of Paul's general attitude: 'The point of difficulty for him perhaps lay in sexual desire, of which he speaks.'[59]

Indeed he does, and in pretty bleak terms. It is not so much that his actual precepts about the *social* situation regarding women and marriage and sex are unusually severe; they are at least no more illiberal than the general Jewish views of his time, and perhaps less so. Women, he said, must obey their husbands; their husbands must repay their obedience, in strict reciprocity, with love: and neither must abuse, by fornication or perversion, the bodies that had been given them by God.[60] These are all injunctions that could be found in earlier and contemporary Jewish writings, enlightened or otherwise, as well as his explanation *why* woman must be obedient (and must keep silent at meetings)[61]: it is because she is inferior, not having been created directly by God but indirectly out of the flesh of his earlier creation, man.[62] But Paul on occasion tentatively contradicts this implication of inferiority, pointing out that theoretically the sexes are equal in Jesus Christ.[63] And he advances beyond Jewish practice in one respect, namely by relying on women not merely as disciples and companions and contributors to the commonweal, as Jesus evidently did in unprecedented fashion, but as very active and constant helpers in his work. They occasionally caused trouble, it is true.[64] Nonetheless, one of his female associates, Prisca or Priscilla, is even on occasion given pride of place before her husband Aquila.[65]

Yet Paul retains a definite, if somewhat guarded, preference for celibacy over the married state. This was in contrast to the general opinion of Judaism,[66] which emphasized the duty of procreation. The Essene* and Qumran* communities (without enforcing total abstinence) would have agreed with him; moreover, according to the Talmud* Moses had voluntarily renounced cohabitation; there was also the recent precedent of John the Baptist, and, it would seem, of Jesus as well.[67] All the same, Paul's preference is expressed to the Corinthians with a grudging sourness which strikes a curiously personal note.

It is a good thing for a man to have nothing to do with women; but because there is so much immorality, let each man have his own wife and each woman her own husband . . . To the unmarried and to widows I say this: it is a good thing if they stay as I am myself; but if they cannot control themselves, they should marry. Better be married than burn with vain desire.[68]

Then Paul goes on to say that, as the time left for the future of the world is short, it is better to concentrate on what is really important – not pleasing one's wife, which is what the married man has to do, but pleasing God, to which the unmarried man is much better able to devote his time.

However, Paul's hostility to sex cannot be entirely attributed to this belief in the imminence of the Second Coming. The harshness of his judgments on sexual offenders seems too marked for that; and so does his general contempt for the flesh and fleshly things.[69] This attitude has made him one of the principal ancestors and models of all the monastic, puritanical self-mortifications which flourished and proliferated during the subsequent centuries of antiquity and through the middle ages.[70]

Since sexual difficulties and problems of various kinds are so common a feature of most societies, it is probably not necessary to go all the way with Havelock Ellis in assailing Paul as a morbid neuropath with a twisted personality who 'trampled on nature when it came in his way, and for the rest never saw it.'[71] Yet his unmistakably pejorative attitude towards sex does raise insistent questions about his own tastes and practices. Evidently, he felt a deep distaste for sex, and (if we leave aside inconclusive speculations that he had once been married) it appears that he refrained from practising it. And this abstinence may partly account for the vast amount of energy he channelled into his work instead, and for the nervous, almost hysterical manner in which this energy was sometimes deployed.

Suppressed and frustrated sexual desire, then, may be the 'thorn in the flesh' of which Paul complains. This 'thorn' has been more generally regarded, however, as referring to some physical ailment instead. That he was not always well we know from what he told the Galatians: 'As you know, it was bodily illness that originally led to my bringing you the Gospel, and you resisted any temptation to show scorn or disgust at the state of my poor body.'[72] Attempted definitions of his illness have included ophthalmia, epilepsy, malaria, erysipelas, and neurotic disorders producing migraine.[73] However, these are only conjectures.

In any case, whatever he suffered from cannot have been altogether crippling, or how would he have accomplished his immense travels? Besides, his own description in *II Corinthians* of the sufferings he had endured makes no specific reference to physical ill-health.

As God's servants, we try to recommend ourselves in all circumstances by our steadfast endurance: in distress, hardships, and dire straits; flogged, imprisoned, mobbed; overworked, sleepless, starving . . .[74]

Later in the same Letter he adds a further and more specific outburst about his missionary journeys.

But if there is to be bravado (and here I speak as a fool), I can indulge in it too. Are they his [opponents in the church] Hebrews? So am I. Israelites?

So am I. Abraham's descendants? So am I. Are they servants of Christ? I am mad to speak like this, but I can outdo them. More overworked than they, scourged more severely, more often imprisoned, many a time face to face with death.

Five times the Jews have given me the thirty-nine strokes; three times I have been beaten with rods; once I was stoned; three times I have been ship-wrecked, and for twenty-four hours I was adrift on the open sea. I have been constantly on the road; I have met dangers from rivers, dangers from robbers, dangers from my fellow-countrymen, dangers from foreigners, dangers in towns, dangers in the country, dangers at sea, dangers from false friends.

I have toiled and drudged, I have often gone fasting; and I have suffered from cold and exposure.[75]

'What is there expressed,' preached Dr John Barwick, Dean of St Paul's, in 1660, 'will make another man shrink at the very reading of it.'

In the all too selective narrations of *Acts*, however, it is impossible to trace more than a small proportion of these hardships. For example, if we consider the five Jewish inflictions of the thirty-nine strokes (the scriptures prescribed forty strokes, but one was habitually omitted in case by a miscount the regulation might be broken), not one of these scourgings is mentioned in the work. Paul also refers to three beatings with rods – a Roman penalty. *Acts* only mentions one of these punish-ments. Paul reports three shipwrecks. The only such event *Acts* men-tions was the adventure at Malta subsequent to the writing of *II Corinthians*. Nor does *Acts* say anything about imprisonment and the other hardships which Paul, elsewhere, declares he experienced at Ephesus.[76] But he would scarcely have provided these very explicit statistics if they could have been shown to be untrue, and we must therefore suppose that he is describing sufferings he actually underwent. Their horrifying nature explains why it was his endurance as a missionary, above all else, which won him the acceptance and admiration of the later Church.[77]

What it was that maintained his tremendous energy, despite every obstacle and hardship, he tells us himself. 'In future let no one make trouble for me, since I bear the marks (*stigmata*) of Jesus branded on my body.'[78] He is not referring to any miraculous stigmata of the Crucifixion but to some visible physical damage or disfigurement resulting from his exacting experiences. But his deliberate linkage of this mark with Jesus Christ is highly characteristic of his thought.

Hard-pressed on every side, we are never hemmed in; bewildered, we are never at our wits' end; hunted, we are never abandoned to our fate; struck down, we are not left to die. Wherever we go we carry death with us in our body – the death that Jesus died . . .[79]

So Paul compared and identified his sufferings with those of Jesus, and it was this identification which inspired him and drove him to carry on. 'We are treated as the scum of the earth, the dregs of humanity',[80] but our hardships, being like Christ's, will eventually bring us to him – and since that is the case, 'in the hope of the divine splendour that is to be ours, let us even *exult* in our present sufferings.'[81]

Paul seems, then, to have conceived his almost ceaseless journeyings and troubles not only as an inescapable slavery, but actually as a martyrdom, like the martyrdoms not only of earlier Jews but of Jesus Christ himself. It was this in a twofold sense. First, it was a martyrdom in the present time, since 'every day I die'[82] – and others too, including the recipients of his letters, have the privilege of dying the same ever-renewed daily death if they take on a share of his sufferings.[83] But it was also, above all, the prelude to a climactic martyrdom in the future, once again in imitation of Jesus. 'If my life-blood is to crown that sacrifice which is the offering up of your faith, I am glad of it, and I share my gladness with you all . . . for to me life is Christ, and death gain.'[84] And so Paul's Letters became the inspiration not only of ascetics in later centuries, but also of martyrs, starting almost at once[85] and continuing throughout the centuries. 'Back to the cloister,' cried Sören Kierkegaard, 'there is only one thing higher, and that is martyrdom!' Paul by no means lived in the cloister. But martyrdom, in the image of Jesus, seemed to him an utterly desirable end. And it was by means of this conviction that he was able to perform such uncanny feats of perseverance and endurance.

II

𝕯

Our Disastrous Past History

1 *The Age-Long Rule of Evil*

Paul was convinced that the world, up to and including a portion of his own lifetime, was a horrible place, plunged in evil. He believed this partly because his own mind and character showed a ready tendency to reject worldly and fleshly considerations with disgust. But he was also, like any other thinker and writer, affected by his own times and by contemporary events.

To us, the Roman Empire in the first century AD, that vast, complex organism, extending from the Euphrates to the Atlantic, seems a relatively peaceful and prosperous place. After the civil wars of the previous century, during which the Republican system of government gradually collapsed, the entire administration had been overhauled and set on a stable basis by the first Roman emperor (*princeps*) Augustus (31 BC–AD 14); and under the successors of his dynasty during the next fifty-four years – Tiberius, Gaius (Caligula), Claudius, Nero – for all their personal aberrations the empire, as a whole, remained flourishing and tranquil. Indeed Paul himself felt it both useless and undesirable to resist imperial authority. Yet he was a Jew, and for the Palestinian Jews this was a period of great and growing unhappiness. For from AD 6 onwards, continuously except for an interval of only three years (41–4), their homeland of Israel or Judaea was a third-class Roman province, ruled with a lack of imagination that was untypical on the whole of Rome's government elsewhere. Indeed, in Judaea this bad government was so conspicuous that unrest and turbulence were on the increase, and it had become possible to foresee the violent outburst of the First Jewish Revolt in AD 66–73, shortly after Paul's death. The Jews felt themselves to be in a trough, with God very remote from them.[1]

Now it is true that Paul was a Jew not of Palestine but of the Dispersion – those millions of Jews who lived not in Palestine but in other parts of the Roman Empire, and principally in the near east. The position of the Dispersion Jews was relatively satisfactory, since they enjoyed, within each of the self-governing pagan city-states of which the eastern provinces were made up, a sort of autonomy protecting their religious customs, under their own local councils. Nevertheless Dispersion Jews remained conscious of a powerful emotional link with the homeland of Judaea, and felt profoundly involved in its troubles. Paul was no politician and does not refer to such matters, but he cannot have been oblivious of the tensions which enhanced and accentuated his already powerful predisposition to see the world around him as evil, as John the Baptist and Jesus had seen it before him.[2] And when Paul pronounced in *Romans* that the world was evil, he explained that it was so because the Fall of Adam made it so:

> It was through one man [Adam] that sin entered the world, and through sin death, and thus death pervaded the whole human race, inasmuch as all men have sinned. For sin was already in the world before there was law [the Law of Moses, or Torah†], even over those who had not sinned as Adam did by disobeying a direct command.[3]

Paul knew from *Genesis*, the first book of the Hebrew scriptures, that God had forbidden Adam to eat from the Tree of Knowledge (of Good and Evil); but he had eaten from it, and in consequence he and Eve had been expelled from the Garden of Eden. It is a theme which has fascinated men and women throughout the ages; and it was the theme of John Milton's *Paradise Lost*:

> Of Man's first disobedience, and the fruit
> Of that forbidden tree, whose mortal taste
> Brought death into the world, and all our woe,
> With loss of Eden . . .

Paul's words in *Romans*, like so many of his utterances, were endowed by later theologians with vast superstructures of doctrine which do not

† For this, see p. 35.

always arise easily or naturally from the actual words he wrote. The doctrine in this case was that of Original Sin, declaring that we have inherited Adam's taint, and are therefore inevitably sinners as Adam, too, was a sinner. Paul, however, says neither of these things in so many words. True, he may wish to assert a direct causal relationship between the sin of Adam and the sin of all subsequent mankind. But if so, he leaves the nature of the causal connection undefined. Does he, or does he not, mean that because of Adam we *cannot help* sinning, however hard we try? This like so much else his own phrases do not clearly reveal.

However, he does intend to remind us that we are the products, whether we like it or not, of the racial history which lies behind us. W. D. Davies assesses his position in these terms:

> The Christian doctrine of sin in its classical form offends both rationalists and moralists by maintaining the seemingly absurd position that man sins inevitably and by a fateful necessity, but that he is nevertheless to be held responsible for actions which are prompted by an ineluctable fate.
> The explicit scriptural foundation for the doctrine is given in Pauline teaching. On the one hand Paul insists that man's sinful glorification of himself is 'without excuse'. 'So that they are without excuse because that, when they knew God, they glorified Him not as God.' And on the other hand he regards human sin as an inevitable defeat, involved in, or derived from, the sin of the first man. 'Wherefore as by one man sin entered into the world and death by sin, and so death passed upon all men for that all have sinned'.[4]

To sin, or not to sin, seems to remain, according to Paul's interpretation, the responsible decision that every human being must take for himself or herself: although it had to be conceded, he felt, that they are gravely predisposed to commit sin, and have been given all too generous facilities for so doing, because they were subjected to the power of wrong which Adam's act let loose in the world. For by this act the world became appallingly vulnerable to the evil in which it has ever since been immersed.

Paul's belief in the essential evilness of man's situation was rejected in progressive nineteenth-century circles as contrary to normal human experience. Indeed, it was denounced as nothing short of a scandal. But the doctrine seems far more reasonable in our own day, after all the harrowing events of recent decades – the most harrowing, both in quantity and quality, that the world has ever seen. As the late Richard

Crossman remarked, there is more evidence today for the Christian doctrine of Original Sin than for the Marxist doctrine of the classless society. To object (with the Marxists) that the former view, by blaming everything on God, surreptitiously sets out to excuse corrupt social institutions does not dispose of its validity, seeing that such horrors have in reality occurred. We have returned to Paul's insight that men do evil because of the evil which has come to be within them. In the unavoidable pessimism of our time, his conviction that there is a fearful flaw in the universe has returned to the eminence it occupied before the progressive optimism of the nineteenth century tried to replace it. Unlike Paul, we are not sure of the origin of the flaw. But like him we are sure it exists.

Paul saw sin as a terrible power implanted and lodged in human beings, an enslaving force which holds them in its power and embraces their whole existence, so that they catastrophically 'miss the mark' – for that is what the Greek term *hamartia*, which he found in his Greek Bible, the Septuagint, signifies. The word occurs no less than sixty-two times in the Letters attributed to Paul – forty-eight times in *Romans* alone. For he is obsessed by the utter, catastrophic degradation of the world. Even the best among men and women, and the best of their accomplishments, seem to him tainted or poisoned at the core.

Nor is there any easy way out: the Greek idea that sin is mainly due to ignorance he cannot accept, for Paul, we must remember, was the man who lamented: 'What I do is not what I want to do, but what I detest . . . when I want to do the right, only the wrong is within my reach.'[5] So, too, had spoken another and very different writer, the Roman poet Horace, but his placid nature was spared the self-tortures of Paul. These agonies are reflected in his constant use of the term 'flesh'. Externally, it is a Greek term, but the 'Dead Sea Scrolls' of the ascetic Jewish community of Qumran* had already employed it to denote the evil part of the mortal endowment. 'Flesh' in such a sense means the common, unregenerate stuff of our inheritance; the lower, debased nature of men and women who have somehow acquired the disastrous impulse to act wrongly.

The problem of evil had always been felt very strongly by the Jews because of their vivid conviction that God was its total, holy, antithesis. Their ancient exile to Babylonia had burnt the sense of sin into the very being and bones of the nation. In particular, the question whether posterity was compelled to suffer for the misdeeds of its ancestors had been much discussed by Jewish thinkers, in whose scriptures apparently conflicting utterances on the subject are to be found. To many of ourselves, this thesis, put in theological terms, does not seem to hold water. Yet it is obviously true from our own historical experience that grave mistakes have to be paid for by subsequent generations; and during the last centuries before our era the belief had grown up that such suffering was inevitable.

This conviction was fostered by the Jewish concept of the solidarity of groups, based on the interpretation of Israel itself as a corporate personality in which the whole community suffers for the sins of one.[6] In this way Adam was seen as a figure representing all humanity to come. For we come into the world not as isolated individuals but as members of the human race, whose undesirable features we cannot fail to inherit. Paul did not differ so very much from his fellow-Jews about Adam and about sin. But he *felt* these beliefs with exceptionally passionate strength, seeing sin not merely, in a legalistic sense, as an act or acts, but as a frightening force, within whose clutches *every* individual, in turn, is inevitably born.

That men and women should be sinful, in other words, was predestined. Paul believed to a considerable extent in predestination – God's foreordainings of everything that comes to pass – and all the controversies which have subsequently raged on the subject are little more than glosses upon his words in *Romans*: 'For God knew his own before ever they were.'[7] This issue of predestination became acute when applied to the question of who would and who would not eventually be saved, a problem that will be discussed in more detail elsewhere. Paul, in such a connection, is prepared to let in a chink of light, since, at times, he seems to admit that what we ourselves do upon this earth will play some part in determining our eventual salvation or damnation. But in regard to the inheritance of Original Sin by each and every one of us, he sees no such way out. We are born with this bequest, one and all.

Orthodox Jewish writers, however, for the most part continued to turn away from accepting this dramatically fatalistic viewpoint. The statement by the English churchman W. R. Inge, Dean of St Paul's, that 'the biblical doctrine of the Fall of Man, which the Hebrews would never have evolved for themselves, remained an otiose dogma in Jewish religion' is quite correct, subject only to one amendment – that it was never a dogma at all. The idea of an Original Sin derivative from Adam

in which all mankind shared made its first appearance in Hebrew literature very late, in *II Esdras** (end of first century AD): 'O thou Adam,
what hast thou done! For though it was thou that sinned, the fall was
not thine alone, but ours also who are thy descendants!'[8] However, in
*II Baruch,** nearly contemporary with *II Esdras*, we find a strongly
implied contradiction of this theory:[9] '. . . Adam is not the cause save
only of his own soul but each of us has been the Adam of his own soul.'
And the Jews in general, though not always speaking with one voice,
tended to agree with the latter view, and were much more careful than
Paul in their insistence upon the full responsibility of every individual
for his sin, despite Adam's Fall and its effects.[10]

Certain Christian writers, too, felt that Paul had moved perilously
near to an excessive rejection of individual responsibility for sin – or
alternatively they tried to pretend that he had *not* done any such thing.
Irenaeus,* in his *Five Books against Heresies* (*c*. AD 185), differed from
those who believed that Adam had fallen and had thereby caused the
whole of mankind to fall with him. Mankind, according to Irenaeus, is
God's raw material still in the dynamic process of creation: God continues to work his purpose out. And recently Teilhard de Chardin and
Austin Farrer, as well as non-religious thinkers, have favoured the same
evolutionary view.[11] But two hundred years after Irenaeus, his optimistic
opinion was superseded by Augustine's ultra-Pauline insistence on the
Fall of the human race resulting in its desperate ignorance, helplessness,
sin and guilt. Augustine's British or Irish contemporary Pelagius disagreed, discarding the Fall and Original Sin, and teaching, like Irenaeus,
that man is able to win eternal life by his own natural powers: 'If I ought
I can.'

Yet throughout the ages it is Augustine's view which has prevailed
among Western theologians and churches. For example, Luther and
Calvin, like Augustine, seized on Paul's insistence upon the terrible,
lasting effects of Adam's Fall, and carried his suggestion of humanity's
helplessness a long stage further. Even if Paul had not *quite* sponsored
the grim idea of total depravity, it proved possible to interpret his words
as if he had. According to the beliefs of Luther:

We must not suppose that the apparent freedom of the will is consistently
experienced. If we appeal to experience, we must not overlook the many
examples of everyday language which testify to a presentiment of the predestination and foreknowledge of God. Moreover, we must bear in mind that
'free will' is a questionable concept. It can represent a tautology, in so far as it

means nothing more than the 'will'. But the will is always committed, always determined by something. Consequently, the concept of 'free will' can also represent a contradiction in terms . . .

Luther realizes that it is a completely abstract mode of thought to speak of an 'absolute' will, that is, the will completely isolated and undetermined. 'The will is always already decided, involved and committed, and is not the natural will in the situation of absolute freedom of choice . . . the will is only the free will to the extent that it is *able* to do what it wishes.'[12]

Calvin's meditations on Paul and the Old Testament led to an even starker point of view, according to which man is 'despoiled of freedom of will and subjected to a miserable slavery . . . Predestination we call the eternal decree of God, by which he has determined in himself of every individual of mankind what he would have to become.' Such a doctrine, Calvin added, though we cannot understand it, or even reasonably expect to do so, is 'productive of the most delightful benefit.' Jacobus Arminius (1560–1609), however, did not agree, arguing that in some way God's sovereignty *must* be compatible with man's free will. But Pascal* felt that the existence of Original Sin had made such a protest impossible to maintain. 'No other religion than ours,' he wrote, 'has taught that man is born in sin, no sect of philosophers ever said so – hence none of these has told the truth.'

Nowadays, the Catholic Church teaches the doctrine of Original Sin in mitigated form, and some modern Calvinists, too, assert that men and women are not wholly condemned to commit evil, but only contain an ingrained bias in that direction. In the Jewish view, the Christian struggle throughout the centuries to strike a right balance has been long and difficult – and inconclusive.

Paul's utterances on Original Sin encouraged an immense diversity of opinion on their meanings because they were essentially equivocal. Some of these ambiguities arise from the random contexts in which Paul threw out his views, with haste and emotion, to meet special circumstances. But others are basic and intrinsic in his thought: these are due to unresolved contradictions in his philosophy. Sometimes, too, one feels some things were left unresolved quite deliberately, because Paul realized, for all his apparent confidence, that some philosophical problems were insoluble.

Besides, in writing of sin, Paul had a further consideration in his mind. The ambiguity we have been discussing relates to the power, or lack of power, of the human will to resist the burden of original evil. But if Paul does not trouble to clear this question up, it is partly because, in his view, it was in any case a subordinate issue. For he had an entirely different cure for the problem of sin, into which the human will did not enter at all. What that solution was we shall see in the next chapter.

Meanwhile what remains, above all, significant for the twentieth century in Paul's attitude to evil is his overwhelming conviction that mankind had always been immersed in it – and that our rescue from this condition was a matter of imperative, overwhelmingly urgent necessity.

To some today, however, it will seem strange that he chose to frame this vital truth, not in the direct language of ethics or current experience, but in a very ancient myth – a myth recounted in those scriptural books which Christians would soon be describing as the Old Testament. This manner of formulating what he wanted to say, which we shall continually encounter, was owed to the gigantically important role which the Hebrew Bible fulfilled in Jewish life. Declared to be the unique and fully adequate expression of the will of God, it seemed to hold all that God has made known of his nature, character and purpose, and all that he would have men and women be and do.

Particularly sacred was the Torah.* Translated as 'law', but rather meaning 'instruction' by means of divine revelation, this was a term which was particularly and specifically employed to describe the first five books of the Old Testament, the five books known by Greeks as the Pentateuch: *Genesis, Exodus, Leviticus, Numbers* and *Deuteronomy*. Reputedly composed before the creation of the world, the narratives and myths in these writings recount the primitive history of man, beginning with the cautionary tale of Adam and continuing with the stories of Abraham and other early Hebrew heroes, the Exodus from Egyptian captivity with Moses, the return as far as the border of the Promised Land, and then the transmission of the Mosaic 'Law' to the Jewish people. For the Law was believed to have been conveyed to Moses on Mount Sinai by God himself, who had inscribed it upon the Tokens, two tablets of stone written with the finger of God.

This act was the supreme event and corner-stone of the Jewish conception of world history, and upon the observance of the directions laid down in these books has depended the whole existence and continuity of Jewish life throughout the centuries. In the words of the Psalmist:

> Thou, Lord, hast laid down thy precepts
> For men to keep them faithfully.
> If only I might hold a steady course,
> Keeping thy statutes . . .
> My heart pines with longing
> Day and night for thy decrees . . .
> O how I love thy Law!
> It is my study all day long.[13]

This intense study, pursued for generation after generation, had an enormous and arresting outcome. It meant, throughout all the ages before Paul was born, and during and after his lifetime as well, that everything which happened, or had happened, or would happen, needed to be interpreted, and was interpreted, as a fulfilment of what was predicted or foreshadowed in these holy scriptures. This typological form of interpretation (from the Greek word *typos*, pattern, example, prefiguration) was already apparent in the Old Testament and continued to be employed by later Jews, and was just as intensely followed by the early Christians – who described every incident in the life and death of Jesus Christ in the light of these same Biblical utterances.

For it seemed to Jews and Christians alike that the course of history was specifically directed by God in such a way that later events corresponded to those earlier ones – which had indeed, they maintained, been expressly designed to anticipate what was to happen later. The Torah, and the books of the Prophets who had succeeded to its inheritance, seemed to contain *the whole of truth*, so that no subsequent developments whatever, apart from what could be interpreted as having been announced and revealed in those writings, were even within the bounds of possibility at all; *everything* that happens reveals something in the Bible. The result was that every conceivable subtlety or ingenuity was held to be justified in extorting the appropriate interpretations from those scriptural sayings. This places a large obstacle in the way of our own sympathy and understanding, since to us it would appear that many of the Old Testament passages quoted in the New Testament as prefigurations cannot possibly, to the objective eye, be interpreted in any such sense[14] – even if we are prepared to grant that the principle of typology is acceptable at all, unlike Nietzsche, for example, who regarded it as plainly ridiculous.

But it cannot be ignored by the historian, since it is a principle which the ancients found both acceptable and inescapable: and Paul, like the authors of the Gospels and other Christian writers, subscribed whole-heartedly to this conviction. In his view, that is to say, the entire Old Testament was replete with prophecies, pieces of information, patterns, examples and warnings, addressed directly to himself and his contemporaries.

Such, then, was the way of thinking which made it possible for Paul to depict the evil state of the world in terms of the part played by Adam. And this, in his judgment, was no mere recourse to literary symbolism or legendary construction, for he was using the role of Adam to describe a situation which, as we have seen, he believed to be intensely terrible and urgent: the overwhelming potency of evil among mankind. That this exists we may feel disposed to agree. But whereas modern intellectuals might speak of the 'power' of evil, he said 'powers' – malignant spiritual powers. For he conceived the unseen in multiple terms that are far more concrete than any which Westerners would overtly employ today – although, even now, many or most other peoples on the earth are haunted by the dread of malevolent spirits of a by no means dissimilar kind.

'Our fight,' he declared, 'is not against human foes, but against cosmic powers, against the authorities and potentates of the dark world, against the superhuman forces of evil in the heavens.'[15] This belief in demons and bad or good angels – *daimones*, spirits, and *angeloi*, messengers – though disconcerting, was a reasonable and logical corollary of Paul's intense monotheistic belief in a single transcendent God. For it was hard to suppose that a God of such exalted remoteness could concern himself directly with the details of men's lives: and so it became necessary to accept the idea that there were intermediaries who would undertake such interventions, and that it was to them, discarnate intelligences in the universe, that we should address our prayers, rather than directly to the inaccessible supreme being. These demons, for example, were capable of giving Paul a sharp physical pain,[16] and their unseen presences could be felt at Christian meetings.[17] Theirs was 'the spirit now at work among God's rebel subjects.' And, indeed, throughout the ages, right up to events in Paul's lifetime itself, 'we were slaves to [these] elemental spirits of the universe'[18] – sinister forces representing the evil which dominates mankind.

Paul saw these forces with a vivid urgency that is all his own. Yet, at the same time, he was speaking in terms which would be fully familiar to his contemporaries, Jews and Gentiles alike. Though it is unlikely that Paul was aware of it, these were beliefs which went back as far as Plato's *Symposium*, in which Socrates is made to say that 'everything which is of the nature of a spirit is half-god and half-man,' and the functions of such beings are 'to interpret and convey messages to the gods from men and to men from the gods . . . Being of an intermediate nature, a spirit bridges the gap between them, and prevents the universe from falling into two separate halves.'[19] And by Paul's time, as E. R. Dodds observes: 'virtually everyone believed in the existence of these beings and in their function as mediators, whether he called them daemons or angels or simply "spirits" . . . And the "daemonic man", who knew how to establish contact with them, was correspondingly esteemed'.[20]

Dodds also specifically includes the Jews in this statement, for even before the Exile they had recognized the existence of many such supernatural beings. And subsequent Jewish thought, increasingly stressing the transcendence of God, and coming under more and more influences from Babylonia and Persia, went much further.

In the Jewish literature of the period we find a highly developed angelology. The writer of the book of *Daniel* (*c.* 165 BC) was the first by whom angels were individualized and endowed with names and titles, and later apocalyptic literature assumed a heavenly hierarchy of stupendous proportions. In *Enoch* seven classes of angels are distinguished . . .[21]

Often such spirits were identified with the astral phenomena in a many-layered universe. But, in particular, Jews of the ages preceding and following Paul came to think that although demons were not *necessarily* evil, it was they, nevertheless, who were responsible for all the moral and physical evil in the world. In the *Testament of the Twelve Patriarchs** each Patriarch warned his children and grandchildren against the influence of evil spirits; and the Sons of Light and Sons of Darkness, whose clashes in the *War Rule** of Qumran reflect the tensions in the hearts of mankind, are human armies guided by rival angels.[22] An apocryphal fragment vigorously illustrates the reality of such concepts in people's minds. It speaks of Egyptian magicians

. . . who, practising their arts, called up devils and sent them against Moses. The evil spirits rushed in hosts upon the holy man: but the power of God and the prayer of the righteous one drove them back as the storm scatters the fire and the wind the smoke. So did the demons fly from the face of Moses . . . As light dispels darkness, so did Moses drive away the wicked ones. Headlong they returned to the magicians by whom they had been hired; and they said: 'We lose our labour against this man, for he is stronger than we, and we cannot get near to the border of the place where he dwells' . . . The magicians therefore set to work: they took some of the hairs and garments of Moses, and made an image of him, and laid it up in a tomb, and set evil demons against it.

Immediately the demons came, and the princes of them: Satan was ready with his hosts, all of them in divers forms, to destroy Moses. They ran against him in a troop. But when they lifted up their eyes to the holy prophet and saw him encompassed by a host of angels, like as it was once with Elisha, they could not bear the look of him, much less attack him, and all together they fled away in confusion with cries and howling.[23]

These demons, originally regarded as the good angel-messengers of God, whom he had endowed with supernatural life, were later asserted, perhaps with reference to Christ's victory over them, to have already been cast down from heaven.[24] Yet, fallen as they may be, they still hold humanity in their grasp and take possession of it – a concrete expression of the evil we all see around us every day.

If man becomes subject to them, then he is fallen to a state of unnatural slavery. The process appears to be after this fashion: the reason of man, being a spark of the divine, knew God and read His law written on the heart; but instead of worshipping God and doing His will, it stooped to adore material forms, and thereby fell under the dominion of the elemental powers. The elevation of the material to the place of God led to the perversion of man's naturally right instincts. Reason itself became 'reprobate' and the whole life of mankind was thrown into disorder.

If the transmitted sin of Adam is the characteristically Jewish doctrine, the theory of elemental spirits starts rather from Greek ideas. Neither can satisfy us, though each has hints of truth: on the one hand, the solidarity of humanity and the incalculable effects of individual transgression; on the other, the peril of exalting the physical and material to a dominance which is not in accord with man's real nature.[25]

Later, the Jewish Christians descended into a welter of angelology, and Augustine,* in his *Confessions*, repeatedly bears witness to the continuing belief in angels and demons, whom he assumed to possess bodies composed of some sort of intangible matter.

This, then, was Paul's further look at the predicament of man: this, remarked C. S. Lewis, 'is practical politics, this is the realism of hell'. But how could man escape from this appalling subjection to demons? The answer was, in Hebrew thought, that the best method of mastering these oppressors was the proper employment against them of the science of angels: and that was why the Jews were regarded by the outside world as magicians and sorcerers second to none. Paul, too, considered the discerning of spirits to be a special, expert, gift; and the charges brought against him and Silas at Thessalonica and Philippi[26] may well have included magic, which was under certain circumstances regarded as illegal. Although his name was not surrounded by a continual aura of wonder-working, he was nonetheless credited with the blinding of a sorcerer at Paphos in Cyprus, and was believed to have performed a number of miracles at Ephesus, involving the expulsion of evil spirits from the sick.[27]

Moreover, the deepest impression made by Jesus himself, as the Gospels make clear, had been his mastery as a healer and an exorcist of demons (a practice which still, amid sharp controversy, continues in the Catholic and Anglican Churches today); and his name was used for purposes of exorcism among Jewish rabbis.[28] Yet exorcism, even when Jesus performed it, was only a palliative, since while it could successfully eject evil spirits from an individual it did nothing to end their reign over mankind as a whole. In Jesus' lifetime, according to Paul, their reign still continued. It needed something greater than individual acts of exorcism to overturn it: and what that greater impetus was, according to Paul's conviction, we shall shortly see. Meanwhile, the world was still plunged in evil.

Moreover, not content with attributing this situation to demons, Paul, like many before and after him, attributed it to their leader Satan or Belial, more frequently described as the Devil (*diabolos*). Here he was responding to a deep-seated popular belief that such a figure existed; but at the same time he was contributing to much subsequent confusion and potential misunderstanding.

Satan masquerades as a good angel, an angel of Light.[29] It is as his messengers that demons torment men's bodies,[30] and offenders are 'given over to him for destruction'[31] just as pagan curses delivered their victims to gods of the underworld. It will be at Satan's doing, too, that terrible hostilities will be directed against us in the times that lie ahead.[32]

Satan, as the Devil, had not explicitly figured in the earliest books of the Old Testament, though his influence is seen behind the serpent who tempted Adam. But during the successive stages of the composition of the scriptures he had changed from an over-zealous member of the heavenly court, not indeed into a second principal power equal to God, but at least into a spirit who, while still God's subordinate, entices men to disobey his commands. Thus in *Job* he roams through the earth like a Persian official who makes adverse reports to the king, acting as an *agent provocateur* permitted to test human goodness under God's authority and control, and within the limits God had set. The bearer of a personal name since *I Chronicles*, in due course he becomes known as 'the Adversary'. That is how Paul sees him. The ancient world was accustomed to personify abstract forces, and Satan is the personification of evil. Although Adam had implanted sin, its continuation, the Bible held, was the product of a push from the supernatural sphere: and the pusher was named as Satan, the Devil.

Satan, together with the demons under his command, was destined to fall. In the words of Milton's *Paradise Lost* where, as in *Revelation*, he is compared with the serpent that destroyed Adam,

> . . . Him the Almighty Power
> Hurled headlong, flaming from the ethereal sky,
> With hideous ruin and combustion, down
> To bottomless perdition; there to dwell
> In adamantine chains and penal fire.

For Jesus had declared, according to Luke,* 'I watched how Satan fell, like lightning out of the sky.'[33] But the vision here was still prophetic or figurative,[34] for meanwhile Satan was still leading his horde of demons in their persecution of mankind. The Gospels have much to say about him, and to *John* he is the 'prince of this world'. 'Your enemy the devil,' says *I Peter*, 'like a roaring lion, prowls around looking for someone to devour'; and to *I John*, 'the whole godless world lies in the power of the evil one.'[35]

The question arises whether these Christian authors (and Jewish writers, too, who likewise saw the Adversary at work) had not, in fact, abandoned the cautious but difficult view that somehow or other he was still God's subordinate. Had they not, that is to say, more or less become dualists, virtually abandoning the cardinal Jewish tenet of monotheism, the belief that there is one God and one only who is directly responsible for everything which has been brought into existence throughout the entire world? By the second century AD, and possibly already in the first century, there would arise – partly under the influence of Judaism and Christianity – the immensely influential Gnostics, whose claim to special knowledge (*gnosis*) was explicitly associated with such dualist beliefs. These sprang from the conviction that the good God could not have been the creator of the evil that so manifestly exists. To call him 'untouched by evil,' in the words of the *Letter of James*,[36] or the one who is 'light, and in him there is no darkness at all,' as *I John*,[37] did not appear to answer this problem. Nor, in response to the pagan critic Celsus who probed the same question, was the explanation of Origen* very satisfactory: 'We affirm that God did not make evils, but that they arose incidentally, just as a carpenter's work produces shavings and sawdust.'[38]

The dualists felt it far more convincing to suppose that all this evil, and the world which is so full of it, must have been created by another power who was not God – and was not necessarily his subordinate at all. For, as Man Friday asked Robinson Crusoe, 'If God much stronger, why God not kill the Devil?' But the Devil, as we see from his torture of our own vile bodies, is manifestly not dead at all. It seemed necessary to the Gnostics, therefore, to conclude that he was God's rival and, up to date at least, his equal. But this view of the universe meant the collapse of the monotheistic theology which was the basis of Judaism and Christianity.

In dualistic systems, forces of good and forces of evil are in conflict, and have been so from eternity. History is simply the continuation of a struggle engaged in before time began: from the very beginning good and evil forces have been locked in conflict. The dualist will have nothing to do with the Biblical formula: 'In the beginning God created the heaven and the earth'; instead he insists that in the beginning there were both good and evil forces, both light and darkness, both God and the devil. The devil is an eternal character.[39]

Does Paul, then, concur with this view, and concede the Adversary equal or comparable powers to God – at least until the battle is finally decided one way or the other?

The answer is that he does not go quite as far as that. He sees God, in true Jewish fashion, as the sole creator of the universe, and his work of Creation is still going on[40] according to 'his design whose purpose is everywhere at work.'[41] To the objection that evil proliferates, and does not look like God's work at all, he gives his response: God's judgments are unsearchable, his ways untraceable; surely the potter can do what he likes with the clay.[42] The Jewish people at Qumran felt the same. The rival angels leading the Sons of Light and the Sons of Darkness against one another are all the creatures of an omnipotent God. This falls short of the dualism that divided the world between two rival powers.

Yet it is also no longer the total, strict monotheism which allowed God total, undivided control. True, it is not a dualism of contrariety; but it could be described as a dualism of subordination. And sometimes it seems, as it must have seemed to Paul, as if Satan has forgotten his subordinate place; for he has abused the degree of freedom granted by God to the creatures of heaven and earth, and for the time being is transformed from unruly servant to active opponent. While Paul rejects the absolute duality of good and evil in which evil is treated as an external principle opposed to God, the horrifying state of the world nevertheless impels him to accept a genuine opposition between God and that which in his created world resists his will, rebelling against him. Certainly, good and evil were not accepted by Paul as equal and coeternal, and Satan, presumably, was believed to exercise his power only by the permissive will of God. But he exercises it all the same!

Paul sought to explain what he meant by a recurrent antithesis between the spirit, which is God's, and the flesh, which is Satan's;[43] 'I know that nothing good lodges in me – in my unspiritual nature, I mean.' 'I bruise my own body and make it know its master . . . In this present body we do indeed groan . . . We know that so long as we are at home in the body we are exiles from the Lord . . . We are no better than pots of earthenware to contain this treasure.'[44] Yet such utterances reveal that once again the daringly questing brain of Paul had given birth to an equivocation: which, like his other obscurities, was to prove a sore trouble for future theologians in search of tidy answers. For, granted that Paul retained a monotheistic belief in God, he also saw the Devil's works very plainly around him. And this disgusted him so utterly that he displayed a harsh disparagement of the body and the flesh which was so abjectly failing to resist such diabolical attacks.

This attitude could readily be seen as an invitation to the dualism which he elsewhere explicitly rejected. It was all very well for Paul to write to the Corinthians, 'As God is true, the language in which we address you is not an ambiguous blend of Yes and No.'[45] No doubt this was his aim. Yet the thoughts he had to convey were so deep, and his manner of conveying them so impetuous and unsystematic, that such ambiguities remained profoundly embedded in his words.

Thus it was to a large extent due to Paul that the doctrines of dualism, so horrifying to the orthodox, rose to a tremendously vigorous life among the generations that lay ahead. Simon Magus, mentioned in *Acts*,[46] was called the founder of this heresy, and a deacon named Nicolaus of Antioch was said to have formulated the doctrine that the visible world was made not by God but by a 'demiurge'. In the second century AD there were great dualist churches such as those of Marcion and of Valentinus,* who claimed to have been taught by Paul's alleged pupil Theudas;[47] and the greatest church of them all, Manichaeanism, was established in about 240. There was a fundamental opposition in the universe, its founder Mani declared, between Light and Dark, two absolutely different eternal substances: at the beginning, Darkness had invaded Light, and Adam, from whom our corrupted selves are descended, contained a portion of both. Manichaeans frequently quoted Paul's antithesis between spirit and sordid flesh. For nine years, too, this was the creed which Augustine embraced, because he found himself unable to believe that the world he saw around him could be God's creation: until finally he turned against the Manichaeans after all, concluding that it was 'a shocking and detestable profanity to make the wedge of darkness sunder the very nature of God.'[48] Besides, if Satan, in the guise of a demiurge, created the world, how and why does the good which, in addition to evil, we still see around us manage to survive in such a corrupt place? And so he receded from Paul's bold speculations to a more completely obedient monotheism.

Religious thinkers have been struggling with the same dilemma ever since. To Luther it seemed that, although this *is* a monotheistic world, in which Satan could be described as 'the mask disguising the absence of God', nevertheless the two powers are locked in a struggle to mount the same horse: the human will. There are two contrasting supernatural spheres, and continual, bitter, strife rages between their masters. 'I must always drum and hammer and force and drive in this distinction between the two kingdoms . . . For the Devil himself never ceases cooking and brewing up the two kingdoms together.' Later, Cardinal John Henry Newman, gazing upon this gigantic struggle, saw that it had been all too faithfully mirrored and imitated by the hostilities between many disputing Christian sects; and he deplored 'that vast Catholic body broken into many fragments by the power of the Devil.' Karl Gustav Jung, however, found the Devil 'a most valuable and acceptable psychic possession.' And the Devil never did a better stroke, it was said, than when he persuaded men to disbelieve in him.[49]

Paul did not display any such disbelief, choosing instead, like others in the ancient world, to see him as a truly existent prime manifestation of the horrific force of evil. The eloquence with which he conjured up this picture aroused conflicts that continued for centuries. What is still important, however, today is his utterly clear-sighted, emphatic recognition that the world is corrupt. And equally significant is his unambiguous resolve that this situation must, as a matter of imperative necessity, be cured. But he believed that what all Jews regarded as the cure, the Torah or Law of Moses, was no cure at all.

2. *The Need for Total Change*

Where Paul sharply differed from his fellow-Jews was not in his belief that the world was evil, a belief which they fully shared, but in his assertion that this state of affairs could not, under any circumstances whatever, be remedied by the Jewish Law. For even if the heterogeneous Judaism of the time held room for reservations on this subject,[1] it was the general Jewish belief that, although the world had been incessantly sinful ever since Adam, careful observance of the Law – including circumcision, and obedience to all the complex regulations concerning dietetic and ritual correctness which minutely regulated daily life – would ultimately cause righteousness to prevail.[2] Paul, however, found himself wholly unable to agree that this could be correct. Such an alienation from his own Jewish background was particularly remarkable because notwithstanding it he persistently continued, and continued for the rest of his life, to make the most careful use in his preachings and teachings of the Old Testament, just like his Jewish contemporaries, in order to display how the scriptures had been, and were being, fulfilled. And yet at the same time he rejected these scriptures in their most essential and insistent claim, their claim to be mankind's ultimate solution.

It is often supposed, because the stories told both by himself and by *Acts* encourage such a view, that this assurance only came upon him suddenly at the moment of his conversion, in a flash. But many others have disagreed. Among them is Samuel Sandmel, who writes:

It is not his Christian convictions which raise the Law as a problem for him, but rather it is his problem with the Law that brings him ultimately to his Christian convictions . . . We quite frequently encounter the view that his nullification of the Law of Moses was the concession which (after his conversion) he made in order to gain converts among the pagans; to re-phrase this vulgarly, Paul was offering a reduced rate to entice customers.[3]

This view, Sandmel continues, he cannot accept; and in adhering to the opposite opinion, and attributing Paul's gradual rejection of the Law to the period before he was ever converted to Christianity at all, he is surely right.

For one thing, Sandmel's conclusion would fit in best with the experience of psychologists, who have concluded that such conversions and the vivid visions which accompany them are generally the sequel and outcome of more or less prolonged earlier periods of anxiety and tension. And so it was with Paul. Even while he, still ostensibly the devout Jew, actively continued to persecute deviations from Jewish orthodoxy, he was doing so under the growing, increasingly harrowing knowledge that for himself, too, just as much as for those he was persecuting, such orthodoxy had become totally insufficient. For the world, according to his belief, was such a completely and desperately bad place that the Law seemed impotent to effect its rescue.

At different points in his Letters, he gives various reasons for this conviction. The Law, he conceded, was useful enough for the purpose of identifying and classifying offences. 'It was added to make wrong-doing a legal offence.'[4] But while performing this secondary task, he maintains, it fails utterly to remove the evil inclination. Certainly, it promotes consciousness of sinful actions: 'except through Law I should never have become acquainted with sin.'[5] But it follows therefrom, Paul startlingly continues, that by creating a consciousness of sin the Torah, far from diminishing the presence of sin in the world, actually increases it, and *multiplies* law-breaking.

> For example, I should never have known what it was to covet, if the Law had not said, 'Thou shalt not covet.' Through that commandment sin found its opportunity, and produced in me all kinds of wrong desires. In the absence of Law sin is a dead thing.

And, 'where there is no Law, there can be no breach of Law.'[6] Here Paul is not merely asserting, as commentators attempt to suggest, that the Jewish Law is a sort of hot fomentation to bring the poison of sin to the surface. For he is openly declaring that this Torah, which is meant to forbid and control sin, instead actually provokes it because of the fatal fascination of the forbidden thing – a phenomenon long since recognized in the story of Adam and Eve. Augustine, after a period when Paul's attack on the Jewish scriptures caused him dismay, became greatly stimulated by this view, recalling the pleasure he himself had experienced as a boy while stealing pears from a pear-tree, merely because he knew it was forbidden: 'I picked them simply to be a thief.'[7] 'Gainsay and the blood's on fire,' said a character in one of Mary Webb's novels. The same impulse to do what one is told not to do is stressed in Jung's teaching of the 'Shadow' – the subversive element within the soul, the rebel self which makes one want to stand up in the middle of a concert hall or theatre during the performance and shout, 'Fire!'

True, Paul denies that he is actually identifying the Torah with sinfulness. 'Is the Law identical with sin? Of course not.'[8] Nevertheless, he goes much farther in his criticisms of the Law, apparently, than Jesus ever had; and by so doing he denies the need, or importance, of the only ethical code the Jews possessed. Indeed, he is actually declaring that this code does more harm than good! True, that impression is contradicted, seemingly, by the careful moral directions which he offers in other passages. Yet his depreciation of the Jewish Law remains on record; and it has caused Jews throughout many centuries to regard him as the arch-apostate of all time. As we shall see later, his attitude is not purely negative, because he has something – something in his view infinitely superior – to substitute in the Law's place. Yet his rejection of the antique, venerated set of rules by which all his co-religionists lived and had lived was revolutionary beyond measure.

To justify this sensational rejection, he brings forward other points as well. One of them, calculated to appeal directly to those versed in the Jewish tradition, is that Abraham, who was the traditional founder of Israel and its monotheism and was regarded as *the* righteous man, managed perfectly well to win the goodwill of God *by his faith alone*,[9] before the Mosaic Law ever existed at all: so the Law cannot be regarded as indispensable for the purpose,[10] and its demotion is merely a return to the original system or covenant granted by God to Moses' ancestor Abraham – but frustrated by subsequent generations.

Paul's next argument to justify the shelving of the Torah is an even more curious one. A Jew, he complains, is required to believe that salvation needs *perfect* conformity with these rules at all points.

Those who rely on obedience to the Law are under a curse; for Scripture says, 'A curse is on all who do not persevere in doing everything that is written in the Book of the Law.'[11]

That purports to be a quotation from the book of *Deuteronomy*.[12] It is, in fact, doubtful whether the original Hebrew version of the passage, or the Greek (Septuagint) version either, had contained the word 'everything'. Nevertheless, Paul felt able to use the passage to make the point he wanted to emphasize. This is based on the commonsense hypothesis that to fulfil all the Law is manifestly impossible for anyone, because 'our lower nature robbed it of all potency'[13] – owing to our propensity to sin, the flesh is too weak to offer complete obedience. Since that is so, and since in any case the scriptures contain so much which, in the course of time, had become outdated, irrelevant and inoperative, Paul saw the alleged injunction that one is accursed if one does not comply with every single regulation as both pointless and cruel: besides, he added, since it is impossible for any man or woman to comply totally with the Law, it cannot possibly be the exhaustive expression of the will of God. Later Jews, deploring this contention, have often maintained that it is based on fallacious assumptions. Even leaving aside the question of the exact text and interpretation of *Deuteronomy*, they deny that observance of the Law involves this rigorous antithesis between complete success and complete failure: God cannot, it is true, expect a perfect performance; a perfect effort is all he can expect. However, Paul employed the argument (in the form of a reminder that no individual can possibly avoid doing wrong) as another of his demonstrations of the incapacity of the Jewish Law to operate effectively as a destroyer of the evil which is rampant in the world.

Jews also complain that he is extremely unfair in his use of the word 'Law'. For he shifts his ground continually and assigns to it, in different passages, a number of considerably divergent meanings. He is helped in these shifts by the Greek Bible he usually had in front of him, the Septuagint, for whereas the Hebrew term 'Torah' went far beyond the merely legalistic significance denoted by the word 'law' – since it embraces also instruction and revelation and all the aspects of God's Covenant with Moses – the Greek translation *nomos*, simply meaning 'law', permits the narrower interpretation: thus encouraging Paul's attack on the whole concept, an attack which takes the form, sometimes, of a distinction between the Law of Moses and the Law of Nature, or between laws and ideals.

Moreover, he equivocates in his definition of what scriptural books this Law, this *nomos* of which he is speaking, represents. At times he duly uses the word to refer to the first five books of the Old Testament, the Torah (in accordance with the usual definition of that term) or Pentateuch.[14] Or he may employ *nomos* to define the Pentateuch starting only from Chapter Twelve of *Exodus*, where the legalistic section begins. Or it can mean the whole of the Old Testament.[15] In a single chapter of *Romans* alone, the seventh, 'Law' is used in a bewildering variety of senses. Origen uncomfortably conceded that he could find six divergent meanings of the word in the Pauline Letters. He explained this on the somewhat curious grounds that Paul (like Jesus himself according to certain commentators) was desirous of concealing truths from the merely flippant. To others, however, it seemed, and still seems, that he was shifting his ground to suit his argument, in a manner not far removed from casuistry.

But, if so, it was casuistry in a passionately sincere cause, for Paul, seeing the inability of the Law to eliminate or even in his view diminish the sinfulness of the world, had concluded that it was a failure. One reason why it failed, he felt, was because it did not bring human beings into direct relation with God. He expressed this point in terms of two current beliefs, that demons and angels were God's intermediaries with mankind, and that Moses, too, had acted as his intermediary in the gift of the Law. For this Law, he says, 'was promulgated through angels, and there was an intermediary: but an intermediary is not needed for one party acting alone, and God is One.'[16] Of this sentence there have been nearly three hundred interpretations. But its general drift is fairly clear. According to a Jewish tradition based on the Greek version of *Deuteronomy*,[17] the angels were the instruments by whom the Law was given at Sinai. This idea had no doubt been meant, originally, to make the Law more glorious; but Paul employs the argument in the contrary sense, to make it *less* glorious and mark its inferiority. And as for the other intermediary, Moses, he had been human, and Paul claims that this use of a human mediator was another element that weakened the sanctity of the Jewish code.

Against the legal covenant of Sinai with its mediator and its two contracting parties, Paul sets the oneness and majesty of God declaring his promise. Such grandeur Paul could not find in the Law, and he says so with great force: lacking the Spirit which alone can give life, 'the written Law condemns to death.'[18] Legalism (which he chose to

49

regard as the chief characteristic of the Torah) is powerless to strike off the fetters of sin with which men are enslaved. For, as Paul adds, quoting the substance of a Psalm,[19] such attempts to be good without God cannot possibly succeed: 'no human being can be justified in the sight of God for [merely] *having kept the Law*.'[20] He therefore believed with the deepest conviction that, in order to end the reign of sin, the claims of the Law to be a fully sufficient guide must be rejected. Mankind, he declared, must instead seek a *direct* relationship with God himself.

For a man who had hitherto made the persecution of deviants from the Law the purpose of much of his adult life, it was a harrowing conclusion. Its outcome was that he himself now felt impelled to join the ranks of those he had persecuted. He was challenging his inherited Judaism at its most central and fundamental point. The patriotic, national aspects of the Law no longer appealed to him. For he, weighed down by the continued dominant presence of evil in the world, was thinking in different and wider terms. The domination by evil had to be stopped, and the Law could not stop it. Nothing, Paul now felt, could stop it except the direct intervention of God, in order to turn history out of all its accustomed courses. These conclusions, it would appear, had grown gradually and formidably in Paul's mind while he was still working for the Jews against the followers of Christ. And then, suddenly, in a single terrifying moment the acute tension exploded and Paul was seized with the overwhelming conviction not merely that God would intervene directly to put an end to the regime of evil, but that *this was just what he had already done*, in actual fact and a very short time ago.

III

The First Act of Rescue

1. The Coming of the Messiah

The direct action by God, rescuing mankind from the disastrous age-long rule of evil, seemed to Paul to have taken place through his sending Jesus to earth. For Paul, in the course of his profound mental and emotional crisis, came to acknowledge Jesus as the instrument of this revolutionary intervention infinitely, the most decisive event of all time.

Paul was able to accept Jesus because he saw him as the Messiah, the Anointed One: the Saviour whose coming had long been awaited by the Jews. The history lying behind this Jewish conviction went back at least as far as *Daniel*, which had been written two centuries earlier. This book presented a collection of legendary popular stories about a Jew of that name, allegedly attached to the Babylonian court at a date five hundred years before the time of writing. Although the tales were attributed discreetly to this remote epoch, Daniel's salvation from the den of lions and the rescue of his three companions from the fiery furnace were intended to refer to the current oppressions of King Antiochus Epiphanes, the Greek monarch of the Seleucid dynasty under whose rule Palestine was suffering at the time when *Daniel* was written.

The book was written to offer hope: everything will come right in the end. And this insistence was elaborated in recognition of the problem, constantly in the minds of the Jews, discussed in the last chapter: why do the unrighteous flourish? Why, although God is omnipotent, do sin and crime prevail? *Daniel's* answer, based to some extent on earlier scriptures, was: do not worry; a Liberator will appear in the near future, when the end of the world is about to come. That final moment will be heralded by 'the appearance of one anointed [i.e. the Messiah], a prince'[1]; and Daniel apparently identifies him (though this is disputed) with the Son of Man or 'One Like a Man', who will take over the rulership.[2] The Jews readily thought in corporate terms, and Daniel may have envisaged the Son of Man as symbolizing their entire Elect Community. Yet the concept was soon interpreted, instead, as foretelling the visitation of a single individual, and a Redeemer; and the herald Messiah was seen in a similar light.

The same themes reappear, at an uncertain date, in the *Similitudes of Enoch* (see *Enoch**), in which once again there is reference to the Son of Man: and now he is more clearly envisaged as an individual Saviour, and as the awaited Messiah himself who had already, moreover, been chosen by God for this role before the world had ever begun.[3] This Messiah of the years following the Old Testament was generally thought of by the Jews as a messenger who would deliver God's final words to Israel at the end of time. He was also the annihilator of the mighty upon earth. With a sidelong glance at Israel's oppressors, the Greeks and later the Romans, faith was placed in his miraculous appearance to lead the hosts of heaven against the kings of the world. At Qumran* there are references to the coming Man[4] but more often to a mysterious Teacher of Righteousness, or Righteous Teacher, a priest and recipient of divine revelation.[5] This Teacher, originally, is quite likely to have been a historical human being who was the founder of Qumran, or at least one of its honoured leaders; and subsequently his memory was cherished by his successors.[6] Later, however, the Teacher, though never regarded as in any sense divine, was probably associated in the minds of the devotees with the *future* Redeemer who was expected to emerge at the end of the world. However, it was also declared at Qumran, with scriptural echoes, that there will not be one Messiah but two,[7] a high-priest of the ancient high-priestly stock, and, below him, a lay king of the royal house of David, to whom, in *II Samuel*, God had prophesied that his descendants would reign for ever:[8] and these Messiahs will be preceded by a prophet who may, or may not, have been interpreted as a future reincarnation of the Teacher of Righteousness.

Messianic ideas, then, were very much in the Palestinian air. There were a number of Jewish religious leaders during the first centuries BC and AD who attracted Messianic or quasi-Messianic hopes, claiming or being claimed by their followers to possess the powers of prophets, healers and exorcists, which they had received by a divine call from God their Father. Such, for example, in the first century AD, was Hanina ben Dosa in Galilee; and there had been Honi the Circle-Drawer (first century BC) and others as well in various regions of Palestine.[9] Among certain of these 'charismatic' religious leaders, particular veneration was centred upon John the Baptist, who was credited with Messianic status by his disciples. When he died they pronounced him to have been raised from the dead, and the tradition of his Messiahship persisted for centuries.[10]

Later, the *Gospel according to St John* explicitly denied that John the Baptist had claimed to be the Messiah,[11] for the Gospels were written in praise of one whom he had baptized, Jesus, who taught and preached in Galilee and Jerusalem in about AD 28–30 (?); and since Jesus was the Messiah, then clearly the same could not be said of John the Baptist. Whether Jesus proclaimed himself to be the Messiah is very uncertain. But at all events he was identified as such by his followers in terms charged with a new and profound emotion, either in his lifetime or very soon after his death. He had been crucified by Roman provincial authorities in Jerusalem, who were acting in collaboration with, or at the request of, the Jewish high-priest and council (Sanhedrin*). But even though he suffered a criminal's death, Jesus' disciples persisted in declaring him the Messiah.

By Jews, the awaited Messiah and the Teacher of Righteousness had never been thought of as God; this would have been inconceivable since the concept of a *second* God could not possibly be reconciled with their monotheism. 'Hear, O Israel,' declared Moses, 'the Lord is our God, one Lord:'[12] in the Shema, which is recited at the beginning of synagogue services, this is the fundamental sentence.

Paul, declaring his belief in the Messiahship of Jesus, did not hail him as the Son of Man – though this was a designation, many think, which Jesus had especially favoured for himself.[13] What Paul declared instead, not altogether abandoning yet somewhat straining the Jewish framework, was that Jesus Christ was not God, but *the Son of* God. It is not unlikely that some of Jesus' followers hailed him by this same designation in his lifetime, though he probably did not claim the title for himself. But Paul shows no such hesitations. 'God sent his own son';

'God chose to reveal his son to me and through me.'[14] This Sonship, however, was not to be taken too literally; it was a metaphor describing a concept not of this world. It could not and did not involve any supposition of a physical or family kinship. For it was 'on the level of the spirit,' and Jesus was not born but *declared* Son of God.[15] Certain contradictions in the metaphor remain unresolved. For Jesus is called the eldest among a large 'family' of brothers[16] – the family being the faithful. Yet, with much more emphasis, he is also God's *only* son.[17]

To the Jews, such formulations obviously implied a grave danger, since it was hard to believe that Paul was not proclaiming the Son of God to be in some sense a second God, which was unimaginable and shocking. It was true that, in the Torah, God had sometimes been defined as the Father,[18] seeing that all Jews, sometimes all mankind, were called the children of God; though this also, on occasion, could be narrowed down to human beings adopted by God for a special mission. It was also true that God, in the second *Psalm*, had said, 'You are my son; this day I become your father'[19]; and it was in the light of such texts that the awaited Messiah was subsequently hailed as the Son of God, though the term is used as metaphorically by the *Psalms of Solomon** as by Paul.[20] Moreover, Simeon ben Shetah, a Pharisee who used the term 'Father in Heaven', compared the preacher Honi's reputed intimacy with God to a son-father relationship (just as Jesus' disciples may have spoken in the same way about him); and even the seemingly un-Jewish idea of a Son of God without an earthly father appears in the Jewish religious philosopher Philo.[21] Yet in the interests of avoiding a possible breach of monotheism, the Jews felt much more general sympathy for the rabbinic commentator who declared that a Son could *not* be ascribed to the Holy One at all.[22]

By the time the Gospels (or their sources) were being composed, certain developments in the Christian way of thinking were on the way. For although it was still possible to say that we are all God's children, the idea that Jesus was *the* Son of God had not only gained strength, but was now being expressed in terms of literal sonship of God with no earthly father at all[23]: the designation was particularly used in connection with his miracles and exorcisms which were the most popular part of the traditions associated with his career.

As for Paul, he was at least dimly and occasionally aware of the peril he was running – which was that people would say he was supposing the existence of two Gods. Moreover, those who accuse him of falling into this trap cannot be entirely satisfied by the methods he uses to extricate himself. Sometimes he seeks to avoid the snare by apparently identifying Christ with God, as a *single* divine entity. True, he never explicitly and categorically declares that they are the same, as his commentators later asserted he had intended to do, since that was the doctrine which they themselves favoured. Yet Paul does pronounce Jesus' nature to be divine,[24] implying not that he was a separate deity but that he shared the divinity of God; and indeed in one passage 'God the Father' and 'our Lord Jesus' both govern a verb which is not plural but singular, as though these are two ways of describing the one deity.[25] Paul also declares 'that at the name of Jesus every knee should bow – in heaven, on earth, and in the depths, and every tongue confess, "Jesus Christ is Lord".'[26] Yet this indication of supreme Godhead is immediately followed by a sort of confused denial: for this confession is to be made 'to the glory of God the Father.'

Here, then, is a distinction, after all, between God and Jesus, and elsewhere, in apparent contradiction to the utterances quoted above, the same distinction is put forward quite explicitly. 'For us there is one God the Father . . . and one Lord, Jesus Christ.'[27] Yet here, with the assistance of a further misunderstanding because the Hebrew terms for God are less abstract than the Greek *theos* sometimes can be, we are right back with what the Jews so particularly disliked. For unless there is a clear understanding that Jesus was human – and Paul said that he was not – these words, by claiming the unheard-of *deification* of a Messiah, precisely involve the breach of monotheism of which Jewish thought was most afraid. Thus Eliezer-ha-Kappar attacked Yeshu-ha-Nasri (Jesus) for declaring that he was God himself; and this blasphemy of calling himself God remained the gist of the Jewish accusation against him for hundreds of years to come.

Paul, in these passages, remains ambiguous and self-contradictory about the relationship between God and Jesus. A remark in *Philippians*, which might at first sight seem to present us with a firmer indication of his viewpoint, does not provide this help after all because its meaning turns out to be by no means clear. 'The divine nature was his [Jesus Christ's] from the first,'[28] says Paul, and according to one interpretation he goes on to say, 'yet he did not think to snatch at equality with God'; but these words may also mean 'yet he did not prize his equality with God', which gives a directly opposite impression. Apart from this controversial utterance, Paul's most decisive definition declares that Christ 'is the very image of God'.[29] The same thought is considerably elaborated in *Colossians*: 'He [Jesus Christ] is the image of invisible God. In him everything in heaven and earth was created . . . In him the complete being of God, by God's own choice, came to dwell . . .'[30] It is in Christ, then, that the complete being of the Godhead dwells embodied. However, *Colossians* cannot, with absolute certainty, be regarded as conveying Paul's exact thinking and phraseology: passages like this look like a working over and working up of his original words.

Nevertheless, there remains his certainly authentic statement that Christ 'is the very image of God'. Paul may have meant by this that Jesus was not himself a divine being, but a human being whose body a divine entity had occupied. But there is no certainty that this was what he had in mind. Did he wish to signify by the term 'image' that Jesus Christ was divine or human, and if the former, as would seem the more natural sense of the phrase, is he not after all suggesting that in some sense there are two Gods instead of one, which is anathema to the Jews, who believe in one single, supreme deity?

These were questions about his teaching which deeply worried subsequent generations. Yet they do not seem to have caused great anxiety to Paul himself. He is concerned with the function rather than the nature of Jesus Christ, whose position in relation to God does not appear to him, as far as we can see, to present any theoretical difficulty or any threat to monotheistic doctrine. Is there a *gulf* between God and Christ which needs to be bridged, or complete *identity* between them, which needs to be explained? Paul shies away from both problems. When the Swiss theologian Karl Barth complained of a lack of unified experience and unified thinking in Paul's concept of Christ, he was right.

It was a lack which among Christians during the years to come prompted countless controversies, so-called heresies and refutations of those heresies, in addition to the Jewish detestation which Paul's failure to allay suspicions that he was accepting a second God inevitably brought down upon his head. Yet he himself felt he had done a great deal better than the Jews had; since, in terms of his own choosing, he had reported and expounded the existence of that medium or mediator between God and man which the lofty, unapproachable character of the Jewish God demanded, and which the demons and angels who had hitherto been envisaged as intermediaries (and whom Paul himself was content to retain in a less central role) failed to provide in any intellectually or emotionally convincing fashion.

How far the various ideas about the Messianic character of Jesus had already developed during the relatively few years, perhaps no more than five, between the Crucifixion of Jesus and the conversion of Paul, is one of the most fascinating and insoluble problems of history. But at all events Paul came to regard Jesus as *Christos*, the anointed or Messiah, and continually speaks of him by this designation. It was a purely Jewish concept despite its Greek translation, and cannot have made the exposition of Christianity to non-Jews any easier. The idea that had to be conveyed to them, and to the Jews as well for that matter, was startling, despite all its roots in tradition. For there had been a change of gigantic significance. The Jewish belief in a Messiah *still to come* had exercised widespread attraction. Yet it paled completely before the allure of a Messiah who had actually appeared on this earth already, within living memory – indeed in the immediate past. This, as events would show before long, was a sensation: a claim with which none of the pagan 'mystery' religions*, with their far remoter saviours, could possibly compete.

Nevertheless, Paul again proves disconcerting. For having once established the truth of this earthly visitation, he astonishes us – if our knowledge of Christianity is based on the Gospels – by preferring to emphasize the spiritual, non-earthly aspects of Jesus instead. And what is most surprising of all to those familiar with modern ideas of Christianity is to discover that Paul, although he recognized that Jesus had come to earth in human form,[31] believed that he had never been the Messiah in his lifetime, but only became this when he was dead. Or rather, after his life on earth was over, he was proclaimed 'the Son of God': 'he was declared Son of God by a mighty act *in that he rose from the dead*.'[32] And that may be the reason for Paul's reluctance to call Jesus by the old Jewish designation Son of Man, which might appear, to some, too reminiscent of his human life on earth – now wholly superseded.

This insistence that Jesus was only recognized as the Messiah after his death and resurrection was reversed by the writers of the Gospels. Thus *Mark* (perhaps depending on earlier sources) already suggests that he had received initiation as Son of God at the very outset of his mission, when he was baptized by John the Baptist[33], (and other Gospels stress that he had always been this). The difference is symptomatic of a very profound contrast between the interpretations of Jesus offered by the Gospel writers and by Paul. For, in sharp contradiction to the Gospels,

Paul's allusions to all the manifold events which their tradition attributes to Jesus' lifetime are extraordinarily few and sparse. Paul knows that Jesus was born of a woman,[34] belonged to David's stock,[35] bore the likeness of a human being, ate the Last Supper, was betrayed, and suffered Crucifixion. *But that is about all*: it is a singularly meagre crop in comparison with the later rich harvest of the Gospels, with all their incidents and miracles and healings.

In regard to Jesus' teaching, which those Gospels were likewise to record (with the exception, for the most part, of *Mark*) the situation is the same, or worse. Certainly, the injunctions offered by Paul, on his own account, have points in common with that teaching. But there are divergences as well, and in any case a historian must hesitate before pronouncing that Paul derived the resemblances from the Gospel tradition rather than vice versa, since the Gospels, whatever their sources, were written later than his Letters. More remarkable, however, is the fact that throughout all those Letters there is only one specific allusion to all the many statements that were later attributed to Jesus, and that is a reference to a relatively subordinate point, his alleged opposition to divorce.[36] All the observations that Jesus was subsequently reported to have made about other matters, and all the characteristic parables that were to be ascribed to him by the Gospels, and all the controversies which he was said to have undertaken with the Pharisees and scribes, receive no direct mention from Paul whatsoever. He shows, as has often been pointed out, an *almost complete lack of interest* in the words and acts of Jesus.[37]

This has caused theologians and others throughout the ages a good deal of shock. And the shock is amply justified. As Jung remarked, 'Paul hardly ever allows the real Jesus of Nazareth to get a word in.' For this arresting state of affairs, two alternative explanations are possible. The first is that Paul *did not know* the facts the Gospels ascribed to Jesus' career, either because these events had never happened at all and were only invented subsequently, or because, although they were true, they had never come to his notice. The second possible explanation is that Paul knew all about these occurrences, including the sayings attributed to Jesus, but he did not think it necessary or desirable to mention them, because his readers already knew them as well as he did, so that this familiar material need not be brought to their notice all over again. There is a good deal to be said in favour of both these views. In support of the first it does seem hard to believe that, if Paul had known the many Gospel stories of Jesus, he would not have said something more about them. But the second explanation, too, is not altogether without plausibility, especially as Paul himself, on occasion, reminds his readers he is telling them of things they already know, or ought to know. Now, at first sight, the two explanations may well seem mutually exclusive. Nevertheless, the likelihood is rather that both of them contain part of the truth. Paul probably did *not*, in fact, know nearly all the things that were said about Jesus in the Gospels: whether they were already current and he just did not know them, or whether some of them had not yet been invented, is a matter beyond the range of this book; but what he *did* know, as far as it went, did not necessarily seem to him worth recording, because his readers themselves, being Christians, were already not without knowledge of some of these matters on their own account.

But in any case this question of how much he knew about Jesus, though vitally important, does not touch upon the deepest roots of Paul's ways of thought. For the essential fact, it appears from his own writings, was rather that he just did not feel very *interested* in the events and teaching activities of Jesus' career: he did not consider them particularly relevant. In this respect, he appears in marked contrast to the authors of the Gospels, and to the vast majority of subsequent Christians. So it is an aspect of his thinking that has to be considered in further detail.

Paul himself offered an important, though difficult, explanation on the subject. Our understanding of men, he has been saying, can no longer be based on their outward lives: and indeed, 'even if we knew Christ after the flesh, we do not know him like that any longer.'[38] The New English Bible recasts this as follows: 'With us worldly standards have ceased to count in our estimate of any man; even if they once counted in our estimate of Christ, they do not do so any longer.' Paul is not asserting here that he had known Jesus Christ personally before the Crucifixion. His point is a different one. What he is arguing is that the *important* kind of knowledge about Jesus is not a worldly, fleshly kind, based on human, secular standards. Jesus as a figure of history – the aspect of him which was to seem to many devotees so much more attractive than the remoteness of pagan saviours – is not his prime concern. True, it could alternatively be argued that 'what Paul is repudiating is not a fleshly kind of Christ but a fleshly kind of knowledge'.[39] But he is repudiating *both*. The Christ he reveres is not to be apprehended by earthly standards from a human point of view, because it is not towards his earthly life that our attention must primarily be directed.

That is what Paul meant by knowledge 'after the flesh'. Far from claiming to have known Jesus personally when he was alive, he is asserting a knowledge about him superior in quality to anything that mere eyewitnesses of his life upon earth could ever claim for themselves. For he had not been among their number, and was anxious to assert his superiority over them. He does not, therefore, think of himself as a disciple of the historical Jesus – as indeed he had not been – but a man commissioned by him after his death; an event and a timing which relegated the actual details of his teaching, during his former earthly life, to comparative unimportance in Paul's eyes.

The whole of Christian theology from the Crucifixion to the present day could be described in terms of an incessant series of endeavours to strike a right balance between the divinity and humanity of Jesus; and any man or woman who, in the opinion of the religious authorities of the time in which he or she lived, seemed to wander in either direction from what they considered to be the central path, was likely to be denounced as the propounder or follower of a heresy. Yet those who denounced such alleged deviations, although they frequently cited Paul, could in fact derive relatively little comfort or certainty from the varying attempted definitions he himself had from time to time thrown out.

The first really significant endeavour to find out what he had been trying to say was the theory of Docetism. This, upheld by Marcion* and the *Gospel of Peter** and Bardesanes,* maintained that, since God could not conceivably have become incarnate in a physical human body, the only body Jesus can have possessed was not a physical one at all, but only an apparent or phantom one, so that his birth, suffering and death were all purely phantasmal and unreal. There was nothing at all human, either, about the concept of Christ in *Revelation* as a terrifying celestial rider on a white horse. Indeed, in early Christian literature in general, it was not for the most part the human, humanitarian Jesus – so attractive to the nineteenth century – who was generally stressed, but the potentate of superhuman might. Nevertheless, Ignatius,* *I* and *II John*, Irenaeus* and Tertullian* all saw that Docetism presented a grave peril to the delicate balance on which Christianity depended for its life. And so they rallied to controvert it by stressing that Jesus' human shape had been authentic.

After the Roman Empire became officially Christian in the early fourth century AD, the battle continued to rage with even greater ferocity. While the Nestorians* divided Jesus' manhood so thoroughly from his Godhead that he became two persons instead of one, the Monophysites and the Monothelites harked back to the old idea that he had not truly been man. At the opposite extreme the Arians, once again citing Paul, pointed out that he had *not* in so many words declared Christ to be God; they themselves, therefore, declared that he was distinct from and inferior to the deity. Amid savage controversy this definition was rejected in AD 325 by the Council of Nicaea, which pronounced that the Son is 'of one substance with the Father', thus declaring him to be all that the Father is – completely and wholly divine. The ruling of the Council was supported by official churchmen, although later theologians, such as Augustine,[40] recognized the intense difficulties still involved in reaching any understanding of the human side of Christ.

Paul himself was too towering a figure to be rejected permanently as an arch-heretic. Nevertheless, his views, unless they could be drastically reinterpreted, undoubtedly presented a picture of Jesus which in the eyes of subsequent generations seemed not nearly human enough. For not only, as we have seen, had Paul described him in terms which in varying degrees seemed to identify him with God – or even, as the Jews complained, to make him into a second God – but he also minimized and ignored the facts of this Saviour's mortal existence upon earth. It was little use for the later Church to declare that Paul's words 'Jesus is the Lord' or 'The Lord is Jesus'[41] indicated a proper recognition of this humanity. For the fact still remained that he had seen his Lord primarily as a divine figure. True, he recognized that Jesus had been brought into humanity for a time. But according to Paul's interpretation, as the German theologian Rudolf Bultmann rightly said, he tended to 'lose his identity as an individual human figure'.

However, Paul endeavoured to explain his elusive point of view further. One idea he explored was that of emptying or pouring out (*kenosis*). Although Jesus' nature was divine, we are told, 'he emptied himself, assuming the nature of a slave.'[42] This is an allusion to a passage of *II Isaiah*,[43] in which a mysterious 'Afflicted One' (of whom there will be more to say later) 'poured out his life to the death,' or, in the rendering of the New English Bible, 'made himself nothing'. This, however, is one of the concepts which have rightly contributed to a widespread belief that the Letters are by no means easy to understand. The idea, observed Dr William Barclay:

... baffles the mind and yet moves the heart. It baffles the mind to see how God could abandon his essential attributes and still remain God. We may make it a little easier for our minds to think of, if we say that in the Incarnation God empties himself of his purely metaphysical attributes, such as omniscience, omnipotence and omnipresence; but not of his moral attributes, his goodness, his justice and above all, his love ... For the heart [this idea] does set out, as no other doctrine does, the unimaginable sacrifice of love which God made in becoming man at all.[44]

Yet it cannot be quite maintained that these ideas of voluntary self-limitation, however welcome to subsequent theologians, were all specifically present in the mind and heart of Paul: though they provide a characteristic example of the somewhat puzzled excitement which one passage after another of his Letters has kindled throughout subsequent ages.

A further line of thinking became apparent in Paul's assertion that Jesus not only possessed a divine nature, but had possessed it *from the first*, before he ever appeared on the earth. This hypothesis of pre-existence is found in the passage of *Philippians* quoted above.[45] It is also elaborated in the *Letter to the Colossians*,[46] who were evidently in danger of undervaluing Christ, regarding him as only one of a number of possible intermediaries between God and mankind. But does this not contradict the *lateness* of his Sonship (p. 57)?

What [writes J. L. Houlden] are we to make of this difficult idea? In some passages it has more doctrinal value than in others. But in other passages, it seems to be frankly mythological, i.e. to be part of a way of speaking in dramatic terms about God and heaven as essentially continuous with life and conditions in this world, however immeasurably greater and more impressive and powerful ...

This theologically crude (though imaginatively impressive and moving) picture of Christ's pre-existence needs much qualification before it can contribute to a satisfactory doctrine about Christ's person ...[47]

The Jews had asserted the pre-existence of objects or men specially representative of God: the Temple, Jerusalem, the Sabbath and above all the Torah, and as we have seen, the awaited Messiah. However,

Paul's application of the same doctrine to Jesus met with a mixed reception. *Acts* never even hints at such a theory. But *John* restated it with celebrated eloquence,[48] and the writer of *Hebrews*, too, formulated the same concept vividly.[49] Origen, too, was impressed by this view. But he formulated it in terms that caused alarm. For Origen saw Jesus as a vision of the divine which, being eternally pre-existent, had already manifested itself in other forms at other times: so that he could be described as potentially multiple!

Paul's idea, then, like so many of his other ideas, was liable to various interpretations and misunderstandings. But he explained it, or elaborated upon it, by the further (and equally difficult) declaration that Jesus is pre-existent because he is God's *Wisdom*.[50] This was yet another way of explaining that Jesus fulfilled an intermediary role between God and mankind: it names him as a sort of appendage of God. And it does so in terms which the Jews, especially in times when Greek thought had seeped in, would understand, since this Divine Wisdom had long since become a Jewish conception. Already in the Old Testament and Apocrypha it was named as a functional, intermediate power operating as a quasi-personal associate of God in the creation of the universe and the history of Israel. Thus according to *Proverbs* the Lord created Wisdom at the beginning of his works, to be at his side each day.[51] In *Ecclesiasticus* it covers the earth like a mist, the special possession of the people whom the Lord had honoured, the covenant-book of God most High.[52] In the *Wisdom of Solomon* it is a fine mist rising from the power of God, a pure effluence from the glory of the Almighty.[53]

And so in an age feeling the need for some toning down of uncompromisingly remote monotheism, this was the lyrical formula on which Paul relied for his explanation of the pre-existence of Jesus Christ. By this association with a historical personage, the already familiar concept of the Divine Wisdom assumed a novel and personal significance, however strange it may seem to us, and however destructive of the human part of Jesus' nature, to see him as a pre-cosmic agent of the Creation.

In *Colossians* as in *John*, the term *Logos*, or Word or Message, is used to convey a similar notion; and this goes back to another phrase of Paul himself. 'Let the Word of Christ dwell among you in all its richness.'[54] The 'Word' of God in Hebrew stood for his irresistible sovereign will, just as in Greek the term signified the meaning and understandable order of the universe. Philo* called the Word the heavenly bread, the cup-bearer and the cup of God. But as Samuel Sandmel observes,

This is neither simple to explain nor to understand. Perhaps an example may clarify matters. There is an electric light within my room and it serves my needs. A power plant is located on the Ohio River about eight miles from my home; I have never visited it, for it is quite remote from me. I myself have no direct contact with the power plant, but only with the electricity which comes into my home; and within my home there are available the effects of what the power plant can supply.

Now let us imagine that the power plant occupies the place of God, who has been conceived of as remote from this world; the electricity entering into my home is an offshoot of the power plant. It is not the same as the power plant, but for me it serves in lieu of the power plant. So, in the time of Paul it was conceived by some that God Himself was remote from this world, but an aspect, or offshoot of God, was within the world, just as electricity is within my home.

This immanent ('within this world') aspect or offshoot of God is called by Philo and by others the 'Logos'. If you start with the belief that God is remote (like the power plant), you deal with or encounter God in the facet which is immanent (like the electricity in my home).[55]

Paul was reaching out, all the time, to find terms and means to express *relationship* with the deity, to use all his vivid powers of language and expression to bring the unapproachable somehow within reach. Yet all these varied conceptions – sonship, image, Wisdom, Word – still remain incomplete and unreal and irrelevant until they are brought into direct relation with what Paul believed to be far the most important event that had ever taken place: which was Jesus' death. And it is to this unique happening, and all the immense implications which Paul derived from it, that we now have to turn.

2. *The Relevance of Jesus' Death*

When the time came (after Paul's death) for the Gospels to be written, they duly stressed, drawing on whatever traditions were available to them, the Crucifixion of Jesus. But they also had a great deal to say about many episodes of his life. In Paul's Letters, on the other hand, there is overwhelming emphasis on Jesus' death, and about his life very little is said. He is the Messiah. But above all else, to Paul he is the martyred, suffering Messiah, who by his martyrdom rescued mankind from the abject evil in which it had been immersed since the time of Adam.

This assertion, which we owe to Paul much more than to anyone else, that Christ died on the cross to save us all, has become atrophied throughout the centuries by incessant repetition, unaccompanied, for the most part, by any adequate explanation (adequate to laymen at least) of an idea that is extremely hard to comprehend; and indeed, to people who have not been brought up in close familiarity with the tradition, the concept of Christ's death for our salvation seems plainly incredible and impossible to accept. Paul himself was well aware that this is so; for in *I Corinthians* he deliberately proclaimed its incredibility to anyone and everyone in his eastern Mediterranean world.

We proclaim Christ – yes, Christ nailed to the cross; . . . this is a stumbling block to Jews and folly to Greeks.[1]

Thus Paul declares the total, staggering paradox, with all the emphasis he can muster. The Hellenic world was familiar enough with 'saviour gods', but they had never been identified with historical individuals, and above all it seemed to the Greeks preposterous that anyone should be credited with the salvation of his followers when he had proved totally incapable of saving even himself. And as for the Jews, they supposed that the Messiah would be a conqueror of the world, not a condemned criminal[2] who had conquered nobody and nothing. For it was their general expectation that the Messiah would establish his triumphant kingdom on earth; indeed this is still expected in the most essential Hebrew prayer, the *'Blessing concerning David'* in the Eighteen Benedictions (apparently not later than the first century AD) in which the one and only reference to the Messiah is formulated in these terms of royal conquest. And immediately after Jesus' death, his disciples referred to their own depression and disappointment, because they too had hoped and believed that he was going to restore the Kingdom of Israel,[3] whereas what had happened was appallingly different.

Paul's Greek word in *I Corinthians* translated 'stumbling-block' (or snare or obstacle) is *skandalon*. And, indeed, that he should request the acceptance of such beliefs seemed, to many Jews, nothing short of a scandal. But Paul, whose mind worked in startling antitheses and contrasts, revelled in this shock, and found it immensely stimulating. It seemed to him that the desperately evil state of the world, which had persisted ever since Adam, could only be ended by something revolutionary; and he believed he had found it. As an answer to the problem, it seemed at first sight nothing short of unbelievable. But the problem was so vast that this is precisely what any answer had to be. The horrors of millennia had been broken by a single, unique, totally irregular event and act.

All the same Paul's proclamation did not fall on completely unprepared soil. True, since he enjoyed the fierce paradox so much, and felt that Christians, if they were to be true believers, needed it in all its starkness, he chose to present it as if it were entirely new. And he is right to point out that the concept of the Messiah dying the humiliating malefactor's death of crucifixion was absolutely no part of orthodox Jewish doctrine. Nevertheless, the Jews also possessed certain traditions foretelling that the Redeemer would meet a violent death – in battle. For this belief was encouraged by specific self-sacrifices by human beings in the past history of Israel. In particular, the Jewish nation had given martyrs to the Maccabean revolt against the Seleucid autocracy (see Maccabees*); and because suffering annuls sin,[4] their voluntary martyrdom in so great a cause appeared destined not only to achieve merit for themselves, but to operate vicariously and hasten on the arrival of universal salvation.[5] Similar speculations, too, were derived from pronouncements that the Messiah, son of Joseph or of Ephraim, would fulfil a text of *Zechariah*[*6] by dying on the final battlefield a martyr's death, whereby the gate would be thrown open to the Son of David. Emphasis was laid on significant passages of the *II Isaiah*, in which the writer envisages a 'suffering servant', standing apparently both for the personified community and for an expected individual destined to bring the community's mission to fulfilment: 'the chastizing he underwent is health to us,' and by his scourging we are healed,'[7] because he is chosen by God to be afflicted in order to provide salvation for others.

It was the Jewish belief in these vicarious torments which prepared the way for the idea that Jesus was not only the Messiah but also the suffering, martyred servant. And that was how the further conviction was born, with the scriptural support which was regarded as so indispensable, that the crucified Jesus was Messiah and martyr in one, the Messiah who was martyred for mankind.

In the immediately preceding century or two, evidence that the amalgamation of the Messiah and martyr and redeemer themes had already been proposed is not entirely absent. For example, Qumran documents such as the Hymn Scroll*[8] may refer to the expectation of a martyred Messiah. That is not entirely certain, but in any case, after Jesus had been crucified, his followers had the Old Testament texts to rely upon for his identification with this double range of ideas. Thus in *Acts* Peter is made to declare (somewhat stretching a point) that God 'had foretold in the utterances of all the prophets that his Messiah should suffer'[9]; while Paul, too, is reported in the same book as 'quoting texts of Scripture which he expounded and applied to show that the Messiah had to suffer'.[10]

When we turn back to his own Letters we find some confirmation that this is, in fact, what he had taught. For he was familiar with the interpretation of Jesus as a servant – 'a servant of the Jewish people to maintain the truth of God'[11]; 'who made himself nothing, assuming the nature of a slave'[12], and it was as servant or slave that he suffered death.

As A. T. Hanson rightly argues,

> One of the conclusions of our study must surely be to put a question mark against the assumption so widely held by New Testament scholars that the identification of Jesus with the Suffering Servant first meets us only in *Luke* and *I Peter*, and that it did not form part of the very earliest preaching. Paul, we must insist, looks on Jesus as the Suffering Servant.[13]

Thus the confluence of the two ideas, Suffering Servant and Messiah, is already complete in Paul's thought. It was a blend of overwhelming significance for the future, since it proved irresistibly attractive, first to the writers of the Gospels, and then to the world. 'If Christ had not suffered,' asks Malcolm Muggeridge, 'do you imagine that anyone would have paid the slightest attention to the religion he had founded?'[14] For unlike the expected Messiah of the Jews and the remoter saviours of other religions, not only had he actually appeared on earth, but he had appeared in sensational guise: not, after all, as one of those mere worldly conquerors, of whom the world had seen enough, but as a conqueror of a far more arresting kind, whose conquest had taken an extraordinary, unprecedented form. For he had suffered like humanity. Indeed, his suffering was *for* humanity's sake.

Paul's presentation of this exceedingly bold conception must now be considered.

> It is notorious that for any Jew the manner of the death of Jesus would be doubly repulsive . . . Not only was crucifixion the most abhorrent of all deaths because of its cruelty and shame, but for the Jew it also involved the curse of the Torah, the curse pronounced on 'every one that hangeth on a tree' [on a gibbet according to the New English Bible].[15] Although Christ died by Roman crucifixion Paul regards his death as on a tree – i.e. it was put

in a Jewish context by him and emphasized as something due to the rejection by the Jews.[16]

The passage in *Deuteronomy*, stating that everyone that hangs on a tree or gibbet is cursed, had at first probably meant that the dead body of a criminal hanging on a piece of wood contaminates the ground. Quoting this passage Paul writes that Christ, by undergoing Crucifixion, 'became for our sake an accursed thing'.[17] This is astonishing language. The death Jesus endured 'was not only a death of shame to Jew and Gentile alike (the death of a slave, a servant), but it also symbolized the fact that the one who hung there was willingly enduring the curse for us.'[18] And in the words of A. M. Hunter, 'We may not say, of course, that Christ was personally accursed, but we must say that he, as our representative, endured all that is involved in being a member of a doomed race.'[19] But perhaps that is to tone down unduly the deliberate harshness and ferocity of Paul's language. He wants to make the Crucifixion as frightful and scandalous a stumbling-block as he can. For only by so doing can he hope to bring out the full, momentous, earth-shaking magnitude of the change that this event brought about.

That it had done so he had no doubt whatever. We do not have the text of the *first* sermon on the subject of Christ's Crucifixion that Paul preached to the community at Corinth, but he tells us subsequently of the plain, concentrated urgency with which he had spoken to them on that earlier occasion.

As for me, brothers, when I came to you, I declared the attested truth of God without display of fine words or wisdom. I resolved that while I was with you I would think of nothing but Jesus Christ, Christ nailed to the Cross . . .

The doctrine of the Cross is sheer folly to those on their way to ruin, but to us who are on the way to salvation it is the power of God.[20]

For the Crucifixion had transformed the entire world: because Christ had died 'for our sake', 'for us', that is to say not instead of us, but on behalf of us. He is our Saviour in a sense the pagan religions never knew. 'He died for us, so that we, awake or asleep, might live in company with him,'[21] incorporated with Christ:[22] so that we shall be *in* Christ, as he continually reiterates. 'One man died for all.'[23] The total evilness of man's situation had received this equally enormous remedy through his death.

The pagan Celsus declared that the crucified Jesus, renewing our own lives, was an impossible belief for any thinking man. Paul, on the

other hand, once declared that, intensely hard though it is to understand, no man, once it had been explained to him in its full glory, ought
to be so bemused that he could miss seeing its immeasurable significance.
He blames the Christian community in Galatia for failing this test.
'You stupid Galatians! You must have been bewitched – you before
whose eyes Jesus Christ was openly displayed upon his cross!'[24]

Yet that is just one of those vivid paradoxes he delighted in, for he
would have agreed perfectly with the later pagan critic Celsus that a
'thinking man' could not possibly accept such a view of Jesus' redemptive death; that is, on any *usual* definition of what a thinking man was.
The Crucifixion was a grossly confounding event, the most confounding
reversal of expectation of all time, a fierce tragic mockery of all the
recognized conditions of human existence: 'a violent tyranny', Calvin
called it: an incomprehensible defiance, in Karl Barth's phrase, of every
correct and natural analogy. It was so grossly anomalous, and so repulsive, that it *had* to be explained, the glaring contradiction simply had to
be solved, and only an equally explosive, outrageous interpretation
could solve it.

'Pain,' said William Temple, Archbishop of Canterbury, 'is the great
binder of hearts.' Yet whatever could possibly be the links ordaining
that the pain of Jesus should have an effect, an overwhelmingly decisive,
revolutionary effect, upon ourselves? Again, death is a situation with
which all human beings can identify. Yet the physical death of Jesus
manifestly delivers no men or women from the prospect of their future
physical deaths. And the idea that it delivers anyone from 'spiritual'
death, either, seems at first sight unintelligible. 'O Death, where is your
victory? O Death, where is your sting?'[25] But *how* did Jesus' death
deliver us from death's sting, and give us life? How did the Crucifixion
conquer the world?

Paul's answer to this most searching of all questions is given in various
ways, at various levels. In the first place, though to us this inevitably
seems dated, he has to express himself in terms of the current belief that
the evil of the world had been operated and perpetuated by the hostile
demons and angels who were between God and man. Since the killing
of Jesus was the climax of all the evil acts of all time, its attribution to
the Jews is, at one point in Paul's writings, forgotten, and instead the
deed is ascribed to these demons and angels, 'the powers that rule the
world':[26] and by this assertion, lifting the death of Christ completely
out of its historical framework into a setting transcending time and

place, Paul intends to declare – taking the risk, once again, that he will be accused of believing in a dualist universe – that God, in Christ, laid himself open to the utmost that all the malevolent powers could do to him. But if the Crucifixion was the work of demons, it also disarmed them and made them impotent, so that later it became the most powerful of magical symbols. 'On that cross he discarded the cosmic powers and authorities like a garment; he made a public spectacle of them and led them as captives in his triumphal procession.'[27] (This was said by Paul, or his editor, to the members of the Christian community at Colossae, some of whom were in grave ideological danger of reducing Jesus to mere angel status.[28]) So the demons, the forces of Satan, were defeated, and a further idea developed too: it was *in order to* conquer him and them that the Son of God had become man. The Fathers carried this notion of victory over hostile powers to remarkable lengths.

Paul had explained the evil condition of mankind by the original sin of Adam, which had let the demons loose in the world and granted them their evil scope. And so it was as a second Adam, who superseded him, that Jesus Christ is envisaged. 'As in Adam all men die, so in Christ all will be brought to life.'[29] Adam had foreshadowed the Man who was to come. But, if the wrongdoing of that one man brought death upon so many, its effect is vastly exceeded by God's gift of that other one man, Jesus Christ.[30]

> A second Adam to the fight
> And to the rescue came.[31]

This second, contrasted Adam, namely Jesus Christ, replacing and far exceeding him – by obedience, in contrast to the disobedience of Adam – had led a new creation, reversing the stream of death and the entire direction of the human race.

But *how*, once again, did the Crucifixion exercise this overwhelming result? How did it make this contact with all or any human beings, bridging the gulf between transcendent God and earthly mankind?

One of Paul's replies was that Jesus' death had been a sacrifice, analogous to the sacrifices which were offered in the Temple at Jerusalem, and indeed directly superseding the Passover sacrifice[32], which was, he believed, abrogated by the Crucifixion. 'We have now been justified by Christ's sacrificial death . . . God designed him to be the means of expiating sin by his sacrificial death . . . Therefore, my brothers, I implore you by God's mercy to offer your very selves to him:

a living sacrifice.'[33] In consequence, there is stress on the blood he had shed, since in all sacrificial activity blood played a central part: since 'the life of a creature is in the blood'.[34] Thus the Passover Lamb, which had in ancient times saved the Jews from the visitation of death,[35] was very early depicted as the symbol of Jesus; and its blood was his.

Among the Gospels, *Mark*, like Paul, bears witness to the sacrificial meaning of Jesus' death.[36] To *John*, too, he is the Lamb of God.[37] But the idea was omitted by *Luke*,[38] and ignored by Ignatius, who became the father of official opinion; and as the second century progressed, the whole idea had receded. Modern critics, too, have often found it distasteful. Nietzsche called such sacrificial concepts a bloody phantasmagoria; H. G. Wells complained that Paul was reviving all the ancient horrors of religious bloodshed; and E. Bloch has recently attacked the Moloch-like God who demands the spilling of his own son's blood. However, Paul and his contemporaries found this sanguinary aspect of sacrifices less revolting than we do, not only for religious reasons, but because, at a time when modern butchers' shops were lacking, the sight of offal and blood from slain animals was too commonplace to arouse repulsion.

More fundamental is the intellectual objection that Paul leaves the significance of Jesus' sacrifice undefined and in the air. It was deemed necessary, we are told, to bring about salvation for mankind. But who demanded the sacrifice, or who was to be its recipient, is not made clear. Had Paul not thought this out fully?

The difficulty is to ascertain what in his opinion was the character of that sacrifice. Did he think of it as *propitiatory*, necessary to turn aside the anger of God justly roused by human sin; or as *expiatory* in the sense in which the atoning sacrifices of Judaism were expiatory, 'covering' sin or the sinner from the view of God; or as *penal* as though there fell upon Christ the punishment for all the sins of the world; or as somehow providing *satisfaction* for the honour of God outraged by sin, or vindicating the moral order which sin had defied?[39]

Each one of these explanations has been offered, and there is something in all of them: but perhaps expiation is often foremost in Paul's mind. This is the covering or blotting out of sin so that it is no longer a barrier between God and man. 'God designed Jesus to be the means of expiating sin (*hilasterion*) by his sacrificial death.'[40]

Now, this alleged claim by Jesus' followers that his death caused the remission of sins could find no answering echo in Jewish Law. It is true that Paul claimed that Jesus' death for our sins was 'according to the scriptures', with reference to *II Isaiah*'s Suffering Servant who was to 'bear the penalty of guilt' for many;[41] and the Maccabean martyrs, too, had been felt, as we have seen, to be contributing to the universal salvation.[42] Moreover, it is possible that one Jewish school of theological thought had developed a similar view of expiatory death from Abraham's plan to sacrifice his son Isaac.[43] Nevertheless, the idea that Christ's death brought about the cancellation of sins remained unacceptable to orthodox Jewish opinion, because it invalidated and destroyed that most essential of Jewish beliefs, God's free forgiveness of the penitent – and about penitence this Crucifixion doctrine had nothing to say.

It has therefore sometimes been felt, and not only by Jews, that its sweeping forgiveness of sins is destructive of morality.

It does not, of course, condone sin, but it almost encourages it by the offer of a free pardon. One of the deep yearnings of the religious man is for the certainty of forgiveness . . . Surely this certainty of forgiveness will encourage sin – a person will feel he can sin with impunity?[44]

'Of course not!' answered Paul, firmly.[45] Yet this possible catch in his argument has been explored with anxiety ever since. In the words of John Donne,

> Wilt thou forgive that sin which I did shun
> A year or two: but wallowed in, a score?
> When thou hast done, thou hast not done,
> For I have more.

Nevertheless, Donne concludes that Jesus' forgiveness of sins is real, and, because of its reality, his own anxieties of a lifetime are set at rest. By this means, even God's original condemnation of man, in the days of Adam, has been set into reverse and transformed into a blessing, 'to which,' as Karl Barth declared, 'we are allowed to submit, to our rich comfort'. And indeed, this belief has moved the world; it has become the very corner-stone of Christianity, and has changed innumerable people's lives. It changed John Wesley's, for example, when, as he declared with wonder, 'the assurance was given me that he had taken away *my* sins, even mine!' We are guilty and deserve death, believers tell themselves. But the penalty has been borne by another. We have been enslaved to sin. But now we are set free. We have failed to realize the extent of God's love. But the Cross has left us in no doubt of its supreme strength.

Paul saw mankind divided into hostile camps 'biting and devouring one another'.[46] But behind that internecine strife, he saw a worse estrangement – of men and women alienated from God, their common Father. However, the Cross had ended all this by bestowing on human beings the gift of Atonement. That term, signifying AT-ONE, the setting at one or uniting of things which had formerly been apart, is employed to translate a Greek word denoting the restoration of unity between estranged persons. In explaining the Crucifixion of Jesus, this was an idea which Paul expressed in terms of Reconciliation. 'We exult in God through our Lord Jesus, through whom we have now been granted reconciliation.'[47] 'God has reconciled us men to himself through Christ, and he has enlisted us in this service of reconciliation . . . no longer holding men's misdeeds against them.'[48] 'Formerly you were yourselves estranged from God; you were his enemies in heart and mind, and your deeds were evil. But now by Christ's death in his body of flesh and blood God has reconciled you to himself, so that he may present you before himself as dedicated men, without blemish and innocent in his sight.'[49] 'Reconciliation,' writes Sandmel,

. . . would seem to mean, if it indeed has some inherently specific meaning' that the final step in ending an estrangement has taken place. Initially there would have been harmony, or relative identity; then departure; and finally, now, restoration. Perhaps the background of this figure of speech is to be supplied from Philo and from the Stoics, that man, in being born into a body on this earth, had left his proper homeland, heaven, and for a time has been away. The true sage, these tell us, is a stranger here on earth. The identical motif is found in the *Epistle to the Hebrews*. The underlying notion may be rephrased in this way: man's soul left the celestial realm and in the consequent alienation was ill at ease in this world; now, however, the soul has become *reconciled* by ridding itself of bodily encumbrances. The Stoics and Philo unite in viewing this attainment as possible by man's exercise of the powers which lie in him; for Paul, however, this attainment comes through the grace of the sacrificial death of the Christ.[50]

This reconciliation could also be expressed in terms of *sharing*. 'For you know how generous our Lord Jesus Christ has been: he was rich, yet for your sake he became poor, so that through his poverty you might become rich.'[51] The idea was taken up dramatically by *John*, where this sharing was seen as a far-reaching reciprocity and union. 'The glory which thou gavest me,' says Jesus to his Father, 'I have given to them, that they may be one, as we are one: I in them and thou in me, may they be perfectly one.'[52]

Another way in which Paul seeks to define the utterly new situation is by asserting that Christ's death has *redeemed* mankind. The phrase has become somewhat blunted by continual reiteration throughout subsequent centuries, but to him it conveyed a specific range of ideas. Men and women, he declares, in the grip of sin, have hitherto been slaves. And now, paradoxically, they are still slaves, but slaves of an entirely different kind: slaves of righteousness, 'in the service of Christ . . . *you were bought at a price*.'[53] Redemption, that is to say, was the process of ransom and emancipation by which a slave could secure his freedom. And now everyone's freedom has been bought and Christ is the buyer.

Ancient Israel had received an advance instalment of redemption when it was freed from slavery in Egypt; but another assertion was that God would eventually redeem the Israelites 'from all their sins.'[54] And now, Christ has given his life as a ransom to release the whole human race from its bondage to inherited evil. 'The price,' declared *I Peter*, 'was paid in precious blood.'[55] But to whom was it paid? To the Devil, replied Augustine. No, to God's justice, as a debt of satisfaction, declared Anselm. But Paul never gives either these or any other answers at all, or even asks the question.

That, then, is one of the various difficulties which he did not try to solve. But he did see that this idea of redemption by ransom (whoever might be the recipient) was likely to strike some of his readers as too legalistic and formal. And so, in a number of other passages, he employs a more intimate image to describe what the death of Jesus Christ has done for the human race. This image is taken from family life, and it is concerned with the practice of adoption. Just as the Israelites had been made God's sons,[56] so God sent his Son in order that we, too, might obtain the status of his sonship; for that is what he destined that we should win.[57]

Adoption in the ancient world was carried out for three main reasons – to ensure the continuation of the family name, to ensure that there was someone to whom the family estates might be passed down, and to ensure that the worship of the family and ancestral gods might go uninterrupted.[58]

The Christian, then, has received a new adoptive father. His new father is God. He himself is a Son of God, in that sense. The reconciliation has brought him as close to God as all that.

And so, in order to explain the significance of Jesus' Crucifixion to ourselves, Paul has used all these ideas: sacrifice, expiation, atonement, reconciliation, sharing, redemption, ransom, adoption. Since the Crucifixion has given us all these gifts of God, it is not a humiliation and a disaster after all. On the contrary, it is a mighty triumph – a triumph for mankind as a corporate whole, and for each one of us as individuals. It totally outshines the expected worldly glory of the Messiah. It is our salvation.

Even after Paul had ransacked the scriptures for all possible precedents, this remains a doctrine of vivid originality; and he expresses it with imagination and eloquence. Nevertheless, the terms in which he conveyed his burning belief have been overlaid and confused by subsequent centuries of dogmatic definition. For such doctrines were, and are, hard to grasp. In consequence, *Matthew*, *Mark* and *Luke* were chary of them, and offered nothing like the fulness and variety of the Pauline view. Indeed, these Gospels generally preferred to show Jesus not as a redeemer at all, but as a preacher and worker of miracles. Besides, beliefs in the immortality of every human soul, long familiar to Greeks and now more and more encroaching upon Jewish thought as well (cf. the passage quoted at note 80 below) seemed to make the idea of special, advance redemption by Jesus unnecessary. And Jews could not see how a man who had lived on the earth, whether Messiah or not, could redeem anybody. In the words of the third century rabbi Johanan bar Nappaha, 'We want no more "deliverance" at the hands of men. Deliverance only comes from God.'

Nevertheless, the saving power of the Crucifixion came to be regarded as the central message of Christianity, and it was this message that the Church councils of the later ancient world were eager, above all else, to interpret and re-announce correctly. Yet the task remained problematical – particularly because we do not yet *seem* to have been saved at all! In the words of Nietzsche, 'Shew me that you are redeemed, and I will believe in your redeemer.' And even Cardinal John Henry Newman was obliged to conclude that the question of precisely *how* Christ's death brought about our salvation 'will ever be a mystery in this life'.

However, Paul's thinking on this deep theme had two parts, and we have only discussed one of them. Christ had been crucified. But after descending to 'the regions beneath earth' (Sheol),[59] it was believed that on the third day he rose again from the dead and came back bodily into the world. And it was this Resurrection following upon his Crucifixion which inspired some of Paul's most moving thoughts, thoughts which changed the direction of the history of mankind.

What Paul wrote to the Corinthians about this corporeal Resurrection of Jesus, his reappearance among mankind after his death, is of the greatest historical importance because it was written, apparently, before the mid-fifties AD, and repeats what Paul had told the same correspondents during his previous visit, which in turn had repeated assertions already current at an even earlier date: so that his words reproduce a belief that was already held less than two decades, perhaps much less than two decades, after Jesus had died on the Cross.

And now, my brothers, I must remind you of the Gospel that I preached to you . . . First and foremost, I handed on the facts which had been imparted to me: that Christ died for our sins, in accordance with the scriptures; that he was buried; that he was raised to life on the third day, according to the scriptures; and that he appeared to Cephas, and afterwards to the Twelve. Then he appeared to over five hundred of our brothers at once, most of whom are still alive, though some have died. Then he appeared to James [the Just, the brother of Jesus], and afterwards to all the apostles. In the end he appeared even to me.[60]

This is a much older written account of what was believed to have happened than the far more elaborate statements in the Gospels about these same appearances of Jesus after his death, coming after the discovery of the empty tomb,[61] to which Paul makes no explicit reference, though he may well have known the tradition. Neither he nor the Gospels directly *describe* the Resurrection. But Paul offers peculiarly valuable evidence for the very early beliefs of the Christian community – formulated by them, no doubt, to refute sceptical doubts about this Resurrection which, as they were assuring their fellow-Jews, had truly taken place.

Earlier Jews had felt that the idea of a man or woman becoming immortal was not to be tolerated because mankind's destiny and God's can never be merged. However, a new belief that bodily resurrection was not impossible had sometimes been hinted at; and by the time of *Daniel** it was clearly detectable. Writing in the second century BC, when the Jews were revolting against their Greek (Seleucid) overlords, he had proclaimed the eventual end of Israel's tribulation, when God would intervene to inaugurate his Kingdom in the world. The outcome of this intervention would be the resuscitation of the dead,[62] their actual re-arising on the earth in their original forms, body and soul together in psychosomatic unity. For the Jews, until Greek ideas began to encroach, refused to distinguish between the survival of the body and the soul; though belief in survival in such terms seemed so incomprehensible to the Greeks, with their notions of spiritual immortality, that when Paul spoke of resurrection (*anastasis*) to the Athenians, his hearers were entirely puzzled and thought he was referring to a goddess of that name.[63]

However, the Jewish sect of the Sadducees* still denied this concept altogether,[64] offering elaborate theological arguments but in fact regarding it as subversive, since its diffusion might encourage the masses to look beyond the secular authorities altogether in search of this promised salvation. The Pharisees,* on the other hand, gradually accepted the doctrine, believing that, in the Last Days, the bodies of the dead would indeed be resurrected on earth.

They claimed to be able to cite earlier scriptural authority,[65] and Paul asserted also (like the Gospels) that Jesus' Resurrection *on the third day* was similarly predicted in the scriptures.[66] Here, however, he is considerably straining Biblical interpretation, just as he had strained it in finding prophecies of the Crucifixion. A text he had in mind was in *Hosea*: 'he has struck us and he will bind up our wounds . . . after two days he will revive us, on the third day he will restore us, that in his presence we may live.'[67] In *II Kings*, too, Isaiah, on God's orders, told King Hezekiah, 'I will heal you and on the third day you shall go up to the house of the Lord.'[68] It was suggested in *Matthew* (who attributes the saying to Jesus himself) that the three days and nights which Jesus, after his death, would spend 'in the bowels of the earth' had been prefigured by Jonah's three days and nights in the belly of the sea-monster.[69] The employment of these three texts, however, is chiefly interesting today as showing the fantastic lengths to which the search for scriptural prefigurations could go.

Since Old Testament days there had been speculations about the precise definition and identity of the group or groups who were destined to enjoy this bodily resurrection. Was it a 'remnant' of all righteous Israelites? Or all Israelites without exception? Or all mankind? Nevertheless, it was generally agreed, in consonance with the Jewish insistence on *the corporate* nature of the community, that the resurrection, too, would be general and corporate, in one or another of these senses. But subsequently the idea of *individual* resurrection had also made its appearance: and speculations of this kind became strongly reinforced among the masses by the belief that John the Baptist, in very recent times, had actually risen from the dead in such a way.[70] Thus by Jesus' time the concept that great individuals could rise bodily from the dead in advance of the general resurrection was no longer wholly unfamiliar. Even though Jesus' disciples after his death argued in bewilderment about what had happened, nevertheless there existed the right psychological conditions for the creation of the belief that his body, too, could be resurrected upon earth.

And that was what Paul understood had happened. Some have said that in his mind the Crucifixion was of primary, and the Resurrection of only secondary importance. But although the Crucifixion receives a greater number of mentions in his Letters, that is not the conclusion which should be drawn. For in Paul's arresting view (unshared by the majority of subsequent Christian thinkers) it was not from Jesus' birth, or even from his Crucifixion, but from the time of his Resurrection that he first became recognizable as the Messiah. 'On the level of the Spirit – the Holy Spirit – he was declared Son of God by a mighty act *in that he rose from the Dead*.'[71] So the Resurrection is as overwhelmingly significant to Paul as the Crucifixion. The two happenings are inseparable in his mind: each owes most of its meaning to the other. The later event did not annul the earlier event, but gave effect to its salvation-bringing powers. Paul even says that the forgiveness of sins, conferred by the Crucifixion, could not have come about at all unless the Resurrection, too, had taken place.[72] For the rising of Jesus from the dead, according to his belief, demonstrated that the conquest of the demonic forces, which had been set in motion by what happened on the Cross, was sealed with triumphant success; and the memory of his death, since it was a victory in that supreme cause, was transmuted from sadness into joy and thanksgiving. Without belief in the Resurrection of Jesus Christ, Paul declared with the utmost emphasis, it is utterly vain and useless to believe in anything at all: '. . . if Christ was not raised, your faith has nothing in it[73]. . . and since he was raised, mankind too will be raised: he is the first to return from the dead . . . the hope of a glory to come.'[74]

Yet once again, like the redemptive Crucifixion, this idea that Christ had already risen from the dead was an utterly radical assault on the categories of our usual understanding. It was nothing short of incredible; and that was why it *had to be* believed, why the faith necessary to believe it had to be mustered. Augustine noted with pleasure that, by his own time, disbelief in the Resurrection had declined: yet this decline he found no less surprising than the event itself had been when it occurred.

> Only a very few among learned and unlearned still remain in stupefied incredulity. If what the world believes is . . . incredible, then surely it is even more incredible that so incredible a thing should be credited! . . . It is incredible that men of no birth, no standing, no learning, and so few of them, should have been able to persuade, so effectively, the whole world, including the learned men.[75]

Thus Augustine saw as clearly as Paul that the Resurrection could only be accepted if ordinary standards of credence were lifted. In the words of Archbishop William Temple, it has been believed in by 'those who love and will practise a chivalry, even a knight-errantry, which to the world must seem grotesque.' Yet, as Pascal pointed out, it was because of this conviction, 'although so contrary to nature, that the Christian religion . . . established itself so firmly and so gently.' For in the minds of those who believed in Jesus' Resurrection, it conferred utterly satisfying evidence of the divine power's sovereign penetration and destruction of the whole man-made fabric of the history of the world. This was the first island-peak rising out of the flat ocean of temporal events: the overpowering guarantee that life is stronger than death, that good is the conqueror of evil. The Incarnation and Crucifixion of Jesus had been huge enlargements of the Jewish religion: belief in his Resurrection was the next stage, the beginning of real, independent Christianity. Without this certainty that Jesus Christ had risen, there would never have been a Christian church at all.

Yet Paul did well to stress so forcibly and frankly the incredibility of this corporeal Resurrection and to insist that nothing short of unquestioning faith would make it possible to accept it. For there were those who asked awkward, prosaic, materialistic questions about *how* this had actually happened: *how* could the decomposition of a human corpse go into reverse, so that the body was able to reappear in its former completeness upon earth? Evidently there were some such sceptical enquirers at Corinth, for it was to his fellow Christians in that city that Paul attempted an explanation:

> But, you may ask, how are the dead raised? In what kind of body? How foolish! . . . What is sown in the earth as a perishable thing is raised imperishable. Sown in humiliation, it is raised in glory; sown in weakness, it is raised in power; sown as an animal body, it is raised as a spiritual body . . . It is in

this sense that Scripture says, 'the first man, Adam, became an animate being', whereas the last Adam has become a life-giving spirit.[76]

Paul, then, had broken away from the simple and obviously untenable Jewish view that the dead would somehow be resuscitated upon earth in their pristine, undecomposed flesh. He believed that Jesus had appeared on earth after his death, but he refused to assert that he had appeared in the customary form of a human body.

Indeed, to have made such an assertion could hardly have been expected of Paul, for personal reasons. For although, as we have seen, he claimed to have been one of those who had seen Jesus, this had happened after Jesus' supposed period of Resurrection upon earth had ceased, that is to say in a subsequent vision when he reappeared to Paul in a spiritual, non-bodily guise, so that to have stressed the corporeal nature of the Resurrection would have been to depreciate his own experience. Later *John* told how Jesus himself, before his Crucifixion, had resurrected a certain Lazarus from the dead. We cannot say whether this account derives from stories dating back to the very earliest days of Christianity or not; but at all events it tells how Lazarus was raised up after four days in the tomb, although, as his sister Martha pointed out, 'by now there will be a stench'.[77] Paul, on the other hand, will allow no such practical problems to interfere with his picture of Jesus' return from among the dead to the earth, for he does not suppose that he returned in ordinary bodily form at all. The 'spiritual' body of which the Letters speak was not, it is true, thought of in any wholly immaterial sense; but, although Paul's words are not very specific, he seems to have envisaged it as consisting of light or air: the objective yet impalpable stuff that he believed visions to be made of.

This was the most feasible interpretation of the Risen Christ available to the metaphysics of the day. It was not, however, entirely new. For the idea had already appeared, although in a somewhat different fashion, in the Jewish *Book of Jubilees*,* in which the ultimate resurrection of the righteous was likewise regarded as something other than bodily:

> At that time the Lord will heal his servants, and they will rise up and see a great peace, and drive out their adversaries ... And their bones will rest in the earth and their spirits will have much joy.[78]

This, like other Jewish concepts of the body metamorphosed into a more glorious organism, was a movement, in a cosmopolitan age, towards the Greek way of thinking in terms of immortal souls, in contrast to the older Jewish conception of body and soul as an inseparable psychosomatic unity.

It seems clear that already by Paul's time Judaism was well used to a variety of conceptions in this matter, so that man could be regarded as a soul, indwelling a body, separable at death, as well as in the older unitary way. And far from immortality of the soul being inconsistent with resurrection of the whole person, including the body, as a way of describing the future life, it was possible to see them as successive phases in the eschatological programme. *II Esdras*,[79] for example, has the two concepts side by side in this way.[80]

And Paul, in his own fashion, was conveying a similar message.

Yet the form in which he launched this belief did not win favour among his contemporaries and immediate successors. The Gospels, for the most part, emphatically prefer the far more popular doctrine of a risen body of Jesus of a very substantial nature, able to speak, eat and be touched. 'Touch me and see; no ghost has flesh and bones as you can see that I have.'[81] 'Reach your hand here, and put it in my side.'[82] And the same point was stressed by Ignatius, in order to confute those who were attempting to depreciate the humanness of Jesus. Thus the Pauline doctrine of transformation had been replaced once again by the older, simpler idea of corporeal revival. Augustine, too, though worried by the stories of the eating and drinking of a risen body, nevertheless accepts, with an explicitness alien to Paul, that they have to be applied literally to the Resurrection of Jesus, with the explanation that 'it is not the ability, it is the need, to eat and drink that will be taken away from bodies like this'. And the only sense in which such bodies will be spiritual is a more or less metaphorical one, that is to say 'not by ceasing to be bodies, but by being supported in their existence by a life-giving spirit'.[83] This is all somewhat casuistical, however, and the technical details of the supposed process, although they perplexed Augustine as much as they had confounded Paul's Corinthian correspondents, are of little concern to ourselves today who are endeavouring to extract what is permanently valuable from Paul.

Yet his formulation, in a more general sense, remains of vast significance. First, it linked the Crucifixion with mankind, since the belief of the new Christian community that Jesus, after his death, had reappeared on earth enabled them to claim that he had been able, on these occasions,

to communicate to them the true significance of his own martyrdom, so that they in their turn could transmit it to the world. And so
Paul's words, despite the near-incoherence which the impossibility of his
descriptive task seems to have imposed on them, and despite the various
modifications they underwent in later times, launched the concept of
Christ's conquest of death which, enshrined in the solemnities of Easter
week, has overwhelmed human hearts for so many centuries.

It is also essential to Paul that the Resurrection was followed by the
Ascension. 'God raised him to the heights,'[84] and 'he ascended far above
all heavens, so that he might fill the universe'[85] – and it is Paul's hope
that one day all mankind, too, will go and live with him there.[86]

Jewish tradition was already very familiar with biblical ascensions,
since they had been ascribed to Enoch and Elijah.[87] But Paul, in order
to stress the uniqueness of Jesus, points out his difference from such
scriptural personages. For whereas they had ascended from heaven
immediately upon the end of their earthly lives, Paul, as we have seen,
recounts (either on his own account, or drawing upon an already existent report) that Jesus had first descended to the 'regions beneath the
earth' during the three days between the Crucifixion and Resurrection,
and only then, after his reappearance upon earth, had ascended to
heaven. It was a contrast that needed to be made and justified, because
whereas the ascension of noble figures to heaven was a common biblical
idea, the re-ascension of a supernatural being, after his temporary
assumption of humanity and descent into the underworld, was far less
familiar.

Yet the sequence of Jesus' Resurrection and Ascension did not,
according to Paul, take place in the same manner or with the same
interval between them as subsequent churchmen were to insist. For the
belief that he ascended to heaven on the fortieth day after the Resurrection[88] is not familiar to him. Nor was it to the writer of the Letter of
Barnabas,* who even asserted that both these miraculous events occurred on the same day.[89] Paul, too, may have had some such idea in mind,
for he did not distinguish between the two reported happenings with
anything like the clarity of subsequent theologians. And indeed such a
tendency towards their fusion was natural enough for Paul, who so
defiantly set up his own spiritual vision of Christ – occurring *after*
Christ's resurrected life on earth was believed to be at an end – in
competition with the earthly appearances claimed by those other

apostles[90] who had actually known the Saviour personally. Indeed, Paul even contrives to combine the two miraculous events in a single phrase: 'Christ was raised from the dead in the splendour of the Father.'[91] Here, it actually seems that what he means by the Resurrection is what we call the Ascension.

Nor was he alone among the early Christians in thus merging or confusing these happenings. For the two ideas, in their writings, are sometimes found alongside each other, without a clear distinction between them; or they even appear in reverse order. Moreover, the Ascension receives curiously few references in the rest of the New Testament: evidently the bodily Resurrection exerted a more compelling appeal. Besides, there was the difficulty, seen by Origen, that if Jesus ascended to heaven, it was hard to accept Paul's claim that he had already been pre-existent there for all time past. However, *Acts* duly stresses the exaltation of the ascended Christ,[92] and *John* carefully distinguishes the Ascension from the Resurrection.[93] But Paul, as we have seen, had been much less explicit.

And yet, whatever the exact nature of the association between the two events in his mind, their combination – the supplementation of the one by the other – was still an essential feature of his thinking. For one thing, their united action placed the final stamp of eternity upon the conquest of the demonic powers which Jesus had won by his Crucifixion. For when he ascended to heaven, God 'enthroned him at his right hand in the heavenly realms, far above all government and authority, all power and dominion, and any title of sovereignty that can be named, not only in this age but in the age to come'.[94] These designations do not refer to earthly governments, but are the titles of the various degrees of demonic and angelic beings, derived from Jewish terminology, and seen as ruling the heavenly spheres. This idea, like its corollary declaring that such beings were defeated by the Crucifixion, is unfamiliar today, except in a purely metaphorical sense – which, however, was by no means how Paul intended it to be taken, or took it himself. Unfamiliar, too, is the concept that heaven is 'above' and an underworld (Sheol and later Gehenna) usually thought of as 'below'.

But, for Paul, the Ascension also has a profounder significance: it seems to him the supreme demonstration of the total reversal which Jesus Christ has brought to the world. The revolutionary redemptive act of Jesus, consisting of the Crucifixion, had to be given these *two* sequels before it could become totally effective. First he had to return to the earth in order to transmit the experience and message of his death to the human race. And then he had to ascend once again to heaven so that his relationship with God would be renewed and his all-powerful force and influence would be established on earth for the remaining duration of mankind.

This is the concept which dominates *Colossians*, in which the supremacy of the ascended Lord is described in terms so superlative that they are thought to go beyond what Paul himself could have written.[95] Yet this emphasis is not so alien to his thought, for it was the Ascension which completes his view of the overwhelming redemptive happening. It was an idea which provided inspiration to Teilhard de Chardin, who saw the *regnant* Christ as the ubiquitous unifying principle, the goal and crown of all movement.

And even to those who stand outside the Christian tradition, Paul's images of the Crucifixion and Resurrection and Ascension are of powerful and permanent significance. For within the range of ideas of his time, but with a force far transcending them, he had produced a description of the total undermining of the powers of evil, in which, not unlike ourselves, he saw the world to have been completely, and but for this irreparably, enmeshed. Yet now it was enmeshed no longer, for these new events, in the words of Karl Barth, brought about '*the great change* in human beings' lives'. Or, as Paul himself expressed it, 'when anyone is united to Christ, there is a new world: the old order has gone, and a new order has already begun.'[96] We have been made ready 'to set our feet upon the new path of life'.[97] This change has come with great suddenness. Friedrich Schleiermacher, in his book *The Coming of Christ*, saw the phenomenon of Jesus Christ as a sharp gust of wind, unexpected, buffeting us; yet, all the same, part of the total phenomena of winds. But in Paul's view it was not part of any previously experienced phenomena at all. God is working his purpose out, but he has *not* chosen to work it out in any gradual process of development. On the contrary, he has cleft an utter breach with the past, of the greatest conceivable abruptness and urgency.

So now there is only one thing to be done: 'at the name of Jesus every knee should bow, in heaven, on earth and in the depths.'[98] As Albert Schweitzer discerned, 'If Jesus has risen, that means, for those who dare to think consistently, that it is now already the supernatural age. And this is Paul's point of view . . . Powers of the supernatural

world were already at work within the created order.'[99] With the Crucifixion, Resurrection and Ascension of Jesus, the Future Age has already
dawned. Here are none of the gradual evolutionary processes, the un-
folding trends and tendencies beloved by historians and by some theologians. For Paul, history as generally understood has abruptly and
completely ended. What has been described as the 'scandal of particu-
larity', the objection that it is impossible to believe God to have inter-
vened decisively only once in all history and then only for the briefest of
durations, did not worry him at all; indeed, it appealed strongly to his
taste for the apocalyptic. Here is total revolution, total glorious crisis in
which the old order is thrown abruptly on the dust-heap to make room
for this unimaginably novel and original beginning.

And just as Paul believed that Jesus' death and its aftermath had
reversed the direction of history, so Paul's views have likewise changed
the entire historical process, both religious and secular, that has unfolded
after him. For they helped to create, indeed to a large extent they
created, a body of belief which means that, in the long run, the Christianity which was so largely based upon his career and writings would
become the most widespread religion in the world: superseding, in this
respect, the Judaism from which it was so substantially derived but had,
nevertheless, deviated in so fundamental a fashion.

Paul's is an elaborate and imposing structure of belief, and in some
though not all of its main lines it has been accepted by countless
millions. But neither Paul nor anyone else, of course, has succeeded in
demonstrating that what he believed is *true*. That Jesus was crucified must
be accepted as a historical fact. But that his Crucifixion possessed
redemptive power, or that his body rose from the dead and walked the
earth, or that he ascended to heaven, are articles of belief which have
not been scientifically proved, and cannot in the nature of things ever
be proved. Of this Paul was very well aware, and indeed he himself
pointed it out, almost ruthlessly. The redemptive Crucifixion, he knew,
seemed incredible: a folly to Greeks and a stumbling-block to Jews.
The Resurrection, in one way, seemed more cogent to the rationalist;
for Jesus' Resurrection appearances, the appearances of his body on
earth after his death, had been witnessed – so it was said, and so Paul
himself testified – by a considerable number of people. These appearances, then, have been described, and quite rightly described, as the
nearest Christians can ever get to providing proof that Jesus was Christ.
To the secular historian, they inevitably fall short of any such effective

demonstration. What they prove, rather, is the overwhelmingly imposing character of the figure, whether he was the Messiah and Son of
God or not, who inspired such heartfelt, continuing, ever-growing
belief.

Paul realized extremely clearly that the historian's approach was not
enough and could never meet his needs. On purely rational grounds,
the evidence testifying to Jesus' miraculous death and the events which
were said to have followed, and which changed the world, could never
be sufficient. Something else was needed as well: and that was faith.

3. *Belief in the Unbelievable*

It was Paul's awareness of the incredibility of the news he had to convey
which caused him to stress so unceasingly the enormous necessity of
faith – faith which had to be strong enough, like his own, to believe in
the unbelievable. Jesus Christ died to bring us salvation. But that salvation cannot reach us unless we come to meet him, by believing. 'Christ
brings righteousness for everyone who has faith.'[1] 'The Gospel is the
saving power of God for everyone who has faith . . . because here is
revealed God's way of righting wrong, a way that starts from faith and
ends in faith.'[2] 'Take up the great shield of faith, with which you will be
able to quench all the flaming arrows of the evil one.'[3]

These were utterances by which John Wesley 'felt his heart strangely
warmed'. And it had been easy for Paul to find scriptural prefigurations
to back them, since the need for faith had been a pre-eminent theme of
the Old Testament as well. *That* faith had been the Jewish community's
utter trust in God's direction of the destiny and history of the nation.
This faith is utter trust in God's revelation of Jesus, trust felt by each
individual. There has been a shift from corporate to personal trust, a
shift which the Greek term used in the Septuagint, *pistis*, made easier.
Paul never defines this word which he so frequently uses;[4] but he means
it in the sense of total, unrestricted, emotional and intellectual willingness to accept what God had vouchsafed to us in Jesus Christ. Like its
Hebrew prototype, *pistis* also carries the connotation of faithfulness,
including a strong element of obedience. Paul saw it as faith and faithfulness and trust and much else, an exalted blend of loyalty and love and
devotion.

A foreign-seeming feature to ourselves, at first sight, is Paul's determined assurance that, if we have faith, it 'justifies' us. This pronouncement of justification (*dikaiosis*) is twice stated by him to be confirmed by

scriptural authority: 'because we read "the man who is righteous (*dikaios*) by faith shall live".'[5] This reference in *Galatians* is to a passage in *Habakkuk*,[6] and it is strange and rather alarming to see how Paul inflicts upon this text a characteristic twist and amendment to suit his chosen interpretation. There is another biblical sentence, too, which Paul likewise finds apt for his argument. It is the declaration in *Genesis* that 'Abraham put his faith in the Lord, and the Lord counted that faith to him as righteousness.'[7] For Paul especially likes the idea that, although Abraham preceded the transmission of the Law and could not be said therefore to have been its obedient adherent, God nevertheless 'justified' him by virtue of his faith alone. And that, Paul says, is how we can be justified too.

This 'justification' was originally a legal term, according to which the person who received it was 'put in the right' or 'vindicated by acquittal'. A judge justified a man when he pronounced him innocent, and so Christ's act in undergoing his noble death justifies ourselves: 'the issue of one *just* act is acquittal and life for all men.'[8] Man can only experience this new life when he gives up trying to provide his own justification of his own self. But theologians have also asked: when Paul says that God justifies human beings, does he merely mean God pronounces them to be in the right – as if they had been on trial before him – or does God do more, and actually *make* them right? In certain passages, at least, Paul clearly means the latter. One such passage is the phrase from *Galatians* that was quoted above. Another is this. 'You have been dedicated to God and justified through the name of the Lord Jesus and the Spirit of God.'[9] So vital a thing is faith that, by its possession, the sinner is not only declared just but actually transformed into a just man, a man who is *dikaios*, enjoying the new status of the Christian before God.

The text of *Habakkuk* used, and misused, by Paul had already been a popular source of reinterpretations before his time; for instance the Qumran Community's *Habakkuk Commentary* linked it with their quasi-Messianic figure, the Teacher of Righteousness.[10] But the belief about Christ which Paul considers necessary for salvation goes much farther than anything that was believed about that mysterious Teacher. For there is no implication in the Dead Sea Scrolls that the Teacher had himself accomplished a redemptive work in any way comparable to the saving act of Christ.

Thus the doctrine that man is justified, is made right, by faith in what God had achieved through Jesus, remains, as far as we can see, Paul's original creation. Indeed, according to Günther Bornkamm's *Paul*, it is the key to everything else he thought and said. The early Fathers, however, were not by any means of the same mind since they detached faith from justification, allowing the latter to fade away. And some modern students, too, prefer to regard it as 'a side crater within the main crater'. But that the concept was important to Paul there is no doubt, for it effectively dramatizes the utter indispensability of faith, without which the entire force of Christ's redeeming martyrdom will remain beyond reach, inapplicable and meaningless.

It was one of the principal complaints of the anti-Christian Celsus* that the religion he was criticizing made its appeal to blind faith and nothing more. Augustine, however, defended Paul's attitude. In this life, he said, we have to take many things on trust: there is a whole host of amazing phenomena in the world which defy all intellectual explanation: yet they exist all the same. When, therefore, unbelievers demand a rational proof for the miracles of God, Augustine maintained that they are speaking illogically, 'seeing that there are these other things in the present which are equally unsusceptible of rational explanation'.[11] So the lack of rational explanation for the objects of Christian belief must not worry us, he concluded: as Paul said, we must disregard their absence and commit ourselves totally, submitting to the overpowering revolution in our whole mental outlook.

Paul's insistence that the incredible must be believed deeply affected his attitude to human knowledge. The sort of knowledge which, as he felt, brought insight into the redemptive truth of Christ was not knowledge of any rational kind: it was a sort of knowledge which was imperatively needed, which could come only by revelation, and not by the workings of the unaided intellect.

In one passage, it is true, Paul appeals to intellectual reasoning to support his beliefs: God's 'invisible attributes, that is to say his everlasting power and deity, have been visible, ever since the world began, to the eye of reason, in the things he has made.'[12] Here, says Bornkamm, he is using 'language of Jewish Wisdom-teaching as influenced by Greece'. But this attempt by Paul to offer a rational, intellectual approach was an isolated endeavour, because it dealt with a special sort of theme: he was for the moment arguing from things that can be seen, whereas for most of the time, the redemptive death of Jesus Christ being his main subject, he had to argue from what cannot be seen at all. And since that is what he was primarily concerned to do, purely intellectual knowledge inspired in him nothing but distant contempt; for it seemed to him wholly irrelevant to everything that really mattered. Thus in *I Corinthians* he writes:

Is there knowledge? It will vanish away . . . Make no mistake about this: if there is anyone among you who fancies himself wise – wise, I mean, by the standards of this passing age – he must become a fool to gain true wisdom. For the wisdom of this world is folly in God's sight . . . God has made the wisdom of this world look foolish . . . As God in his wisdom ordained, the world failed to find him in his wisdom, and he chose to save those who have faith by the 'folly' of the Gospel.[13]

'Godless, wicked men', he declared, 'when they boast of their wisdom, make fools of themselves',[14] and traditions of man-made teaching only result in 'hollow and delusive speculations'.[15] Nor did Paul find it difficult to locate scriptural support for such pronouncements, since there had been very similar assertions in the *Psalms*.[16] Moreover, responsible Jews, both before and after Paul, often expressed themselves severely against Greek secular learning and philosophy; he was only too glad to echo the same censure, especially after his speech to the sophisticated Athenians had proved comparatively unsuccessful.[18]

It was he, therefore, who crystallized in memorable form the rejection of rational knowledge which would in due course gain the passionate agreement of many powerful religious groups, and then, eventually, break down classical culture and set up medieval irrationalism in its place. Before that time, however, there was to be a prolonged and determined dialogue and dispute. How much secular knowledge should the Christian try to take with him on his earthly journey? 'The symphony of Christianity,' in the words of Schweitzer, 'began with a tremendous dissonance between faith and thought.' A scholarly Christian, Clement of Alexandria, contradicted Paul by declaring that philosophy was 'God's special covenant with the Greeks as a basis for the philosophy according to Christ'.[19] Origen, too, believed that belief based on philosophical reasoning was better than its unreasoned counterpart. But Origen also declared that his opponent Celsus, who like other pagans deplored the Christians' contempt of empirical knowledge, had misrepresented Paul by calling him a depreciator of 'wisdom in this life', and a man who looked favourably on foolishness.[20] Augustine, too, tried to argue from that single appeal to the 'eye of reason' in *Romans* that

Paul had mitigated his attacks on philosophy; though in fact, as we have noted, the reference was isolated and highly untypical.

Anselm aimed at rational, inexorable proof that his own religion was true. But Pascal saw that this was something which Paul, in his more usual moods, had not even attempted to achieve: 'Jesus Christ and St Paul have the order of charity, not of the mind, for they desired to warm the will, not to instruct.' Sören Kierkegaard felt the same: 'in order to become a Christian one must commit oneself by leaping in the darkness and acting from faith in the absurd'; no rational proof can ever be forthcoming, and it is on the basis of faith alone that the individual has to make his choice between Christ and the world. Karl Barth, on the other hand, was dissatisfied with Kierkegaard's irrationalism, and, like Anselm nine centuries earlier, defended the rational reliability of the human knowledge of God.

Paul's attitude on the whole was nearer Kierkegaard's; and their arguments were cogent. Revealed religion in general, and Christianity in particular, cannot aim at demonstrating its truth in terms that would be acceptable in a court of law, or a philosophically composed textbook (though many textbooks have made such attempts). How, for example, could Paul possibly prove that the vision he claimed to have seen on the road to Damascus had been an objective fact? Christianity must inevitably rely upon faith in the irrational – upon faith in what Paul knew and declared to be outrageous by any purely intellectual standard. That being so, there is no advantage in opening the door even to reveal a chink of the rational, for rationality is wholly beside the point: and that is why so many highly intelligent Catholics fail to share the Protestant enthusiasm for Pope John XXIII, who seemed willing to let that chink appear. On just one occasion Paul had done the same, when he argued that the 'eye of reason' could detect the power of God. At that moment he was arguing, as we have seen, from visible objects. For the rest of the time he was not; and therefore he urged far more frequently the irrelevance of reason, and the overriding, overwhelming need to possess faith in its place.

Paul was so supremely impressed with the importance and efficacy of faith that in comparison he regards the significance of mere Works (meaning good deeds, good behaviour) as secondary and altogether subordinate and subject to its possession. To say that, however, is to state all too briefly one of the most sensational features of his teaching, which has aroused controversy throughout the ages and has provoked great movements of support and opposition.

Obviously, Paul declared over and over again, one must behave decently. This is summed up, in his sentiments if not in his actual words, by *Ephesians*: 'For we are God's handiwork, created in Christ Jesus to devote ourselves to the good deeds for which God has designed us.'[21] In other words – and this is the essential feature of his belief – Good Works are not the *cause* but the *outcome* of salvation: salvation by faith comes first: according to the injunction the Gospels were to attribute to Jesus, 'Set your mind on God's kingdom and his justice before everything else, and all the rest will come to you as well.'[22] True, the Last Judgment will judge men's works and deeds.[23] But decent conduct in itself justifies nobody in the eyes of God: the words and deeds that are going to be judged will only, *can* only, have been good at all if there has been a sufficient measure of faith. The point is made abundantly clear (though with the usual not obviously apposite scriptural quotations)[24] in *Romans*: 'Israel never attained righteousness . . . because their efforts were not based on faith, but (as they supposed) on deeds.'[25] And the *Letter to Titus* reiterates the same principle by speaking of Christians who have been saved by God's mercy, but 'not for any good deeds of our own'.[26]

This seemed a strange and heretical doctrine to the Jews, who, despite their own far from insignificant emphasis on faith, nevertheless observed a religion of deed rather than creed. The Pharisees, for example, for all their eulogies of faith, believed also in an unending struggle to *do* God's will. It is true that the Hymn Scroll[27] and Community Rule*[28] at Qumran approach the doctrine of Paul by stressing the insignificance of human righteousness compared to God's, while *II Esdras** and certain scribes agreed with him that God will have mercy on those who have no store of good deeds to their name.[29] But most of the later rabbis still emphasized with great force that right conduct is more than just desirable; it is of paramount necessity.[30] To these Jews, Paul's relegation of Works to second place perilously sapped man's moral initiative and responsibility.

His attitude also aroused incomprehension, if not alarm, among some of the Christians who came after him. In the whole of *Acts* there is only one tribute to his teaching about faith,[31] and even that is strongly mitigated by a subsequent assurance by Paul, speaking to King Agrippa II, that he himself had been accustomed to urge Jews and non-Jews alike 'to prove their repentance by *deeds*'.[32] Meanwhile, the *Letter of James*, possibly written at about the same time, issues a remarkably emphatic comment on the inadequacies he detected in Paul's attitude:

> My brothers, what use is it for a man to say he has faith when he does nothing to shew it? Can that faith save him? Suppose a brother or a sister is in rags with not enough food for the day, and one of you says, 'Good luck to you, keep yourselves warm, and have plenty to eat,' but does nothing to supply their bodily needs, what is the use of that? So with faith; if it does not lead to action, it is in itself a lifeless thing ... The kind of religion which is without stain or fault in the sight of God our Father is this: to go to the help of orphans and widows in their distress and keep oneself untarnished by the world.[33]

The author of *James* is not exactly contradicting Paul, for the latter would have agreed that faith ought to lead to good conduct. But their emphasis is entirely different. Paul had placed faith first and good behaviour afterwards as its outcome and consequence on a lower plane. The *Letter of James* feels that this does not represent a proper balance, since to its writer, as to the Jews in general, good conduct was the essential thing. Paul and the writer of *James* looked at the two concepts through different eyes. Faith, to *James*, could easily become the merest lip-service. Works, to Paul, could readily degenerate into a mere striving for credits in the ledgers of heaven.

Most of the early Fathers emphatically sided with *James* against Paul, for in the latter's teaching they saw an unconscious invitation to lax behaviour and moral anarchy. Indeed, Tertullian went to the opposite extreme from Paul, describing all religion as right attitude and conduct. Origen is more non-committal. Faith alone, he concedes, can bring salvation. Yet at the same time he seems to regard it less as a glorious blessing than a regrettable necessity! Moreover, he devotes himself to the uphill task of trying to argue that Paul's *Letter to the Romans* had clearly enunciated the principle of judgment by Works – the only Works it minimized, Origen maintained, were merely ritual procedures.

The fourteenth-century English poet, William Langland, agreed with *James* that 'faith without fact is nothing worth, as dead as a door-tree [door-post] unless deeds follow.' But in the next generation the opposite view, Paul's doctrine of justification by faith, was elevated to lofty heights by the Reformation. To Martin Luther, disgusted by what he regarded as the barren, legalistic, ceremonial repetitions by which current Catholicism sought to acquire salvation, the doctrine seemed literally a godsend. And so, when he was translating Paul's words, 'a man is justified by his faith,' he added the word *alone*. 'Understand,' Luther said, 'that we do not reject Good Works, but praise them highly' – and yet 'unless a man is already a believer and a Christian, his works have no value at all. They are foolish, damnable, idle sins . . . the dung of one's own merits, the filthy puddle of one's own righteousness.' When, therefore, he read about Paul's preference of faith to works, he declared 'I felt myself to be reborn and to have gone through open doors into Paradise.' And Pascal, too, wrote rapturously about the utter uselessness of human effort.[34]

The background of Paul's comparative lack of enthusiasm for good works was his far more marked lack of affection for the Jewish Law, the Torah. Seeing that the world was plunged in evil, he had, as we have seen, become convinced that the Law was proving impotent to perform the imperatively needed act of rescue. At the same time, therefore, as this hitherto devout Jew set about persecuting followers of Jesus Christ for deviation from the Law, he himself was gradually coming to the overpowering conclusion that it was totally inadequate, and that something else must be put in its place. The dilemma had become terrible and schizophrenic: the intolerable tension between these two simultaneous sets of circumstances, his persecution of the Christians for anti-Law thinking and his feeling that the Law was after all totally inapplicable and therefore wrong, resulted forcibly in his declaration for the latter attitude, and in the complete reversal of his view of Jesus Christ. The motive power behind this reversal was faith: and faith, Paul proclaimed, faith in the gigantic change that had come about for himself through Jesus, was above all else what everyone else in the world, too, imperatively needed from now on. Good behaviour, though also important, was not the primary consideration: it would follow easily enough once there was faith.

This relegation of Good Works to the second place was the consequence of his disillusionment with the Torah or Law – and made it sharper still. It was the consequence because, since so much of the Law was concerned with works, Paul's recognition of its ineffectiveness meant that he rejected the paramountcy of good behaviour as well. And, in turn, the arguments which he thus developed against that paramountcy made him all the more eager to believe and point out that, in comparison with faith in the new order of Jesus Christ, the Law had faded from the foreground and become insignificant. It was not only, he felt, that far too many people merely paid ostensible, superficial respect to its code, or were ludicrously complacent about the detailed exactitude of its observances. The problem was more fundamental than that. For Paul had come to feel an utter distrust for any righteousness that did not come direct from God: and the Law, presented through intermediaries, did not seem to him to be able to claim such origins.

He also tried to explain what he meant in another way. The Law, he said, had merely been the *paidagogos*, the slave who accompanied children to school: a necessary stage in the procedure, but by no means the same as the schooling itself; and 'now that faith has come, his charge is at an end.'[35]

This was because 'now, quite independently of Law, God's justice has been brought to light. The Law and Prophets both bear witness to it.'[36] For, as we saw above, these sacred books could be made (by something of an effort), to provide suitable forecasts of Christ; though it remains a strange paradox that Paul, in the same breath as rejecting the Law, should have wanted these sacred writings to fulfil that role, continuing, in spite of his conversion, to insist that God's revelation in Christ was in continuity with the Old Testament revelation.[37] The curse which Paul quoted or misquoted from *Deuteronomy*, directed against 'all who do not persevere in doing everything that is written in the Book of the Law',[38] had now been removed by Jesus Christ. 'Christ brought us freedom from the curse of the Law by becoming himself an accursed thing'[39] – a startling phrase which refers obliquely to that other passage of *Deuteronomy*[40] asserting that he who is hanged on a tree or gibbet is the object of a curse.

These references to the scriptures seem to us arid and strained. But the essential point is Paul's insistence on the supersession of the Torah or Law. 'Christ is the end of the Law as a way of righteousness (*dikaiosyne*) for everyone who has faith.'[41] 'If righteousness comes by Law, then Christ died for nothing ... 'When you seek to be justified by way of law, your relation with Christ is completely severed.'[42] And the point is elaborated in *Colossians*: 'He has cancelled the bond which pledged us to the decrees of the Law. It stood against us, but he has set it aside, nailing it to the cross.'[43] To put it differently again, there is an altogether *new* Law now – the Law of Christ.[44] To people imbued with Judaism, this was a startling conception. True, Paul himself, at least when he was associating with his co-religionists (though not otherwise, cf. chapter V, section 1) maintained personal conformity with the provisions of his ancient Law regarding diet and uncleanliness and the Sabbath and so on – for the sake of expediency, as some have noted with disapproval. 'To Jews I became like a Jew, to win Jews: as they are subject to the Law of Moses, I put myself under that Law to win them, although I am not myself subject to it.'[45] And yet he does not scruple to describe that old Law – from which 'in Christ Jesus the life-giving Law of the Spirit has set you free' – as *the Law of sin and death*.[46]

Those are harsh words. And there are still harsher words to come. Paul tells the community at Philippi:

I have been a Pharisee, in my attitude to the Law faultless and impeccable. But all such assets I have written off because of Christ. I would say more: I count everything sheer loss, because all is far outweighed by the gain of knowing Christ Jesus my Lord, for whose sake I did in fact lose everything. I count it so much garbage, for the sake of gaining Christ and finding myself incorporate in him, with no righteousness of my own, no legal rectitude, but the righteousness which comes from faith in Christ, given by God in response to faith.[47]

So Paul dismisses the Jewish Law and all it stands for as mere garbage. The New English Bible cautiously allows 'dung' as an alternative translation; but the real equivalent for what Paul meant is a nastier word. He wants to reject the Law by the grossest, most violent term he can muster, just as, a few verses previously, he had used a coarse term, mutilation, for circumcision.

This virulent abuse was meant to separate Christianity from Judaism: to sever the new dispensation from the old. And that is just what it did. The Old Law had yielded to a New Law; or, to put it differently, the Old Covenant (the same word is translated 'Testament') bestowed upon Moses at Sinai had been replaced by a New Covenant. And this was by God's deliberate wish and initiative, because of what had happened on the Cross. 'It is God who has qualified us to dispense his New Covenant – a Covenant expressed not in a written document, but in a spiritual bond . . . Only in Christ is the old Covenant abrogated.'[48] And it had been described to Paul how Jesus himself, after the Last Supper, on the night of his arrest, took the cup and declared: 'this cup is the New Covenant sealed by my blood.'[49]

Now, it was not altogether unknown for Jews to speak of a new Covenant which would eventually supersede the old one granted to

Moses. *Jeremiah*, for example, unimpressed with the full technicalities of the written Law, had forecast that such a development would take place: 'the time is coming, says the Lord, when I will make a New Covenant with Israel and Judah.'[50] Much nearer Paul's time, too – in the days of the Maccabean revolt against the Greeks – there had been Jews prepared to surmise that the Old Covenant, and the Mosaic Law with it, might be abolished at the future advent of the Messiah. And the devotees of Qumran called themselves 'the Faithful of the New Covenant'.[51] But it was one thing to engage in such airy speculations about the future, and entirely another to say, as Paul did, that the New Covenant, graven, as *Jeremiah* had promised and forecast, not on stone but on the hearts of men, had arrived here and now, conferred by the Crucifixion of Jesus – so that the question of the supersession of the Mosaic Law no longer lay in the future, *for it had already happened.*

This was what seemed to the Jews to be intolerable. They were not so much worried by the declaration that Jesus Christ was the Messiah – though of course they did not accept this – as disgusted by the argument that, because of this alleged visitation in the recent past, the Mosaic Law had somehow been abolished. For in their eyes the Law continued, perpetually, to proclaim God's holy will: and all Paul's arguments about 'works' and 'justification' did not seem to them to erode this essential point in any way. His insistence that the Law had been totally superseded and shelved by the New Covenant which Jesus' death had brought drove a shattering wedge between Christianity and themselves.

After the First Jewish Revolt, the Pharisees, who had by this time gained control of the Hebrew community, decided that it was essential to concentrate wholly on the Law; and Paul, who had died not long before, was attacked (though not by name) for having interpreted it falsely: 'he has no shame in the world to come.'[52] Indeed, he was denounced by Jews as the greatest apostate of all time; and rightly, from their point of view, because had it not been for him Christianity might have been absorbed into Judaism. In which case, the Christian faith might have gradually disappeared, like other deviating Jewish groups; or it could have modified the content of Jewish belief from within. Perhaps there would have emerged a united front fulfilling an even greater role in the ancient, medieval and modern worlds than the two religions have fulfilled as separate units. But those are unprofitable might-have-beens. What is certain is that, by his radical rejection of the

Law, Paul took a step which, as time went on, came to exercise an almost uniquely decisive effect on the course of history, religious and secular alike.

It was not, as we have seen, that Paul minimized the importance of good behaviour. But not only was this, in his judgment, a secondary derivative from faith, but his injunctions about morality – like those attributed to Jesus in the Gospels – are for the most part, perhaps to the extent of ninety per cent, closely analogous with the standard moral demands of the Old Testament and Apocrypha. They are also very similar to the regulations laid down for the community at Qumran. The assertions of Paul and Qumran alike were probably derived from current Jewish ethical codes, though they also, unconsciously, incorporate certain additions derived, through these codes, from the Hellenistic Greek world that lay all around.

The ethics of Christianity, in other words, are not very original. 'Its ideas,' as Sir Walter Raleigh observed, 'are all to be found elsewhere, and are not, it would seem, part of the attraction.' There was virtually no such thing as a distinctive Christian moral system. What was distinctive is that such ethical instruction as it offered was now linked, not with the Torah or on any code dependent on it, but with Christ. Every Christian has to aim at conformity with him: for which enterprise Paul, though careful to disclaim perfection for himself, boldly offers his own person as the intermediary: 'Follow my example as I follow Christ's.'[53]

The real novelty of Christianity, then, was not any system of good conduct, but the new *motive* it supplied for this: namely, the motive deduced from God's revolutionary action through Jesus Christ. This, to Paul, was what was important; the good conduct would follow from it. Paul looks to the inspiration of Christ to make the fruits of the spirit flower in the soul. Where, then, is the need for a *code* of conduct? The question of having one just does not arise. Paul, observed Albert Schweitzer –

. . . arrives at the idea of a faith which rejects not only the works of the Law, but works in general. He thus closes the pathway to a theory of ethics. This is the price which he pays for the possibility of finding the doctrine of freedom from the Law in the doctrine of the atoning death of Jesus . . . Ethics are brought in a natural way into connection with the idea of the forgiveness of sins and of redemption in in general . . .

What he wants this subsidiary doctrine [of righteousness by faith] for is to enable him . . . to conduct his controversy with the Law by means of the argument from Scripture. More he does not ask of it. But those who sub-sequently made his doctrine of justification by faith the centre of belief have had the tragic experience of finding that they were dealing with a conception of redemption from which no ethic could logically be derived.[54]

So faith came first, and ethics were wholly subsidiary. But how could that faith be acquired?

Paul did not for a moment believe that human beings were able to acquire it on their own account. They could only do so by an act of God, that is to say by grace (*charis*), the gift of divine favour. It is a gift which, by virtue of the Crucifixion, believing Christians have already received. 'All are justified by God's free grace alone . . . The grace of our Lord Jesus be with you.'[55] 'It is by his grace you are saved.[56] 'You have received the grace of God: do not let it go for nothing.'[57] Grace is prior to faith, for without this free, unmerited kindness of God to sinners, without the abundance of this inexhaustible, loving generosity, man is powerless even to begin to form the belief that confers salvation. Accord-ing to Luther, man has no more power to turn to God than a stone, unless God makes the first move. And Francis Thompson wrote, in the *Hound of Heaven*,

> Naked I wait thy love's uplifted stroke.
> My armour piece by piece thou hast hewed from me.
> I am defenceless utterly.

It was argued by Paul's successors that he had meant grace not only to be a gift but a responsibility, and that a man, before acquiring it, must intend and endeavour to become what it requires. Nevertheless, no such deduction can be made from his words. He expressed himself almost as unequivocally as Francis Thompson about the helplessness of man to acquire grace on his own account.

This idea of the total humbling of the heart ran contrary to the attitudes of the Jews, since, for all their belief in absolute dependence upon God, his doctrine seemed to them to strike at the roots of all morality, by paralyzing the human will. Furthermore, Paul's attitude was just as violently opposed to the cardinal Jewish doctrine of repent-ance. This tenet of Judaism, to which reference was made in the last section, proclaimed that God, out of Love, forgives the *sincerely penitent* sinner. No Old Testament writer suggested that God loves the sinner before he repents: on the contrary,[58] and John the Baptist and Jesus, if as is probable we should accept the Gospel version, likewise believed that repentance should come before forgiveness.[59] But if grace, as Paul suggests, is going to be handed out by an entirely free, unilateral gift of God, then it is no longer of any relevance whether the sinner has first become penitent or not. It is true that Paul – like Peter, according to *Acts*[60] – asserts the need for repentance.[61] But it is an isolated allusion, and in any case refers to something quite different. For in Paul's eyes repentance is not merely, as it was to the Jews, the human ability to turn away *from* wicked actions: it is rather a fundamental turning away *to* salvation in Christ.

To him, then, in contrast to the central doctrines of his inherited Judaism, the expiatory death of Christ eliminates the idea of God's free forgiveness for the penitent sinner: since the Crucifixion has brought forgiveness already. By this gift, God has shown himself freer still – too free altogether, in the Jewish view: for he has awarded his grace without any such conditions, indeed without any conditions at all. Later commentators were nervous about the starkness of this doctrine, and stressed (against the evidence) that Paul had *meant* to link this divine grace with a free human response. The controversy broke out again, with redoubled force, between Augustine, who revived Paul's doctrine of all-powerful grace in extreme form (denying free human response), and Pelagius who denounced this idea on the grounds that it undermined human endeavour. John Bunyan, in the opening sentences of *The Pilgrim's Progress*, laid a Pauline, Augustinian stress on our helplessness to save ourselves, and Martin Luther, likewise, disagreed with Erasmus' too humanistic interpretation of the Pauline doctrine: 'I fear that he does not promote the cause of Christ and God's grace sufficiently.' Calvin, too, in the same spirit, emphasized the *mysteriousness* of the grace of God, who saves sinners although they are unworthy.[62]

The argument put forward by Paul's opponents, that his doctrine of grace, buttressed by the subordination of works to faith, fettered the human will and deprived it of any power to take effective action, may seem to possess some cogency. Yet it would have been utterly rejected by Paul, who believed his doctrine brought liberation. The redemption bestowed by Jesus had been like the emancipation of a slave, and Paul's demotion of the Law seemed to him a uniquely liberating process. Indeed its proclamation in *Galatians* has made that Letter appear to many the noblest blow for liberty that has ever been struck, the manifesto and Magna Carta of Christian freedom against thraldom to Law, sin and death. 'Christ set us free, to be free men.'[63] 'All are justified by God's free grace alone, through his act of liberation in the person of Jesus Christ.'[64] 'In him we have access to God with freedom.'[65] 'Where the spirit of the Lord is, there is liberty.'[66]

Then Paul's love of antithesis comes into play once again. We have become free because we have become slaves, but in a totally different sense from our former slavery to sin. Now, it is slavery to Christ – as 'captives in his triumphal procession'[67] – which has given us true freedom and self-mastery. Before this intervention of God's grace, declared Augustine, man had been 'free' only in the single sense of being free to believe: now there is an infinitely wider freedom, since 'it is where the spirit of the Lord is that there is true liberty.' It was the inspiration of Paul that led him to this conclusion; and a passage in *I Corinthians* on the same theme affected Martin Luther too, with tremendous force, and prompted his essay *On the Freedom of a Christian*: 'I am a free man and own no master; but I have made myself every man's servant, to win over as many as possible.'[68]

By the same token, Paul emphasized, in a sense unfamiliar to the Old Testament, the existence and free operation of the consciences of all human beings, whatever their faith. 'When Gentiles who do not possess the Law carry out its precepts by the light of nature, then, although they have no Law, they are their own Law, for they display the effect of the Law inscribed on their hearts. Their conscience is called to witness.'[69] And how much more notable was this 'freedom' of conscience among Christians. It is a concept which may seem hard to understand in the light of mankind's helplessness before the grace of God. But that was all part of the instructive paradox, for this very helplessness was what, as Paul declared, endowed human beings with freedom from *every other* sort of dependence – and thus made their consciences free in the only sense that was authentically meaningful.

Paul claimed that his own conscience was entirely clear,[70] and he stressed that the consciences of others must not be hurt.[71] And then, in Luther's time, it was from a renewed emphasis on these Pauline ideas that novel, more respectful attitudes towards the liberty and inviolability of people's consciences gradually developed – the attitudes which mark the transition from medieval to modern times.

However, Paul's critics were always able to point out that liberty could mean licence, and that this was precisely where the supersession of the

Law by Grace and Faith was likely to lead; and so was the perilous belief that the merit of one, namely Jesus, was available to swell the merit of others. Indeed, these criticisms had at once become vigorously apparent in Paul's lifetime. For when we consider all that the Law meant to the Jews, who revered it as a comprehensive guide to their moral conduct every day of their lives, it was not hard to foresee what practical results would flow after Paul had announced that this guideline was no longer operative. The results included an immediate and rapid increase of lax behaviour and immorality in the Christian communities – on Paul's own admission. There was sexual misbehaviour at Corinth, theft at Ephesus, drunkenness at both, and troubles, too, in the communities of Galatia and Rome. Nor was this surprising, for the deliberate refusal to apply the traditional sanctions of the Torah encouraged people of unexacting moral standards to join this apparently easy-going movement.

At a later date, the sect of the Carpocratians interpreted Paul's remark 'except through Law I should never have become acquainted with sin'[72] as an invitation to unrestricted orgies, at which, according to Clement of Alexandria, 'they overturn the lamps and extinguish the light . . . and have intercourse where they will and with whom they will'[73] – even arguing that this behaviour was necessary for their salvation!

> Free from the Law!
> O Happy Condition!
> I can sin as I please,
> And still have remission.

Paul, of course, denied strongly that this was where his opinions could be regarded as leading. To the Galatians he wrote: 'You, my friends, were called to be free men: only do not turn your freedom into licence for your lower nature.'[74] And to the Corinthians he expanded the point: '"I am free to do anything", you say. Yes, but not everything is for my good. No doubt I am free to do anything, but I for one will not let anything make free with me.'[75] To the community at Rome, also, who had evidently tried to justify their misbehaviour on theological grounds, he delivered an equally sharp rebuke. 'Are we to sin, because we are not under Law but under grace? Of course not! . . . No, no! We died to sin: how can we live in it any longer?'[76] And these corrective words were all the more necessary because there were some people in the imperial capital who explicitly blamed Paul's permissive teaching for what was going wrong: 'some libellously report me as saying "do evil that good may come".'[77]

He had laid himself open to this misinterpretation by his extremely sweeping remarks about the Law: and they had been made, as far as we can tell, on his own original initiative. Although the evidence on both sides is contradictory and biassed, there is no reason to suppose that Jesus had already spoken in equally scathing terms. Jewish critics did later maintain that Jesus had denigrated the Law, and asserted that this had helped to bring about his execution. But that was emphatically not the opinion of the *Gospel according to St Matthew*, whose author quotes Jesus as saying: 'Do not suppose that I have come to abolish the Law and the prophets: I did not come to abolish, but to complete'[78] – the saying is preserved in an alternative form in the Talmud, probably from an Aramaic original: 'I am come not to detract from the Law of Moses, but to add to it.' *Matthew*'s defensive language on the same lines, whether it accurately reproduces a tradition going back to Jesus or not, shows that at least *some* Christians of the time when this Gospel was written, in the later years of the first century AD, very strongly condemned Paul's doctrine that the Crucifixion had abrogated the Law. Indeed, Jesus, according to *Matthew*, actually went on to emphasize that meticulous observance of the Law in all its details remained a necessity. To *Acts*, likewise, Paul's doctrine of justification by faith, accompanied by the suspension of the Jewish Law, seemed incomprehensible; while *Hebrews*, too, deliberately toned down the Pauline tension between Law and Gospel.

Yet as Gentile Christianity became stronger and its links with Judaism weakened, support for Paul's view spread; and the Church, which had hitherto held the Law second only to its own new scriptures, began to share Paul's antipathy towards it: that Christians were not expected to adhere to its rulings was taken by this second generation as a matter of course. Thus the *Letter of Barnabas* (*c.* 130) explained that the Jews' literal interpretation of the Law was based on a radical misunderstanding;[79] and that when Paul described it as 'ordained by angels through an intermediary', he had meant it was a snare created by the wiles of a demon. And then the Letter went on to deny, in total contradiction of *Matthew*, that there was any link whatever between Judaism and Christianity. Marcion's* *Antitheses*, too, quoted and exaggerated Paul's sayings in order to draw the sharpest contrast between the Law and the

Gospel – which, in his view, superseded the Law more thoroughly than even Paul himself had intended it to.

But then came the great cover-up. For the churchmen of the second century AD were shocked by Marcion's extremism, and anxious to reinstate Paul; yet they were anxious to do so without subscribing to what seemed his more outrageous conclusions. For the Church was eager, like most second or third generation churches and missions of any and every faith, to base its activities on a firm foundation of moral teaching. Paul's ideals could not survive, this school of ecclesiastical thought maintained, without the meticulously laid down code of behaviour which disciplines people to live up to such principles. About all this, it was now felt, Paul had written in terms that were very much less than satisfactory. Or, better, the terms he had employed could perhaps be stretched somewhat and reinterpreted into meanings which at first they had not seemed to possess. And so it was insisted that, after all, his fierce criticism of the Law was not quite what it seemed to be. His association of the Law with sin (the commentators maintained) does not really depreciate the Law at all – Paul was only saying that it is the *revelation* of sin. They seized, with approval, on his comparison of the Law to the attendant taking children to school; since such an attendant, even if of subordinate status, is a good man. They also claimed that Paul had intended to distinguish between *two* Laws: one comprising cere-monial requirements and the like, which cannot be fulfilled perfectly; and the other including the ethical demands, which are capable of fulfilment. And pointing out that Paul had written of the '*Law*' of Jesus Christ, Clement of Alexandria argued that he had meant *not* that Christ meant the end of the Law, but that the Law had reached its perfection in Christ.

Yet in none of these assertions were these Christian thinkers faithful to what Paul had said and intended. Their aims were well-meaning, in regard to their conception of what the church ought to be, but mis-guided, if not at times positively dishonest, in their interpretation of Paul's words. For he had been a great deal more radical than they were prepared to suppose. Even if he had refrained from carrying his conclu-sions to quite the extreme standpoint of the *Letter of Barnabas* and Marcion, he did genuinely believe, and assert, that the Jewish Law was totally superseded – by faith in what God had done through Jesus Christ.

Faith or good actions, which must come first? Which counts the more? The controversy has continued to rage throughout the centuries. Its answer is partly a matter of temperament. Some people, for example, are capable of behaving decently without any faith at all. Paul, however, did not acknowledge the existence of such people, since for him faith came absolutely first, and good behaviour could only follow as its consequence. Today, there will be many prepared to say that during the present century we have had more than our fill of faith, much of it directed, by millions, to appalling causes such as Nazism. Others will disagree, feeling that in the present critical state of the world an increased amount of faith could move mountains. It would be on their side, and among their leaders, that Paul, were he alive, would be. For one of the most startling achievements of his own career, perhaps the most startling of all, was this pronouncement of the complete conquest and supersession, *by faith*, of the Jewish Law – with which, therefore, countless millions of Christians since his day have had nothing to do. Whether you consider this a good thing or not depends on whether you are a Christian or a Jew. But what cannot be denied is the incalculable effect of Paul's utterances on the course of events from that day to this. By breaking with the Jewish Law and Covenant and ethical creed, and seeking to replace it by the God-given redemptive power of Jesus' death, Paul became one of the most influential historical figures who ever lived.

4. *Direct Contact with the Deity*

The reason why Paul possessed the faith to believe and convey to others his belief in this astonishing, revolutionary, world-overturning power of the Crucifixion, Resurrection and Ascension, was because of his certainty that Jesus Christ had appeared to him in a vision: an experience which converted him from Saul, a savage opponent of Christianity, to Paul, its passionate follower.

Did I not see Jesus the Lord? . . . In the end he appeared even to me. It was like an abnormal birth; I had persecuted the church of God . . .[1] I persecuted the church of God, and tried to destroy it . . . but then in his good pleasure God, who had set me apart from birth and called me through his grace, chose to reveal his Son to me and through me, in order that I might proclaim him among the Gentiles. When this happened, without consulting any human being, without going up to Jerusalem to see those who were apostles before me, I went off at once to Arabia, and afterwards returned to Damascus.[2]

That is how Paul himself described his conversion in the Letters. *Acts*, having been written so much later, cannot necessarily be trusted to provide as reliable a testimony about what really happened on the road to Damascus. Yet is it remarkable that this otherwise unrepetitive work describes the conversion of Paul in no less than three separate passages. That shows the significance attached to the event: to *Acts* it seemed the supreme example of the argument that the book was above all trying to develop – that nothing can stand in the way of the Gospel. And this triple account also conveys to us, if not what Paul himself, in every detail, had believed to have occurred, but at least how this mighty happening *seemed* to have occurred, to the generation immediately following his lifetime. The three passages of *Acts* are as follows:

1. Meanwhile Saul was still breathing murderous threats against the disciples of the Lord. He went to the High Priest and applied for letters to the synagogues at Damascus authorizing him to arrest anyone he found, men or women, who followed the new way, and bring them to Jerusalem. While he was still on the road and nearing Damascus, suddenly a light flashed from the sky all around him. He fell to the ground and heard a voice saying, 'Saul, Saul why do you persecute me?' 'Tell me, Lord,' he said, 'who you are.' The voice answered, 'I am Jesus, whom you are persecuting. But get up and go into the city, and you will be told what you have to do.' Meanwhile the men who were travelling with him stood speechless; they heard the voice but could see no one. Saul got up from the ground, but when he opened his eyes he could not see; so they led him by the hand and brought him into Damascus. He was blind for three days, and took no food or drink.[3]

2. And this is what happened. I was on the road and nearing Damascus, when suddenly about midday a great light flashed from the sky all around me, and I fell to the ground. Then I heard a voice saying to me, 'Saul, Saul, why do you persecute me?' I answered, 'Tell me, Lord, who you are.' 'I am Jesus of Nazareth,' he said, 'whom you are persecuting.' My companions saw the light, but did not hear the voice that spoke to me. 'What shall I do, Lord?' I said, and the Lord replied, 'Get up and continue your journey to Damascus; there you will be told of all the tasks that are laid upon you.' As I had been blinded by the brilliance of that light, my companions led me by the hand, and so I came to Damascus.[4]

3. In all the synagogues I tried by repeated punishment to make them renounce their faith; indeed my fury rose to such a pitch that I extended my persecution to foreign cities. On one such occasion I was travelling to Damascus with authority and commission from the chief priests: and as I saw a light from the sky, more brilliant than the sun, shining all around me and my

travelling-companions. We all fell to the ground, and then I heard a voice saying to me in the Jewish language, 'Saul, Saul, why do you persecute me? It is hard for you, this kicking against the goad.' I said, 'Tell me, Lord, who you are'; and the Lord replied, 'I am Jesus, whom you are persecuting. But now, rise to your feet and stand upright. I have appeared to you for a purpose: to appoint you my servant and witness, to testify both to what you have seen and to what you shall yet see of me. I will rescue you from this people and from the Gentiles to whom I am sending you. I send you to open their eyes and turn them from darkness to light, from the dominion of Satan to God, so that, by trust in me, they may obtain forgiveness of sins, and a place with those whom God has made his own.' And so, King Agrippa, I did not disobey the heavenly vision. I turned first to the inhabitants of Damascus.[5]

Most painters have found it too hard to attempt to depict this almost uniquely influential event, though Murillo, Camuccini and Caravaggio tried to do so. Michelangelo, too, in the Cappella Paolina of the Vatican, depicted it strangely and startlingly, with a multitude of the heavenly host gazing down upon the scene.

On the whole, the discrepancies between these three accounts in *Acts* are not serious enough to deserve much notice. It is clear that they represent minor variations from an identical tradition. Whether this goes back as early as the briefer allusions to his conversion made by Paul himself is another question. The first two of the quoted passages of *Acts* indicate that he must proceed to Damascus and receive further instructions; there, these stories go on to tell, a disciple named Ananias restored his sight, baptized him, and according to one version informed him of his future missionary duties.[6] Yet this is in marked contradiction to Paul's own repeated insistence that he received his commission solely from Jesus Christ himself, on behalf of God, which was a vital part of his claim that his apostleship was equal or superior to the status of the apostles who had known Jesus in his lifetime and had then seen his risen body while it was still on earth, before the Ascension. However, the revised statements which appear in *Acts* can be easily explained because, as we shall see elsewhere, that book was concerned to tone down and eliminate Paul's evident remoteness from the Jerusalem church. And for the same reason one particular aspect of the record, namely his mission to the Gentiles, which Paul himself so emphatically links and synchronizes with his conversion, received very much fainter emphasis in these three narratives of *Acts*, and indeed does not appear directly in two of them at all, and even in the third only rates a subsidiary mention after a reference to his mission to the Jews.† But apart from this easily explainable discrepancy between Paul's Letters and *Acts*, it seems as though the versions in the latter work are derived from his Letters, and not based on any independent account.

This threefold reiteration in *Acts* shows that the early Church attached enormous importance to Paul's conversion as the supreme example and prototype of all the conversions that Jews ought to be experiencing. The repetition of so many of the same details in each of the three accounts suggests that the tradition was a firm one, and therefore early in date; and although these details do not appear in Paul's own surviving allusions to the event – which are, after all, not intended as descriptions of his conversion, but only refer to it in passing – they may well go back to statements composed by himself, whether oral or written down in writings that have not survived.

As for the voice, writes Stewart Perowne:

A voice was the *normal* method of learning of the divine will. Adam heard a voice, St Augustine heard a voice, Joan of Arc heard several; and Bunyan heard one '. . . that would sound so loud within me, yea, and as it were call so strongly after me, that once, above all the rest, I turned my head over my shoulder, thinking verily that some man had, behind me, called me.'[7]

But the exact nature of Paul's violent, overwhelming experience has been the subject of endless discussion. *Acts* strongly stresses the presence of a blinding light; and indeed Paul himself had probably been referring to his own vision when he wrote in *II Corinthians*: 'For the same God who said "Out of darkness let light shine," has caused his light [*photismos*] to shine within us, to give the light of revelation.'[8]

Perowne suggested that Paul encountered one of the ferocious storms of thunder and lightning which occur in those parts of the world and seemed to the ancients a terrifying manifestation of divine power. That is perfectly possible; yet, even without flashes of lightning, psychologists have noted radiant light as the most frequent of all accompaniments of visions and especially conversions. According to William James' *Varieties of Religious Experience* (who gives details of the modern visionaries he mentions):

† Elsewhere in *Acts* the first statement of the Gentile mission is attributed to later occasions; cf. chapter 5, section 1, p. 141

There is one form of sensory automatism which possibly deserves special notice on account of its frequency. I refer to hallucinatory or pseudo-hallucinatory luminous phenomena, photisms, to use the term of the psychologists. Saint Paul's blinding heavenly vision seems to have been a phenomenon of this sort; so does Constantine's cross in the sky. The last case I quoted mentions floods of light and glory. Henry Alline mentions a light, about whose externality he seems uncertain. Colonel Gardiner sees a blazing light.

President Finney writes:

'All at once the glory of God shone upon and round about in a manner almost marvellous ... A light perfectly ineffable shone in my soul, that almost prostrated me on the ground ... This light seemed like the brightness of the sun in every direction. It was too intense for the eyes ... I think I knew something then, by actual experience, of that light that prostrated Paul on the way to Damascus. It was surely a light such as I could not have endured long.'

Such reports of photisms are indeed far from uncommon. Here is another from Starbuck's collection, where the light appeared evidently external:

'I had attended a series of revival services for about two weeks off and on. Had been invited to the altar several times, all the time becoming more deeply impressed, when finally I decided I must do this, or I should be lost. Realization of conversion was very vivid, like a ton's weight being lifted from my heart; a strange light which seemed to light up the whole room (for it was dark).'[9]

And Aldous Huxley, too, envisaged the experiences of his first wife Maria in terms of the same brilliant illumination:

In the desert [they had had a house in the desert in California earlier], and later under hypnosis, all Maria's visionary and mystical experiences had been associated with light. In this she was in no way exceptional. Almost all mystics and visionaries have experienced Reality in terms of light – either of light in its naked purity, or of light infusing and radiating out of things and persons seen with the inner eye or in the external world. Light had been the element in which her spirit had lived, and it was therefore to light that all my words referred.[10]

Paul's experience was apparently of a similar nature, stimulated perhaps by heat, exhaustion, thirst: who knows what hardships of this kind he may not have suffered on a middle-eastern journey? It was easy for a Jew to conceive the divine spirit not only as sound but as light – visible, material and palpable. In Paul's conversion, therefore, as F. Van Hügel suggested, 'we get Christ or the Spirit conceived as an element, as it were an ocean of ethereal light, in which souls are plunged and which penetrates them.'[11]

But why did Paul's spectacular conversion occur at all? What prompted it? Our evidence is too fragmentary, and enigmatic, to allow us to do more than guess at an answer. But what we can surmise is that, even if not (as some have believed) an epileptic, he was already in an extremely nervous, anxious state, which made him highly suggestible. For that is the sort of emotional climate in which such conversions generally happen; and they are not infrequent. Man's extremity, it has been said, is God's opportunity. People living on the ragged edge of consciousness lose control of their normal response to stimuli. In order to recover their life and energy, what they do is to plunge into self-surrender. And such sudden conversions, it has been found, usually bring a strong urge to make them known to others – which was what Paul, for ever after, felt the most pressing impulsion to achieve.

He was liable to harrowing tensions. 'What I do is not what I want to do, but what I detest . . . when I want to do the right, only the wrong is in my reach . . . Miserable creature that I am!'[12] These self-tortures continued throughout his life. But it was before his conversion that they had reached the most intolerable heights. This was because of his growing, acute dissatisfaction with the Jewish Law on which he had been brought up: a dissatisfaction founded upon its apparent incapacity to rescue the world from abysmal evil. Seemingly abrupt conversions are often based on long previous periods of unconscious, subliminal incubation and cerebration, and Paul was in a state of such desperate, confused discontent that either he must break down completely or some utterly radical psychological solution would have to be found.

What the solution was, we know. It was an amazing one, paradoxical like all Paul's thinking, since, as he himself declared, he had been a savage persecutor of the infant Christian community, proclaiming the unalterable intention of stamping it out of existence. Why, then, did he go into complete reverse, and passionately find his salvation, and the salvation of the whole world, in this very same community which he had hitherto been attempting to annihilate? *Acts* suggests, by implication, that the reason lay in his admiring observation of the martyrdom of Stephen.[13] For shortly before Paul's conversion, there had been this other Jewish follower of Jesus, who had likewise clashed with the Law of his people. It is not certain whether Stephen, like Paul afterwards, had advocated preaching to non-Jews or not; his primary point was not the same as Paul's, since what he had particularly objected to was the allegedly excessive Jewish devotion to the Temple.[14] For this, he had been stoned to death in Jerusalem by the Jews, either in the course of a riot or after a more or less legal trial. As he died, *Acts* reported him to have cried out, 'Lord, do not hold this sin against them!'[15] But that was very like what the dying Jesus, too, was reputed to have said;[16] and this reminiscent echo by the writer of *Acts* is so manifestly deliberate that it arouses suspicions about the detailed veracity of the whole story of Stephen – suspicions which are deepened by the content of the speech attributed to the martyr, since surely no one can have taken down in detail what he said at the time – and besides, the version given here bears many specific signs of later literary invention.

Doubts are also inspired by *Acts*' statement that Paul was present at Stephen's death: 'the witnesses [at the trial?] laid their coats at the feet of a young man named Saul . . . And Saul was among those who approved of his murder.'[17] This makes a highly suitable and dramatic prelude to his conversion from persecutor to apostle, which follows very shortly afterwards. But suspicions that his link with Stephen's martyrdom is a literary device rather than a historical fact are sharpened by Paul's own statement that before his conversion he had experienced no contact at all with the Judaean Christians. Indeed, even after it, he at first only got to know Cephas (Peter) and James the Just, the brother of Christ. Apart from them, 'I remained unknown by sight [*or*, personally] to Christ's congregations in Judaea.'[18]

Attempts have been made to get round this awkward point by suggesting that Paul was only referring here to the regions of Judaea *other than* Jerusalem, its capital. But it is far easier to suppose that he means what he said: he was a Jew of the Dispersion who did not come to Jerusalem until after he had been converted, so that the statement by *Acts* that he was an onlooker at Stephen's death in Jerusalem must be regarded as fictitious. However, the nexus of cause and effect insisted upon in *Acts* may not be as wholly irrelevant as this might suggest. For it is reasonable enough to believe that Paul's revulsion against the Torah of the Jews, a feeling already very powerful in his heart because of the palpable failure of this code to cure the world, was intensified to fever heat when news came to him, in the north, about how they had treated Stephen. And this, in turn, would help impel him to reverse his previous view of Jesus Christ. For not only had Stephen himself been a devotee of Christ, whom he was believed, during his last moments, to have seen in a vision standing at God's right hand,[19] but he had suffered a fate which closely resembled the Saviour's; and *Acts*, as we have seen, took trouble to stress the comparison.

Besides, Paul's mind always throve on contrasts of the most vivid possible type. He had previously persecuted the Christians; and now, not content with merely ceasing from this course of action, he was characteristically determined to go to the very opposite extreme and become one of their most ardent fellow-members. He told himself, and others, that this had been predestined since his birth:[20] just as the *II Isaiah* and *Jeremiah* reported claims that their writers or heroes, too, had been predestined to their prophetic missions ever since their births, or even since the moment when they were conceived in their mothers' wombs.[21] Such a comparison with the Prophets was yet another of Paul's paradoxes, although perhaps an unconscious one, because even while breaking away so radically from the Jewish Law he still could not help framing his breakaway in traditional Jewish terms.

His conversion radically altered the direction of the world: had it not been for his Letters and missionary work, how could Christianity ever have conquered the West? 'Without the conversion of Paul,' wrote E. W. Hunt, 'the movement that had begun at Pentecost might well, after surviving for a brief period as a Jewish heresy, have dissolved, leaving behind it only a memory of an idealistic visionary named Jesus of Nazareth.'[22] But what happened on the road to Damascus meant that everything would now be different. The event has been hailed, notably in Lyttelton's *Conversion of St Paul* (1747), as proof that Christianity was the true religion. Such a proof it does not and cannot in itself suffice to provide. Nevertheless,

His conversion proved the power of Christianity to overcome the strongest prejudices and to stamp its own type on a large nature by a revolution both instantaneous and permanent. Paul's was a personality so strong and original that no other man could have been less expected to sink himself in another; but, from the moment when he came into contact with Christ, he was so overmastered by his influence that he never afterwards had any other desire than to be the mere echo and reflection of him to the world.[23]

Paul's apprehension of God and Jesus was not a rational, philosophical tie. On the contrary, it had been communicated by visionary revelations. The blinding vision vouchsafed to him at his conversion was not his only experience of this kind: others followed later.

I shall go on to tell of visions and revelations granted by the Lord. I know a Christian man who fourteen years ago (whether in the body or out of it, I do not know – God knows) was caught up as far as the third heaven. And I know that this same man (whether in the body or out of it, I do not know – God knows) was caught up into paradise . . .[24]

That man was himself. It is true that theologians would sometimes like to minimize the visionary nature of Paul's contacts with the deity, which is so out of keeping with modern everyday institutionalized religion. However, his Letters compel us to accord these experiences full weight; and *Acts* faithfully reproduced this tradition by telling how he claimed, in Jerusalem, to have seen Jesus in a trance.[25] But the process can more accurately be described not as occasional but continuous, since the effect of these visions was a state of exaltation by which Paul felt he was transfigured all the time: 'the life I now live is not my life, *but the life which Christ lives in me.*'[26] Thus Paul was always 'in Christ'. Sometimes this constantly repeated term, when employed about the community as a whole, merely refers to the medium in which the everyday life of Christians was lived, just as a fish lives naturally in water. But the words, as applied to himself, meant more to him than that, involving an absolute identity of personality, a total organic union, with Jesus.

And so Saul, or Paul, is 'I – yet not I.'[27] It was his experience, anticipating Karl Gustav Jung, that a man may cease to rely on his own will and come to a way of living which seems to be directed from a centre that is not himself. Whether this is to be called mysticism or not depends on what precise meaning we attach to that term. One favoured definition is Lalande's:

Mysticism is belief in the possibility of an intimate and direct union of the human spirit with the fundamental principle of being, a union which constitutes at once a mode of existence and a mode of knowledge different from and superior to normal existence and knowledge.[28]

What is characteristic of the mystics is their claim to a widening of normal consciousness, a release of latent powers, which brings them into immediate contact with this fundamental principle: if they link their experience with a religion – as some but not all mystics do – their belief is that the human will can feel itself moved by the transcendent without the acknowledgment of any rational intervention. C. H. Dodd seeks an analogy in people's closest relationships with each other.

You have a friend, dear as your own soul, the very embodiment of that which you admire and aspire to. Now you may sit in the room and converse with your friend, and his spoken word, or act, or look may exert upon you the influence of his personality. Or you may be apart and he may exert that influence by letter. Or without letter you may recall him so vividly that the memory serves as a potent source of influence. All this is still the friend without. But when once the influence is established, there is a somewhat abiding in the central places of your own mind which is yet not yours but your friend's. You may even be unconscious of it, but it shows itself in count-less ways. Someone will remark, 'I seemed to hear X in what you said just now'; or 'The way you did that was so exactly X that I could have fancied him here.'[29]

Yet to apply this sort of interpretation to Paul risks, once again, depre-ciating the visionary or, as non-Christians might say, hallucinatory, aspects of his experience. For these are indeed very evident.

Yet, even so, it is doubtful whether Paul – or any other early Christian for that matter – can be legitimately described as a mystic. Among these men, writes E. R. Dodds,

> . . . There is much talk of *assimilation* to God, especially where Platonic influence is strong, and even, in certain authors, of 'divinization' while still in the body . . . The *Sentences* of Sextus* tell us that 'in seeing God you will see yourself', and conversely that 'the soul of the wise man is God's mirror': for this way of talking there are two sources, in the *First Alcibiades* attributed to Plato, and in St Paul's *Second Letter to the Corinthians* ('for us there is no veil over the face . . . we are transfigured into the Lord's likeness, from splendour to splendour.')[30] But while there is the same general trend towards mysticism in the wide sense that we have observed in pagan authors, so far as my reading goes I have not found in any Christian writer of the period a single explicit reference to the possibility of *mystical union* in this life.[31]

Although, therefore, Albert Schweitzer wrote a valuable book called *The Mysticism of Paul the Apostle*, it would probably be right not to consider Paul a mystic in any acceptable sense of the word.

Yet he was equally not a person who operated on a purely rational level: he was a man, that is to say, of highly nervous temperament who believed that he experienced periodical visionary visitations, acting upon him as enlivening, exalting stimuli which spurred him on to bridge the intervals between one such experience and another: 'if we died with him, we shall live with him.'[32] In this he was like others of his age: and above all he was like the prophets of ancient Israel. They, too, should scarcely be described as mystics. Stanley Spencer, though reluctant to come to this conclusion, nevertheless concedes its reality in the following terms:[33]

Although their experience involved a quickening of the spiritual consciousness, an awareness of the supreme reality of the Transcendent, and can in this sense be regarded as possessing a mystical quality, it is true that there is a certain distinction between the experience of the prophets and that of the mystics generally.

Hocking has said that the prophet is 'the mystic in action.'[34] The revelation which he claims to receive is a message specifically related to the circumstances and events of his time. He is called as a prophet to proclaim that message. His union with God is a functional union; he is identified with God as his messenger to men. With mystics generally, the case is different. What they seek is union with God as an end in itself. Such union carries with it the transformation of their being, but it does not involve a specific task or type of work.

This functional union of the prophet, rather than the more general union of the mystic, is the background of the exalted language of *Ezekiel*, who after one of his visions remained for a week in a state of stupefaction, 'dumbfounded.'[35] And that, according to Paul, was what happened to himself. The writer of *II Isaiah*, too, had borne witness to similar experiences, and a passage in that work is adapted by Paul in *I Corinthians*. 'Things beyond our seeing, things beyond our hearing, things beyond our imagining, all prepared by God for those who love him.'[36]

And Paul is deliberately echoing *II Isaiah* once again, and *Jeremiah* as well, when he insists that his mission was predestined from his birth.[37] It was an integral part of the Jewish tradition that God equipped chosen leaders with prophetic abilities in which trust must be placed. After the last Old Testament prophets had spoken and were silent, orthodox Judaism believed that prophecy had ceased. Many Jewish adherents to Messianic doctrines, however, expected that it would eventually be revived;[38] and the Qumran devotees, who fervently studied scriptural prophecy, believed that it *had* already been revived in their Teacher of Righteousness, the prophet of the Last Days to whom was revealed even what had been hidden from the prophets of old.

When John the Baptist appeared, and baptized his converts in the Jordan like the prophet Elisha, and supposedly ascended to heaven like the prophet Elijah, it seemed clear to many that the divine moratorium on prophecy had ended. Jesus, too, was regarded as an heir to the prophets, as the Gospels confirm: people were already saying in his lifetime 'he is a prophet like one of the old prophets,' and a prophet was what he was called immediately after his death.[39] This prophetic concept of Jesus did not take very strong roots in the Christian tradition, because a plethora of pseudo-prophets in Palestine during the first century AD[40] cheapened the whole idea in the eyes of orthodox Jews and Christians alike. Yet, in spite of this, there was a continuing Jewish tradition that *some* prophets were authentic and deserving of obedience,[41] and the idea that Paul had inherited this prophetic role played a prominent part in his idea of his own conversion and mission. And so he speaks with admiration and awe of prophetic gifts, since 'it is prophecy that builds up a Christian community.'[42]

Yet prophets were not the foremost of its leaders. For, as Paul himself declared, 'within our community God has appointed in the first place apostles, in the second place prophets, thirdly teachers.'[43] However, that did not relegate Paul the Prophet to the second place, for he was perpetually insistent that his conversion had elevated him to the rank of apostle as well. The term, meaning 'messenger', has a Jewish background, and the apostles of Jesus were twelve in remembrance of the twelve Israelite tribes.[44] These twelve had known Jesus personally during his lifetime. But Paul had not. It was therefore with great intensity that he explained how his vision on the road to Damascus raised him to the same status as theirs. For there were clearly very many who sought to deny this. Most prominent of all among such recalcitrants were the Jewish Christians, the community centring round the twelve apostles.

Although he recognized their claims to have known Jesus during his lifetime, as he had not, and although he even accepted that some of them had seen his risen body upon earth – another experience he himself had not been allowed to share – nevertheless Paul reacted very indignantly against the Jewish Christian rejections of his claims to apostleship. 'Am I not an apostle? Did I not see Jesus our Lord?'[45] Because he had seen Jesus – not, admittedly, during his resurrection on earth, but in a subsequent vision – he declared that he had no need to be 'made' an apostle by the Jewish Christian church at Jerusalem – or indeed by any mortal man at all; about *Acts'* assertion that he was baptized at Damascus after his conversion, he says nothing whatever. For he was an apostle, he maintained, 'not by human appointment or human commission, but by commission from Jesus Christ and from God the Father'.[46] He was in no way less of an apostle than Peter, as the church dignitaries at Jerusalem, he claimed, had themselves fully recognized.[47]

'Have I in any way come short of those superlative apostles? I think not! . . . Look facts in the face. Someone is convinced, is he, that he belongs to Christ? Let him think again, and reflect that *we* belong to Christ as much as he does.'[48] And so, besides making uncomplimentary remarks about the heads of the Jerusalem church in general,[49] he implicitly depreciates the twelve by only once mentioning them by this term in all his surviving Letters.[50]

His fanatical insistence on his own special position eventually bore fruit – after his death. For before long the early Fathers were describing him by precisely the term he wanted: 'the Apostle.' Though nervous about many of his views, they hailed him by this designation because his missionary activity seemed to them so admirable. Paul agreed that this task of spreading the word was a duty that fell to the apostles above all others. But the reason why he had called *himself* an apostle, this noblest of all titles, was not because of his missionary work at all, but because of his vision before the gate of Damascus, since this was what had brought him into direct contact with Jesus Christ.

Such contact was something right outside the ordinary things of this world: it was an initiation into the sublime, into a mystery. For if Paul cannot accurately be described as a mystic, he was nevertheless emphatic in describing Christianity as a mystery, in the sense of a secret that had been disclosed to him and had brought him the gift of supernatural knowledge. 'I speak God's hidden wisdom, his secret purpose.'[51] 'It was by a revelation that his secret was made known to me'[52] – 'a revelation of that divine secret kept in silence for long ages but now disclosed.'[53] 'That secret is Christ himself: in him lie hidden all God's treasures of wisdom and knowledge.'[54] It is not necessary to turn to the Greek mystery religions (or at least not directly) for the origin of Paul's concept of this *mysterion* for the initiated. In *Daniel*, as in later Hebrew books, the word represents the Aramaic *raz*, secret: to Jews in general, the concept called to mind their apocalyptic literature, being found, for example, in the *War Rule* of Qumran.[55] Paul, not unlike the writers of the Gospels, regards the metaphorical initiations of his fellow-Christians into these mysteries as a progressive affair, and writes to the imperfectly enlightened Corinthians: 'for my part, my brothers, I could not speak to you as I should speak to people who have the spirit.'

This widespread idea of secret, salvation-bringing knowledge, confined only, as Origen declared, to 'a very few among the few,' reached its climax in the second century AD among the leading Gnostic churches, the sects whose designation comes from *gnosis*, which is knowledge of this peculiar, significant kind:

> . . . hidden and esoteric, known only to the initiates. By this special knowledge man may become spiritual and, therefore, good, according to Gnostic ideas. The soul is thought of as liberating itself progressively from its imprisonment in matter . . .[56]

Though we cannot say for certain how early this Gnosticism began, Valentinus, its most influential leader in the second century AD, was said to have received his esoteric traditions from Theudas, a supposed pupil of Paul. And the Gnostics frequently quoted Paul's own references to secret and hidden wisdom: though *Colossians*, and *I Corinthians*, with its reference to 'knowledge breeding conceit',[57] seem to be criticizing people who became altogether too arrogant in their claims to this spiritual superiority.

In view of Paul's insistence on the visionary unreason of his faith, he does not find the same difficulty that most moderns find in recognizing the validity of ecstatic speech, uncontrolled by the utterer, like the utterances of the early Quakers, Wesleyans and Irvingites. This is a theme to which he reverts several times in writing to the community at Corinth. It is true that he regards this gift as less valuable than the power of controlled prophecy of the future; unless, indeed, like a prophet, the man who gives forth this ecstatic speech 'can explain its meaning and so help to build up the community' by offering valid instruction or revelation: since 'if I do not know the meaning of the sound the speaker makes, his words will be gibberish to me, and mine to him.'[58]

Such warnings against the misuse of the talent are in the correct prophetic tradition.[59] Nevertheless, Paul declares – once again with the scriptural support which the frequent ecstasies of the early prophets readily afforded – that the appointees of God include 'those who have the gift of ecstatic utterance of various kinds.'[60] And indeed he himself claims this ability and experience for himself. For although (he says), 'in the congregation I would rather speak five intelligible words, for the benefit of others as well as myself, than thousands of words in the language of ecstasy . . . *thank God, I am more gifted in ecstatic utterance than any of you.*'[61] (Or perhaps the words mean: 'I use ecstatic speech more than any of you.') Paul, then, in pursuance of his belief in a religion based upon direct visions of God and Jesus Christ, was prepared, if he could convert it to his needs, to practise this rapturous form of cult which is so alien to the major sections of institutional Christianity today.

The miracle of Pentecost immediately after the Ascension of Jesus, a miracle emphasized at the outset of *Acts* as the inauguration of the Christian Church of the future, tells the same story. For the disciples 'were all filled with the Holy Spirit and began to talk in other tongues, as the Spirit gave them power of utterance.'[62] According to *Acts*, although some said contemptuously 'they have been drinking', these disciples were in fact speaking in foreign languages. Yet the original tradition had probably maintained that they were pronouncing unintelligible ecstatic utterances, like those referred to by Paul – utterances among which foreign-sounding words may have been haphazardly included.

Anyone who has been present when others have been subject to strong emotional and spiritual or even alcoholic pressure or stimulus may have observed that words of complete gibberish together with words suggesting a foreign tongue are mixed up when the 'censors' of the psyche are removed.[63]

Paul's willingness, under the appropriate circumstances, to respect ecstatic speech in others and employ it himself was bound up with the conviction that people are inhabited by demons and angels and spirits, supernatural yet less than God. This idea we have already encountered in connection with his belief that the world is infested with sin, which these spirits are instrumental in stimulating. This they do, it was understood, by introducing themselves into the bodies of human beings, as numerous stories describing their exorcism and expulsion by Jesus himself testify: and Paul too, it was declared in *Acts*, had on occasion expelled such spirits on his own account.[64] But it was not always easy to discern if a spirit was good or bad. This needed considerable care, as *I John* points out: 'do not trust any and every spirit, my friends: test the spirits, to see whether they are from God.'[65]

There it is spirits *from* God which are mentioned; but they can also, when authentically of this divine origin, be thought of as parts or elements *of the* spirit of God – of the Holy Spirit or in, the Authorized Version's obsolete phrase, the Holy Ghost. Paul's definition of the Holy Spirit was not always entirely clear. But it was a dynamic and potent concept in his mind, for he saw it as the vital, indispensable link which brought the true faith into the hearts of human beings. 'God gives you the Spirit and works miracles among you.' 'All who are moved by the Spirit of God are Sons of God . . . Through our inarticulate groans the Spirit himself is pleading for us.'[66]

The idea was already an ancient one, for the Jews had long believed that the spirit (*ruah*) of God was a divine power or energy poured out into the hearts of the prophets, revealing God's truth to them, and enabling them to recognize it when it was revealed: so that they became henceforward vehicles of the divine purpose.[67] Paul invokes this tradition with highly emotional eloquence, but he also innovates dramatically by connecting the Spirit, no longer only with extraordinary persons and occasions, but with the everyday existence of every Christian.

The Holy Spirit helps our infirmities. It is through the power of the Spirit that we abound in hope. It is by the power of the Spirit that we are sanctified. The Spirit is the source of Paul's own power . . . The Spirit is life because of righteousness . . . The beginning and the middle and the end of the Christian life all depend upon the work of the Spirit.[68]

However, its association with superior beings remained in the forefront of his mind, for he associated it especially with Jesus. It had long been believed by Jews that, when the Messiah eventually came, this Spirit would have entered into him.

The consciousness of Spirit-possession carried with it the consciousness of authority. The Jewish prophets ascribed this possession to the future Messiah and (later) to the people of Israel; a general outpouring of Spirit was expected to come in the days of the Messiah.[69]

It was therefore inevitable that Paul should link the Holy Spirit with Jesus. In his farewell benediction to the Corinthians he places the two names together with God's: 'The grace of the Lord Jesus Christ, and the Love of God, and fellowship in the Holy Spirit, be with you all.'[70] This is the familiar formula which was subsequently developed into the doctrine of the Trinity. But elsewhere, instead, he makes the Holy Spirit an *aspect* of Jesus, asserting that 'the Spirit of Jesus Christ is given me for support.'[71] This is explained: 'for through him [Jesus] we both alike have access to the Father in the one Spirit.'[72] The Spirit, Paul believes, is an aspect of Jesus in the rather difficult sense that it is his corporate personality, the Church: this Spirit is what Jesus has left behind him so that it can carry out his work and gradually reshape mankind more and more in his image. After he left the earth, the Spirit dwells on as the fulfilment of God's promise to stay with his people: a continuing, quickening source of the new life which Christ had created. It is by this means, through the Holy Spirit, that his divine presence goes on for ever: and so it can even finally be inferred that the Holy Spirit *is* Christ.[73]

Yet this veering between the partial differentiation of the Holy Spirit from Christ and its identification with him was productive of confusion, and became one of the many Pauline ideas which left a legacy of deep puzzlement. In *Colossians*, the Holy Spirit is already much less emphasized in order not to appear to set up a competitor to the unique glory of the Saviour. *Acts* recorded that some of the converts at Ephesus had not even heard that there was such a thing as the Holy Spirit at all,[74] for Paul's emphasis on this Spirit had to be underplayed when it was an overriding need to distinguish between good spirits and bad. This difficulty made the presence in a man or woman of the Holy Spirit or its opposite embarrassingly hard to determine. That is what the writer of *I John* meant when he emphasized that spirits must be elaborately scrutinized, to see whether they are truly from God or not:

> This is how we may recognize the Spirit of God: every spirit which acknowledges that Jesus Christ has come in the flesh is from God, and every spirit which does not thus acknowledge Jesus is not from God.[75]

The *Gospel according to Matthew* echoed Paul's benediction framed 'in the name of the Father and the Son and the Holy Spirit'.[76] Indeed, most Christian theologians have found it barely possible to describe the biblical interpretation of the nature of God without resorting to something like the dogma of the Trinity, though, in later antiquity, the precise relations between the three were a subject of loudly reverberating controversy. In the course of these, Paul's utterances were meticulously examined. But they were not always a great deal of help, for, as so often, he had offered visionary suggestions and appeals, rather than exact definitions.

Such, then, was the gift of the Holy Spirit which, by God's grace and the faith that this conferred, was available for mankind. But how was one to gain this grace and faith? By means of what later became known as the 'sacraments': Baptism and the Eucharist.

'Baptized into union with him [Jesus Christ], you have all put on

Christ as a garment.'[77] 'Have you forgotten that when we were baptized into union with Christ Jesus we were baptized into his death? By baptism we were buried with him, and lay dead, in order that, as Christ was raised from the dead in the splendour of the Father, so also we might set our feet upon the new path of life.'[78] Paul is very concrete. To him, baptism imitates the act of dying (immersion) and rising from the dead (coming up out of the water):[79] indeed the baptized individual *experiences* death with the Lord, and resurrection in his company. It was because of this that the Holy Spirit, which Jesus had left to continue his work in the world, was able to exercise its influence, which acted potently upon those who had been baptized in his name.

'Have you forgotten?' asks Paul, and this may mean that he had inherited the tradition from even earlier Christians. (His use of the word *mysterion* may have come, through Jewish intermediaries, from the pagan mystery religions of secret initiation and dying and rising gods: but the link is only superficial, since no significant part of his conception is owed to that source.) The baptisms by John the Baptist – including his baptism of Jesus himself – were still remembered and famous; *Acts* tells us of people at Ephesus, including the distinguished Alexandrian Apollos, who did not know about the baptisms in the name of, or by, Jesus, but had heard of the baptisms of John.[80] But those rites had not been by any means what Paul is talking about. John's baptisms had not been thought of as a dying and rising, but were (with differences) the symbolic, ritual ablutions common in middle eastern societies: a washing, a cleansing in the waters where the prophet Elisha, too, had long ago ordered a cleansing, symbolic of 'repentance' (a total change of attitude) and the forgiveness of sins.[81] John's practice displayed certain themes in common with the purifying ritual baths taken by the Qumran community,[82] but they had taken these baths themselves, whereas the Baptist innovated by bathing others.

The sort of baptism which Paul proclaimed was likewise administered by one person to another, but it was seen by him not merely as a cleansing but as a solemn means of admission to fellowship with him whose Crucifixion and Resurrection they were thus permitted to share. They themselves, in their own persons, were called upon to participate in the sacred drama. Yet Paul did not believe that this ritual acted magically without the need of faith. It was, from one point of view, a symbolical re-enaction and justification of Jesus' death. But it was also a good deal more than that. For it was also an *effective* sign, like those signs in which the Old Testament had abounded, not only representing something else but at the same time causing what they represented to come about. And what this baptism represented and brought about was the direct operation of God's grace in its most effective manifestation of all time, his saving action apparent in the death of Jesus Christ.

As regards his own rule, however, Paul comments in *I Corinthians*: 'Christ did not send me to baptize, but to proclaim the Gospel.'[83] This specific disclaimer provides a valuable key to Paul's thinking. His point is that the significance of baptism as such, although considerable, was only secondary all the same:

His remarks, although they were written when he was in a highly emotional state because of the divisions in the church at Corinth, suggest that there were moments when he did not attach so much importance to the act of lustration as many Christian theologians think; and indeed, the whole tenor of all his references to it as to emphasize the significance of the ceremony rather than the ceremony itself.[84]

The reason why baptism was not, in itself, of primary importance in his eyes was because faith in the events it enacted had to come first. This attitude was also reminiscent of the Qumran community, which likewise insisted that baptism must be preceded by humility and obedience. To Paul, this ceremony was the *mechanism* which enabled faith to bear its fruits. Without faith, baptism was useless. The Jews of the Exodus, he wrote, had 'all passed through the Red Sea: and so they all received baptism into the fellowship of Moses in cloud and sea . . . And yet most of them were not accepted by God, for the desert was strewn with their corpses.'[85] This was because in various ways they had *not* displayed the right approach to God. And now, too, baptism will be of no avail without prior faith in God – which meant, under the new order, belief in the redemptive death of Jesus Christ. Because this belief lay at the very centre of baptism, which depended on it utterly, Paul was most anxious that no one should consider that he or she had been baptized 'in the name of Paul', which might have given misleading impressions about the nature of the rite. And that was why he himself preferred to baptize scarcely at all.

Was it Paul who was crucified for you? Was it in the name of Paul you were baptized? Thank God, I never baptized one of you – except Crispus and Gaius. So no one can say you were baptized in my name. Yes, I did baptize the household of Stephanas; I cannot think of anyone else.[86]

For the same reason – in order not to set the baptizer in the centre of the scene, where he did not belong – Paul never tells us by whom he himself had been baptized. *Acts* later reported that this took place immediately after his conversion at Damascus.[87] But Paul himself has nothing to say about the matter.

As for Jesus, he had been baptized with John's baptism for the remission of sins (quite different from Paul's later concept dependent on the Crucifixion), and that event was in some sense the start of the Gospel story. But thereafter, like Paul after him (and this no doubt influenced Paul's caution), Jesus himself, according to *The Gospel According to St John*, after a preliminary period of baptizing others, had discontinued the practice: 'It was only the disciples who were baptizing, and not Jesus himself.'[88] Jesus' decision not to baptize any longer, or the Gospel's statement that he made such a decision, was no doubt due to a desire to distinguish his mission from the Baptist's (especially as the latter, after his death, continued to have a strong, independent, personal following). Indeed, *Acts* still continues to see baptism as John the Baptist rather than Paul had seen it, in the guise of a washing away of sins.[89] *I Peter*, however, seems to combine the two conceptions. Citing the precedent of Noah's ark, which brought a few persons to safety through the water, the writer declares: 'Baptism is not the washing away of bodily pollution, but the appeal made to God by a good conscience: and it brings salvation through the Resurrection of Jesus Christ.'

Later, the Greek Fathers, in Pauline spirit, declared that baptism prepared Christians for their own resurrection. But subsequently the Nicene creed declared instead: 'We acknowledge one baptism for the remission of sins.' This definition lost sight of the Pauline concept, and so did Augustine's pronouncement that by conferring supernatural grace upon those who received it, whether infants or adults, the ceremony expunged their original sin. The Anabaptists, the radical wing of the Reformation founded in Switzerland in the early sixteenth century, were closer to Paul when they required a baptism which followed faith and was not thought to create it. And the Baptist denomination of the Church stresses the same point when they insist that baptism be administered to adult, responsible believers only.

After the essential prerequisite of faith, then, the initial formal stage in the establishment of a relationship with God and with Jesus was baptism. This ritual of inauguration was undertaken once only. But the second, the other means of coming into contact with God and his Son was repeated over and over again. This was the Eucharist (Thanksgiving), which came to be known also as the Lord's Supper, the Breaking of Bread, the Mass, Holy Communion. It is Paul, in *I Corinthians*, who gives us a written account of this ceremony for the first time.

> The tradition which I handed on to you came to me from the Lord himself: that the Lord Jesus, on the night of his arrest, took bread and, after giving thanks to God, broke it and said: 'This is my body, which is for you; do this as a memorial of me.' In the same way, he took the cup after supper, and said 'This cup is the New Covenant sealed by my blood. Whenever you drink it, do this as a memorial of me.' For every time you eat this bread and drink the cup, you proclaim the death of the Lord, until he comes [again] . . .
> When we bless 'the cup of blessing', is it not a means of sharing in the blood of Christ? When we break the bread, is it not a means of sharing in the body of Christ?[90]

To Paul, the Eucharist – like baptism – was essentially a participation in Jesus Christ's death, standing in relation to faith as act or word stands in relation to thought. But, unlike baptism, the Eucharist was to be performed repeatedly by every Christian man or woman. And it went back to a profoundly significant moment of Jesus' life on earth, shortly before it came to an end. At the Last Supper, Jesus had warned his disciples of his death, and had no doubt assured them of its redemptive quality. Moreover, the tradition had grown up, though probably only after his death, that he had broken bread in order to give his followers his broken body, and he had taken the cup to bestow upon them the blood he was so soon to shed by his sacrifice;[91] for that was what the wine represented.

There are many suggestions about what sort of Jewish meal this Last Supper had been. Paul said: 'our Passover has begun: the sacrifice is offered – Christ himself.' So was the meal the annual celebration of the Passover*, that ancient Jewish feast commemorating the passing over of the Israelites' houses when the Egyptians were smitten? Or was it a social sacred meal (*kiddush*) in anticipation of the Passover? Was it a meal of sanctification? Or the communal *haburah* supper eaten weekly by Jewish groups? Even after the most careful study of references to the Last Supper in the Letters and the Gospels, no certain answer can be given, though some association with the Passover remains probable. But whatever the nature of this particular meal, it was the custom for Jews, before they ate or drank, to bless God's name; and the blessing or thanksgiving (the terms are synonymous) possessed particular solemnity when the occasion was of a social character. A special thanksgiving significance was attached to the bread broken by the host or presiding figure at the start of a meal, and to the cup of blessing drunk at its close. But there seems to be no exact Jewish precedent for a ritual meal at which the bread and wine enabled believers to commune with the deity; and the drinking of blood was alien to the practice of the Jews.

Nevertheless, Paul professes to find a number of scriptural prefigurations for his concept of the Eucharist. In particular, he finds it prefigured by the traditions in *Exodus* about the Jews led by Moses.

They all ate the same supernatural food, and all drank the same supernatural drink; I mean, they all drank from the supernatural rock that accompanied their travels – and that rock was Christ . . .[92]

The miraculous food to which Paul refers was the manna gathered by Moses' people in the wilderness, and the drink came from the rock in Horeb.[93] Perhaps these Mosaic reminiscences are uppermost in Paul's thinking about the Eucharist. But it was also the liturgical anticipation of the Messianic banquet foretold in *Isaiah*; and in this respect it resembled meals at Qumran, accompanied by pronouncements that 'this bread is the Messiah of Israel'; of whom, in anticipation of his coming, one of the participants at the meal acted as the personal representative. In this spirit, the celebrations of the ritual laid down by Paul, when the early Christians broke bread and gave thanks, not only looked backward to the Last Supper which terminated Jesus' first coming to earth, but looked forward to his Second Coming as well. It was also a 'sharing', the common meal of love (*agape*), the outward and visible sign of the united community and church: Holy Communion was holy communism.

Once again, as in baptism, all the benefits of the Eucharist were held to be thrown away if the right disposition did not exist.[94] Faith, total belief in the redemptive death of Jesus, must come first, and Paul, who explicitly refrained from claiming that baptism was of overriding importance, considered the Eucharist, too, as much less important than the faith which had to precede it. Nevertheless, Paul had to pay careful attention to the details of the Eucharist for the sake of his flock. For this highly dramatic means of maintaining contact with God and Jesus Christ played a part in their daily lives infinitely more important than any amount of theological doctrine. And so Paul was at great pains to ensure that the ceremonial was properly conducted, carefully warning against abuses such as over-indulgence at the sacred meal by those able to afford it.[95]

The sacramental repasts of the pagan mystery religions offer certain resemblances to the Eucharist, though no doubt, if we knew enough, we should find that (as in the case of baptism) these apparently pagan features were incorporated in the Christian ritual through the mediation of contemporary Jewish thought. Nevertheless, the similarities were unmistakable, and proved a thorn in the flesh of the propagandists of Christianity, who felt compelled to explain them away as tricks of the Devil determined to imitate Christ: indeed some of the early Fathers, rejecting pagan priority, claimed that the ceremonies of the contemporary pagan mysteries were borrowed instead, unscrupulously, from Christianity.

In the Eucharist as described by Paul, the breaking of bread came first, then the meal itself, and then the thanksgiving. At an uncertain date after his death, however, the meal and the thanksgiving were separated, and the latter became a separate, rearranged, ceremony at which only the necessary token quantities of bread and wine were consumed. This concentrated emphasis on the significance of the rite. And yet as time went on, Christians began to be afflicted by doubts about its exact meaning. The question which, in particular, worried them to distraction was this. In the passage quoted above from *I Corinthians*, Jesus was reported to have said: 'This is my body' ('is' for *esti* in Greek; though if, as is probable, Jesus was speaking in Aramaic, no such verb appeared). Did he mean that the bread actually *is* his body (as Catholics believe) or that it only *represents* it (the Protestant view)? The ambiguity remains insoluble. Augustine wrote: 'If you are the body of Christ and its members, it is the mystery of ourselves that is laid on the altar. It is the mystery of yourselves that you receive. If you have received well, you are what you have received.'[96] But this does not provide a solution to the mystery. Confronted by it, John Henry Newman felt that discussion was of no avail:

> Enough, I eat his flesh and drink his blood.
> More is not told – to ask it is not good.

What is clear, however, is that in Paul's mind the body of Christ had two different but related significances:

We are all there gathered at the common table and eating the common food. What is that food? The body of Christ. What are we? The body of Christ. We, collectively, have become that of which we have partaken. On the verbal level, St Paul's conception may be regarded as the world's most tremendous pun. Christ's body has become the body of Christ – the sacrificial merges into the social meaning.[97]

This identification between the two meanings of the body of Christ was already explicit in Paul, who repeatedly describes the Christian Church and community in this manner – metaphorically, it would seem to us, but to him, a Jew accustomed to corporate solidarity, it appeared true in a completely objective sense. 'When we break the bread, is it not a means of sharing in the body of Christ? Because there is one loaf, we, many as we are, are one body, for it is one loaf of which we all partake.'[98] 'For just as in a single human body there are many limbs and organs, all with different functions, so all of us, united with Christ, form one body, serving individually as limbs and organs to one another.' And in Letters which were written by Paul later on or were elaborated from his words, namely *Ephesians* and *Colossians*, the idea is developed a good deal further in order to describe the gradually rising and institutionalizing Church. In *Ephesians* it was declared that by this solemn ritual 'all of us are the parts of one body', or, in the Authorized Version, 'we are members one of another'.[99]

The last remnant of this majestic inheritance which survives in the conscious thought of Protestant Europe is this phrase, which still lingers on as a moralistic cliché in popular parlance. Such language is nowadays written off as unreal uplift or utopian idealism. But for St Paul, it was a matter, not of idealism, but of fact.[100]

Paul himself believed he enjoyed access to the salvation conferred by Jesus Christ's death, not through baptism and the Eucharist, but by visionary experience. These had given him faith in Jesus' redemptive power, and he felt it was the grace of God which had conferred the gift. Others, too, he was convinced, had to be imbued with faith in these incredible events, and it was his life's work to ensure that they were. Once they possessed such faith, there were solemn means which completed their sharing of Jesus Christ's death and Resurrection, and sharing of the mighty benefits that they conferred, and sharing of his fellowship. Those means, though he did not need them himself, were baptism and the Eucharist.

But there was still one very serious problem, indeed perhaps the most serious problem that any thinking Christian had to face. For Jesus had visited the world, they were told to believe, and had saved it. And yet, as Nietzsche pointed out and Newman noted with perplexity, it manifestly is not saved. And it was already clear to the early Christians, too, that *their* world, and they themselves, had not been saved in any perceptible sense. For the evil from which mankind and they personally were suffering, far from having been removed, was as prevalent as ever – indeed, increasingly prevalent, as the situation of Rome's Jewish province continued to deteriorate into anarchy. Christ had been crucified, yet there were no results to be seen. Upon a solution of this dilemma, the whole future credibility of the Christian faith depended; Paul had to address himself to the problem.

IV

𝕯

What the World Still Has to Wait For

Paul had identified Jesus with the Messiah, and according to Jewish tradition the coming of the Messiah would bring the world to an end and bestow salvation upon the faithful. And yet Jesus had come and died, and the end of the world had not arrived, and the faithful seemed no better off than they had been before. According to the Gospels, they complained of this themselves. 'We had been hoping that he was the man to liberate Israel.'[1] But it was now clear that this had by no means been his role, not in any sense that they were able to understand. Paul dealt with this grave situation by a striking expedient. Although the Messiah had indeed come, as he explained in *II Thessalonians*, that had only been his *First* Coming: it was a mistake to suppose that the promised Day of the Lord had already arrived,[2] for he would come again. His Second Coming, when all that had been hoped for and promised would duly take place, still lay ahead.

Perhaps even earlier Christian leaders than Paul, including, reportedly, Stephen,[3] had dealt with the harrowing doubts of their followers by proposing the same doctrine. In any case, its formulation was greatly assisted by developments in Messianic thought which had been occurring in contemporary Judaism. These are described by W. D. Davies:

There were two main currents of eschatological thought in Judaism. First there was the Messianic expectation of the prophets, both pre-exilic and exilic, according to which there would arise a scion of the House of David who would judge the nations and then allow the righteous who survived the sifting of the judgment to enter His Kingdom. This Messianic Kingdom would be the consummation of world history and its scene would be this earth, albeit an earth transformed in various ways. According to the earliest sources only those alive at the advent of the Messiah would be judged and could therefore participate in the blessings of the Messianic Kingdom, but later it was held that there would be a resurrection of the dead at the advent of the Messiah in order that they too might be judged and be partakers of the Kingdom.

Secondly, on the other hand, there arose what we may conveniently call the Danielic eschatology, according to which the Kingdom of God is made manifest not through the advent of a Messiah but through that of the Son of Man, a supernatural being. The inauguration of this kingdom is marked by a general resurrection of the dead, and their judgment. The kingdom itself is of a supernatural character.

We cannot here trace the various vicissitudes of these two views of the end in order to show how now one and then the other predominated; we merely point out that Judaism had somehow to harmonize both. This harmonization was accomplished ingeniously in the first century AD, when we find that the Messianic Kingdom comes to be regarded as one of temporary duration preceding the final consummation of the historical process, which was supernatural, the Age to Come.[4]

This amalgamation of the two ideas was now translated by Paul, under the impulsion of the Crucifixion, into Christian terms. And from this process it emerged that, although the Messiah had already come to the world, the overwhelming, total, material changes which he had been expected to bring would now be postponed until the consummation of the historical process in his *Second* Coming: a concept which Paul endeavoured to back up by citing five passages of *Isaiah*.

'Our Lord, Come!' he wrote in Aramaic (*marana tha*) at the end of *I Corinthians*:[5] but even earlier, in *I Thessalonians*, he had already enlarged on the theme of this awaited Second Coming.

This we tell you as the Lord's word: we who are left alive until the Lord comes shall not forestall those who have died; because at the word of command, at the sound of the archangel's voice and God's trumpet call, the Lord himself will descend from heaven . . . About dates and times, my friends, we need not write to you, because you know perfectly well that the Day of the Lord comes like a thief in the night . . . But you, my friends, are not in the dark, that the day should overtake you like a thief . . . We do not belong to night or darkness, and we must not sleep like the rest, but keep awake and sober . . . armed with faith and love for coat of mail, and the hope of salvation for helmet.[6]

These are urgent words, and gave the impression that the Second Coming might be expected any day. Yet later, in *II Thessalonians*, Paul was at pains to correct this expectation.

And now, brothers, about the coming of our Lord Jesus Christ and his gathering of us to himself . . . Let no one deceive you in any way whatever. That day cannot come before the final rebellion against God . . . You cannot but remember that I told you this while I was still with you.[7]

What had happened, apparently, was that the Christians of Thessalonica, inspired by the urgency of his first Letter to believe that the Second Coming would occur almost at once, had begun to neglect their ordinary daily activities (a development which, incidentally, risked attracting unwelcome attention from the Roman authorities). This misunderstanding needed correction, which Paul's Second Letter to them was designed to provide. Perhaps Paul himself, after further reflection, had changed his mind. For although, like all other Christians, he always believed that the Second Coming would not be too long delayed – 'the time we live in will not last long'[8] – he may now have concluded that it was not going to take place as promptly as he and others had expected. Or possibly he had never expected that Jesus would return in the absolutely immediate future, and had only expressed himself in *I Thessalonians* so forcibly ('in, may I not say, incautious language,' as Coleridge put it) in order to emphasize the certainty that *there would be* a Second Coming, so that those confounded by the apparent ineffectiveness of the First Coming could take heart.

In any case Paul, seeing one Coming of Jesus behind him and the other ahead, believed that he himself and his contemporaries were living in an extraordinary, unique, harrowing period of abrupt change in which the processes of history were temporarily suspended: 'this crooked age', 'a time of stress', 'a time of troubles'.[9] 'Up to the present, we know,' summed up Paul, 'the whole created universe groans in all its parts as if in the pangs of childbirth'.[10] For although the Crucifixion had routed Satan, the war was not yet over, the final battle against him still had to be fought: somehow or other, he was still plaguing the earth, even if he had fallen, or would fall, to a dungeon in hell from which he would be released, in the end, to fight his last desperate rebellion against God.

This, then, was the interim time of troubles that had to be lived through: a time in which, as *I Peter* declared, Christians were 'aliens in a foreign land'.[11] And yet it was no mere meaningless vacuum, for what would take place during this transitional period was supremely important. So important is it, indeed, that earthly matters like getting married or being a slave or not being a slave were of altogether secondary significance. Something far more vital, indeed something overwhelmingly conclusive, was happening every day: the universe was full of continuous, decisive, movement and development. This is an idea congenial to our modern epoch; and we shall also see before long how, in successive past generations as well, this theory of a transitional age exercised a gigantic effect on the history of the world – through Paul himself, whom it prompted to make the utmost urgent use of the years available, by attempting the conversion of the whole world before time ran out.

Yet there remained an extraordinary contradiction between the things that Christ, we are told, had already achieved – things declared by Paul to be overwhelmingly vast – and the achievements which, nevertheless, still remain for him to perform when he comes into the world for the second time. Jesus has conquered: and yet he has not conquered. In this two-layer discussion in Paul's Letters, about the First Coming of Christ that has already taken place and the Second Coming that is expected, there is a sharp, unremitting tension and conflict between discontinuity and continuity, between the decisiveness of the recent revelation and the alarming fact that it nevertheless was not final after all: a conflict between the 'already' and the 'not yet'. It was a conflict which Paul must have inherited from Jesus, or from the tormented thoughts of the disciples immediately after his death, and which he bequeathed to his successors. It remains apparent in all the Gospels. In *John* it is left unresolved, in words ascribed to the Saviour himself: those who believe in himself, Jesus is made to say, have 'already passed from death to life': and yet, all the same, 'the time is coming' when the final reckoning will be made.[12] *II Peter* seeks to tackle the dilemma and console those who are disappointed because the Crucifixion appears to have changed nothing.

There will come men who scoff at religion and live self-indulgent lives, and they will say: 'Where now is the promise of his Coming? Our fathers have been laid to their rest, but still everything continues exactly as it always has been since the world began' . . . But here is one point, my friends, which you must not lose sight of . . . It is *not* that the Lord is slow in fulfilling his promise, as some suppose, but that he is very patient with you, because it is not his will for any to be lost, but for all to come to repentance . . . Look eagerly for the Day of God – and work to hasten it on.[13]

In general, however, the early Church dwelt more happily on Paul's references to the transitional present than to his forecasts of the eventual Second Coming and Day of the Lord. For in this way they could make his Letters more easily applicable to the practical problems of their flocks.

But *when* would this Day of the Lord come? The Gospels cited the supposed view of Jesus, related to that of *I Thessalonians*, that the end was indeed already at hand.[14] But this Gospel evidence is far from unambiguous on the subject, and although the expectation of the apocalypse is never explicitly denied, the 'interim period' is, in fact, already beginning to take on the aspect of an Age of the Church, which will be of great length: later, the *Book of Revelation* announced that the final struggle would not take place until the Crucifixion was a thousand years past.[15] By the mid-second century AD, the eschatological hope had become less important, though it was revived again before long, and at intervals ever afterwards.

When the End of the World comes, Paul believed that there will be a Final Judgment accompanied by a general resurrection of the dead, leading to the final consummation of a perfected, divine kingdom when God will be all in all. These are doctrines which were integral to the thought of Paul's time, and were accepted by vast numbers of his contemporaries, but have retained comparatively little significance in our own age, when most people have ceased to accept them in anything like a literal form. W. R. Inge, writing in the 1920s, remarked that the greatest change in Christian preaching in his own lifetime had been the virtual disappearance of the 'other world'.

The general resurrection of the dead, destined to take place at that final hour, was directly deduced by Paul from Jesus' Resurrection, and he was disgusted by denials, at Corinth, of the validity of this logic.[16] For that will be the time for the fulfilment of famous passages in *Isaiah* and *II Isaiah*, which Paul adapts: 'Awake, sleeper, rise from the dead, and Christ will shine upon you'[17] (the text of a sermon by Charles Wesley which became the most famous Methodist book). And Paul described what would happen:

As in Adam all men die, so in Christ all will be brought to life; but each in his proper place: Christ the first-fruits, and afterwards, at his Coming, those who belong to Christ. Then comes the end, when he delivers up the kingdom to God the Father, after abolishing every kind of domination, authority and power.[18]

The Last Judgment, which will take place at the End of the World, is a particularly alien concept to many today – or perhaps only an unwelcome one. But it formed, from the start, an essential feature of Pauline and apostolic teaching. Its most important feature was the message, conveyed for example in *Daniel*, that, although all alike will rise from the dead, the blessed will be separated from the damned.[19]

This belief that in the Final Judgment there were some who would win through and achieve eternal salvation was the wonderful grounds for something that Paul expounds with great fervour: namely, Hope. This was a possession peculiar to the Christians which no pagans could effectively acquire. For their minds, he declared, 'are set on earthly things. We, by contrast, are citizens of heaven, and from heaven we expect our deliverer to come, the Lord Jesus Christ.'[20] He 'in his grace has given us such unfailing encouragement and such bright hopes.'[21] It is hope for the hereafter: 'the hope of salvation is our helmet'.[22] 'The secret is this: Christ in you, the hope of a glory to come.'[23] 'I reckon that the sufferings we now endure bear no comparison with the splendour, as yet unrevealed, which is in store for us.'[24] That was why Paul was always searching for biblical predictions of Christ: the scriptures were given us to 'maintain our hope with fortitude'. And so he triumphantly adapts *Hosea*: 'O Death, where is your victory? O Death, where is your sting?'[25]

Nietzsche declared that Paul had turned the Gospel into 'the most despicable of all unfulfillable promises, the most immodest doctrine of personal immortality'. But it was this hope of eternal bliss after our deaths which, throughout the ages, has gripped and held the hearts of Christians, and particularly Christians who are hopeless and desperate. For to understand Paul's Gospel, it has been said, one does not need higher criticism; but one needs despair. That is what he demolishes, and in its place, he erects a soaring, immense structure of hopefulness. The old Israel, too, had felt a deep faith in the future. But that had been mainly a hope for the community as a whole. The forecasts of the Prophets included no clear reference to the individual, no message of light for his or her encouragement. To Paul on the other hand, in spite of and in addition to his strong feeling for the corporate Christian community, this hope is an essentially, profoundly personal thing which belongs to individuals and uplifts them. And so another of his recurrent words is Joy. It appears in the Letters time after time.

How, then, to ensure that we are saved? For the alternative is unspeakable. It is damnation. No wonder Paul speaks of the *terrors* of Judgment to come, from which only Jesus Christ can deliver us.[26] 'If indeed our Gospel be found veiled, the only people who find it so are those on the way to perdition.'[27] For the damned would not only include Satan and his dark angels, but enormous numbers of human beings.

The *Community Rule** of Qumran went into explicit detail about the appalling punishments that would fall on the wicked 'in the fire of the Dark Regions'.[28] Paul, however, never refers directly to this penal Hell, either under the name of Hades or of its Hebrew equivalent: not the shadowy Sheol, but the place of punishment, Gehenna; and in regard to the specific nature of the penalty to which sinners are exposed, he has little to say. But in any case it will involve catastrophe, and exclusion from the presence of God, for very many.[29] That is a prospect which has often seemed repulsive to later readers – to John Stuart Mill, for example, who declared that in comparison with such a doctrine any other objection to Christianity sinks into insignificance. Furthermore, this traditional belief seemed to contradict Paul's own concept of divine grace as free, unmerited forgiveness. Shock has also been caused by his scriptural assignment of the ultimate vengeance to the Wrath of God,[30] a term which the translation in the New English Bible prefers to avoid. Paul sees this divine anger, which is not fatherly but rather judicial and impartial, as the reverse side of love, the eternal reaction against evil without which God would not be the governor of the world: for blots on the order of the universe he cannot ignore. Luther called God's wrath his 'strange work', as mercy was his 'proper work.' But Ernest Renan said that Paul is obsolete, and that we can put our trust in an unindignant God. Berdyaev, too, declared that anger in every shape and form is foreign to the Deity.

But on what basis does Paul suppose that this distinction will be drawn between the damned and the saved? Here as so often he displays a large degree of ambiguity. In a matter of this kind, totally defying proven knowledge, it was inevitable, no doubt, that there should be uncertainties. But it would have been easier for us if Paul, who in different passages offers alternative, contradictory answers, had listed them all in one place instead of presenting each of them, in its momentary turn, as the single definitive solution. One difficulty has already been foreshadowed in discussing his attitude to sin (chapter 2, section 1). For, up to a point, like other Jews, he regarded this as predestined; it is only within certain limits that he believed that man can determine his own actions. By the same token, the choice of the men and women who would eventually achieve salvation often seemed to him to have been predestined as well. Just as Paul himself had been called to his mission before his birth, so, in general, 'the gracious gifts of God and his calling are irrevocable ... God knew his own before ever they were.'[31] Paul is eager to refer man to his proper and most humble place where the very idea of seeking rights from his creator is seen to be absurdly presumptuous. This attitude seemed utterly convincing to Augustine: 'Will any man presume to say that God did not foreknow those to whom he would grant belief?'[32] To Calvin, too – with whose followers John Wesley later crossed swords – God had determined from eternity the men and women he would save and damn, totally regardless of their merits or demerits:

For the seed of the word of God takes root and brings forth fruit only in those in whom the Lord, by his eternal election, has predestined to be children and heirs of the heavenly kingdom. To all the others (who by the same counsel of God are rejected before the foundation of the world) the clear and evident preaching of truth can be nothing but an odour of death.

In Calvin's view, then, the actions or decisions of men and women were wholly irrelevant even as a secondary causal factor in determining their eventual fates.

So all these theologians seized with approval upon Paul's pronouncements accepting God's predestination of those who would be saved and those who would be damned. But such a view stimulated an obvious reaction: if my destiny is determined already, what is the point of my trying to behave decently at all? That was also an argument which had impressed the prophet Amos, for he was at pains to point out that God's election of the Israelites as his chosen people would not save them from punishment for their wrongdoings.

Paul, too, was aware of this dilemma, since elsewhere in his Letters it is disconcerting – though many will be relieved – to find that he contradicts his own view of predestination completely. For in these other passages he stresses that God, or Jesus Christ, will take his decision about the salvation of each man and woman on the basis of their good or bad deeds in their lifetimes – 'God is not to be fooled: a man reaps what he sows.'[33] 'Before the tribunal of Christ . . . each must receive what is due to him for his conduct in the body, good or bad.'[34] 'My dear friends, do not seek revenge [yourselves], but leave a place for divine retribution: for there is a text which reads: "Justice is mine," says the Lord, "I will repay".'[35]

This doctrine of an eye for an eye and a tooth for a tooth, of just rewards for good behaviour and punishments for bad, was deeply ingrained in the Jewish mind. The writers of Qumran, however, had already foreshadowed Paul's contradiction between salvation or damnation predestined and salvation or damnation decided on personal merit. For on this subject their *Thanksgiving Psalms** and *Community Rule* speak with similarly discordant voices.[36] In these works:

The destiny of the righteous as well as of the sinners is already determined by God from the womb. Nevertheless, the sinners are punished for their wicked acts because they have wilfully separated themselves from the Covenant of God and chosen what God hates. The good, on the other hand . . . are rewarded by God . . .

Thus the question still remains open whether the Qumran Essenes* believed in a doctrine of absolute predestination. If this was the case, it was by no means consistently thought out. One rather gains the impression that for them everything – including the acts of men – is determined in the knowledge of God, but that this still does not absolutely determine man, for he is able either to go on sinning or to repent. But he who has already abandoned sin and turned to God also knows that because of that act he belongs to those who have been chosen from the beginning to be the elect of divine good pleasure.[37]

That analysis could also be applied to the same contradictory posture in which Paul, too, places himself, with scarcely even an attempt at self-extrication. Moreover, he displays a further complexity. For in certain passages, the persons whom he reserves for salvation are not those who have been predestined to be saved, and not even those who have earned such a reward by their behaviour, but 'those who belong to Christ' or 'those who have faith'. If a man accepted or rejected God's invitation to believe, it counted to his merit or demerit just like his good or bad deeds – but even more effectively.

This, at first sight, is a bewilderingly direct rejection of the doctrine, found elsewhere in his Letters, that men and women reap what they sow. Even so, the rejection is not so complete after all; it is more a question of priorities. For, essential though Paul considers good moral conduct to be, he has all along basically regarded it as subsidiary to, and dependent upon, faith in Jesus Christ's redemptive Crucifixion. It was in this spirit, pervading all his thought, that he pronounced God's selection to be founded 'not upon men's deeds but upon the call of God';[38] and the same point had been made at Qumran, where the good are good because they belong to the faithful congregation.

Another old concept, which Paul likewise shares with Qumran, is the idea of the Remnant. Throughout every tribulation in their history as a chosen people, the Jews were proud to believe that an Elect Remnant had won through. And in just the same way, said Paul, in the new, Christian dispensation, a new sort of the old Remnant has come into being, selected by the grace of God; and just as *Isaiah* had declared about the Remnant of which he, also, had spoken, it is this body of privileged persons that will be saved at the Final Judgment.[39]

It seems, however, that in *I Corinthians* Paul makes a reference to a subsequent and final stage in which no longer a Remnant but *all the world* will be saved: 'As in Adam *all* men die, so in Christ *all* will be brought to life.'[40]

In this word *all*, the unconverted dead must be included. Further support for this interpretation is to be found in *I Corinthians* 15, 25–28 and 3, 13–15. In the former passage Paul prophesies the destruction of all evil by Christ and the subjection of the whole universe to God. Obviously an essential element in this process is the conversion of the unconverted dead. In the latter passage, speaking of the condemnation of sinners at the Final Judgment, Paul emphasizes that the fires of Judgment will be purgative, destroying the evil that is in them, but preserving their personalities. This suggests that the conversion of the unconverted dead will take place at the final consummation.[41]

For in making all mankind prisoners to disobedience, God's purpose was to show a mercy that would likewise be universal.

For a moment at least then, Paul, like *Isaiah*, discards the old combative exclusiveness, and concludes that since Jesus died for the whole human race, somehow God will save it in its entirety. Yet this all-important point on which Paul himself presents such an equivocal front continued, after his time, to be hotly disputed: and the more ancient and grim idea of a division of mankind's fate between morally black and white displayed tenacious powers of survival. It took the Christians a long time to outlive ideas of a chosen Remnant. *Matthew*, in particular, paints a bleak picture of the departure of the righteous to everlasting life, and the relegation of everyone else to everlasting punishment: 'The curse is upon you! Go from my sight to the eternal fire that is ready for the devil and his angels!'[42] In the famous words of *Hebrews*: 'It is a terrible thing to fall into the hands of the living God.'[43] And the *Apocalypse of Paul** (like the *Apocalypse of Peter**) tells with gusto of the various excruciating penalties which, under the apostle's own gaze, were inflicted on the malefactors in Hell: an elaboration which was almost justified by some of his declarations, but did a grave injustice to others.

Later Origen called into question not only the eternity of hell but also the reality of the fiery punishment which it was believed to inflict; and his doubts on this subject influenced Ambrose and Jerome. But the majority of the Fathers adhered to a more literal and ferocious interpretation of the scriptural warnings. Origen also supported Paul's alternative view that there would, eventually, come about a universal restoration of all without exception, including sinners. But the Catholic Church, like the Orthodox Church, did not accept this doctrine, preferring Augustine's reiteration that the damned were destined to unending punishment.[44] Prosper of Aquitaine* objected, asserting that when Paul declared it God's will that all men would be saved, he meant just what he said. Calvin, however, did not agree, insisting particularly upon the idea of an Elect and upon his own Election, though many later Protestant thinkers preferred to supersede the eternal hell by a temporary hell which would be disciplinary and remedial, the same sort of solution already adopted by the Mishnah.*[45] Karl Barth and Emil Brunner admitted the existence of hell, at least as a state of separation of the wicked from the good.

But we must now turn to Paul's other, opposite argument, in favour of *universal salvation*, since his ideas about this are linked with the universalist views which he held in other connections, and which have left their permanent imprint on the world.

V

While We Wait

1. The Unification of all Human Beings

We have seen that Paul's vision of the after-life led him cautiously and amid contradictions to the understanding that eventually all would be saved. But he also believed that the Second Coming and the End of the World, even if as time went on they seemed decreasingly imminent, would nevertheless be upon mankind before very long. He therefore interpreted it as his urgent duty to prepare for that final event by spreading salvation as far and wide as he could.

But there appears to be a difficulty here. For if all men and women were in any case intended to be saved, or even, for that matter, if the identities of those who would be saved were already predestined, then why was it necessary to make such enormous efforts to make sure that everyone should be converted? Paul would probably have answered, on the basis of emotion rather than logic, that since it appeared to be God's will not only that some should be saved whose identities he knew already, but that *all* should eventually be saved, it was the imperative function of his apostles to further this sacred intention by every possible means.

That being so, it was necessary for Gentiles as well as Jews to be imbued with the redeeming faith, and this was the task to which Paul passionately devoted himself. It was a task, *Ephesians* declared, which had been laid down by God in the most ancient of times past.[1] God announced it to Paul, he told the Galatians, in the vision which brought about his conversion. For it was on that road to Damascus that 'in his

140

good pleasure God, who had set me apart from birth and called me through his grace, chose to reveal his Son to me and through me, in order that I might proclaim him among the Gentiles.'[2]

It has been surmised that Paul, looking back, is dramatically concentrating into that single tremendous moment a decision – the decision to convert the Gentiles – which was in fact subsequent and perhaps gradual; in the words of A. D. Nock, 'Memory foreshortens the course of events.' On this subject *Acts* speaks with voices that are conflicting. On the one hand, it echoes Paul's assurance, in *Galatians*, that the Gentile mission was laid upon him at the time of his conversion. Yet this aspect does not emerge very forcibly from the three descriptions of the event in *Acts* itself: which is scarcely surprising, for two reasons. In the first place, the same book, like the Gospels, contains suggestions that there had already been earlier conversions of Gentiles by others.†

Secondly, in spite of the reminder that God had entrusted Paul with this Gentile mission at the time of his conversion, we learn from a further passage in *Acts* that he did not actually make the decision to carry out these instructions until a subsequent date, while he was at Pisidian Antioch, and, five chapters later on, much the same assertion is made once again when he was at Corinth.[3] And indeed it is likely enough that his mission to the Gentiles took shape, not at once but during the course of his journeys, at Pisidian Antioch or Corinth or both, and that it grew in his mind as his career continued amid increasing rejection from the Jews.

At all events, this became his life's work, as is repeatedly proclaimed in his Letters. Do you suppose, he asks the community at Rome:

God is the God of the Jews alone? Is he not the God of Gentiles also? Certainly, of Gentiles also, if it be true that God is one . . .

There is no distinction between Jew and Greek, because the same Lord is Lord of all, and is rich enough for the need of all who invoke him . . .

It falls to me to offer the Gentiles to him as an acceptable sacrifice, consecrated by the Holy Spirit.[4]

And the message is reiterated and re-emphasized, on the basis of Pauline utterances, in the great ecumenical *Letter to the Ephesians*:

Gentiles and Jews, he [Jesus Christ] has made the two one, and in his own body of flesh and blood has broken down the enmity which stood like a

† See notes 56–8 below.

dividing wall between them . . . This was his purpose, to reconcile the two in a single body to God through the Cross, on which he killed the enmity.[5]

'Never before or since Paul,' said the nineteenth-century theologian Dean Stanley, 'have the Jew and Gentile so completely met in one single person.'

Paul's view was part of a mighty conviction of the essential *unity* of the growing Christian church. It seemed to him out of the question that the people who had been converted to one and the same indivisible faith in the redemptive Jesus, and who were therefore all 'in Christ' (a phrase which appears 164 times in the Letters) should, or indeed could, be anything other than a unity. And he conveyed his conviction by comparing and identifying the Church with one single body: the body of Jesus Christ himself.

Now you are Christ's body, and each of you a limb or organ of it . . . If one organ suffers, they all suffer together. If one flourishes, they all rejoice together . . .[6]

He is the head, and on him the whole body depends. Bonded and knit together by every constituent joint, the whole frame grows through the due activity of each part, and builds itself up in love.[7]

In order to appreciate the deeply felt meaning of this 'body' of which Christ is the head, the Body of Christ:

It is necessary to understand the Hebrew, as distinct from the Hellenic, way of looking at things. The Jew, unlike the Greek, was not interested in things in themselves but only in things as they are called to be. He was not concerned with an object as such but with what it becomes in relation to its final reference according to the divine purpose. The meaning of an object therefore does not lie in its analytical and empirical reality, but in the will that is expressed by it.

Hence Jesus could say of a piece of bread: 'This is my body.' The bread does not cease to be bread, but it becomes what it is not, namely the instrument and organ of his presence, because through his sovereign word he has given it a new dimension. Similarly the Church is the Body of Christ because its true nature rests upon its relation to God's purpose. The Church is the organ of Christ's presence uniting his members to himself and in him to one another. So Christians are 'limbs of his body'; they are 'the body of Christ, and severally members thereof.'[8]

This idea of the body of Christ was the most vivid possible expression of the *solidarity* which Paul required of the Church. 'No other age,' said

Sir Samuel Dill, 'felt a deeper craving for some form of social life, greater than the family, but narrower than the state.' Paul's fellow-Jews, who had long thought of their community as the assembly of the people of God,[9] bequeathed to him this intense feeling of unitedness. But they had never expressed themselves in this particular fashion. To convey the difference between his ways of thinking and theirs, he retained from describing his churches as synagogues, but instead used the term *ecclesia* (assembly), which the Septuagint had employed in general terms to describe gatherings together of the people. In Paul's Letters, *ecclesia* refers to religious congregations (not to a building, for no special Christian meeting-places were to be built for two hundred years to come). These congregations were 'churches', each with its own organization, though the exact forms which this assumed have been disputed and cannot be deduced with any confidence from Paul's writings.[10]

Paul sees each one of these individual churches as part of one single Church.[11] His Letters to its members show the beginnings of ecclesiastical worship and discipline and consciousness. It is in *Ephesians*, however, that there appears a particularly well developed sense of the Universal Church, one, holy, catholic and apostolic; and that is one of the reasons why the letter has sometimes been regarded as a subsequent elaboration of Paul's own opinions, which are likely to have been rather less highly organized and detailed. But even if *Ephesians* contains post-Pauline additions, its main ideas are his. The Church is Christ's Body, and is therefore One. Not so long afterwards, these Christians were to display the biggest attempt that the ancient world had ever known to create a real community which was both geographically inside the framework of the secular Greco-Roman system, and yet wholly apart from it. A new kind of society with no parallel in the history of religion, this Church proved successful because it was a far more tightly coherent organism than the pagan mystery religions of Isis and Cybele and Mithras, with whom it had to compete.

This tight unity was largely the concept of Paul, and it was a powerful enough concept over the course of centuries to surmount a good many (though never all) of the innumerable divisions which continually threatened to fragment the unity of the growing Church. These divisions had not been healed – indeed had been partly caused – by Paul himself, and by his passionate determination that his own line was right, and everyone else's wrong. This determination prompted him to utter a never-ceasing stream of denunciations of rival views within Christianity itself; views which, according to his belief, must inevitably be murderous and blasphemous, since they are tearing Christ's Body apart. Why, he asks his co-religionists at Corinth, are you divided between different Christian sects? – 'Surely Christ has not been divided among you!'[12]

I implore you, my friends, keep your eye on those who stir up quarrels and lead others astray, contrary to the teaching you received. Avoid them, for such people are servants not of Christ our Lord but of their own appetites, and they seduce the minds of innocent people with smooth and specious words . . .

I now repeat what I have said before: if anyone preaches a gospel at variance with the Gospel which you received, let him be outcast! . . .[13]

And Paul, so jealous of his own claim to be regarded as an apostle, is extremely touchy about the effects of this Church disunity upon his own position, thus somewhat belying his protests that there was no room for personal rivalries and vanities.[14]

I shall go on as I am doing now, to cut the ground from under those who would seize any chance to put their vaunted apostleship on the same level as ours. Such men are sham-apostles, crooked in all their practices, masquerading as apostles of Christ. There is nothing surprising about that; Satan himself masquerades as an angel of light.[15]

Nevertheless, in spite of all such abuse and entreaty from Paul, there remained what he stigmatized as heresies on every side. Indeed, anything else would have been surprising. For the religions which had so far appeared in the course of human history had not, for the most part, been monolithic; and contemporary Judaism in particular comprised a great variety of divergent schools of thought. But Paul did not intend, if he could help it, that Christianity should follow this heterogeneous pattern. In consequence, his Letters are full of violent exhortations directed against every shade of opinion that was at odds with his own particular interpretation of Christianity, thus setting a tragic precedent to the secular persecutors of later centuries, who transmuted his hostile words into repressive deeds. Yet the incarnation of Jesus Christ and all the matters relating to it did raise very difficult questions, about which complete agreement was almost impossibly hard to achieve. And these events and their implications had been preached in profoundly divergent fashions even during the few years before Paul ever appeared on the scene, and continued to receive discordant treatment, from a variety of preachers, throughout his career. It is not surprising, therefore, that he found a great deal to censure. And because he was a highly combative man with an insistent, lofty conception of the unity of the Church, he never shrank from the task of launching onslaughts against any and every Christian who disagreed with him.

In pursuing his ideal so untiringly, Paul was inspired by a mighty overriding idea, one of the greatest ideas to have animated any of the world's religions. That idea was love. It is one of the numerous paradoxes surrounding the career and character of Paul that the man who spent so much of his life battling fiercely against the 'heretics' who disagreed with him should have been the most passionately convinced and eloquent standard-bearer of love. But so it was. The apparent hatred which he lavished on those who held different opinions from himself was only the reverse side of the coin of love: it was because the deviators failed to enrol themselves under his standard of universal love that he attacked them.

True, his sharp criticisms of others invited retaliation. Thus Tertullian could call him 'the favourite apostle of the heretics',[16] because some of his own views were dangerously near those which were denounced, after his lifetime, as heresies. And not only after his lifetime, for already while he was alive those whom he proclaimed to be utterly misguided were loudly saying that it was he, not they, who was destroying the unity of the church. But the written arguments of these contemporaries who disagreed with him have vanished, whereas his own writings not only survived but eventually became part of the Holy Bible itself. Besides, even if the works of his opponents had been preserved, it is exceedingly unlikely that they can have rivalled Paul's extraordinary eloquence: and, in particular, the eloquent exposition of the idea of love which dominated his concept of the unified church.

His term for love, *agape*, is curiously rare in pre-Christian writings. The verb and adjective are found often enough, but the noun only occurs very sparsely. However, it does appear in the Septuagint, where it denotes loving feeling of any and every kind. That is why Paul chose it; it is the most comprehensive word for love that existed in the Greek vocabulary, and therefore seemed to him the most appropriate designation for the vastness of the new, Christian love which he wanted to communicate to the world. Jesus, too, had urged men and women to love one another, and even their enemies, and to turn the other cheek: because he had felt that anything short of this was an irrelevant distraction to those seeking admission to the kingdom of God. But Paul spoke of love with a passion which seems all his own.

Agape was rendered 'charity' in the Authorized Version of the Bible. That is now misleading, but the magnificent seventeenth-century rendering of Paul's praise of love to the Corinthians can never be bettered.

Though I speak with the tongues of men and of angels, and have not charity, I am become as sounding brass, or a tinkling cymbal.

And though I have the gift of prophecy, and understand all mysteries, and all knowledge; and though I have all faith, so that I could remove mountains, and have not charity, I am nothing.

And though I bestow all my goods to feed the poor, and though I give my body to be burned, and have not charity, it profiteth me nothing.

Charity suffereth long and is kind; charity envieth not; charity vaunteth not itself, is not puffed up.

Doth not behave itself unseemly, seeketh not her own, is not easily provoked, thinketh no evil.

Rejoiceth not in iniquity, but rejoiceth in the truth.

Beareth all things, believeth all things, hopeth all things, endureth all things.

Charity never faileth: but whether there be prophecies, they shall fail; whether there be tongues, they shall cease; whether there be knowledge, it shall vanish away.

For we know in part, and we prophesy in part.

But when that which is perfect is come, then that which is in part shall be done away.

When I was a child, I spake as a child, I understood as a child, I thought as a child: but when I became a man, I put away childish things.

For now we see through a glass, darkly; but then face to face: now I know in part; but then shall I know even as also I am known.

And now abideth faith, hope, charity, these three; but the greatest of these is charity.[17]

Although Paul writes so eloquently about love, he does not say very much about men and women loving *God*. Ancient Israel had been summoned to love God;[18] but it is only rarely that Paul echoes such appeals.

Augustine was, I think, the first to refer to the fact that Paul, who says such great things about the love of men between themselves – that is to say, as members of the Church of Christ – says very little about the love of men to God. This is all the more strange, since from childhood he had heard every-day in the summons 'Hear, O Israel' the commandments to love God with his whole soul, and indeed he knew also the saying of Jesus in which this was called the first commandment of all. The rare use which Paul makes of the word *agape* (love in the religious and ethical sense) in the sphere of the relation of men to God has been explained by the fact that for him 'love' is charac-terized as 'made known through the cross of Christ', and that accordingly human devotedness to God, unspontaneous and uncreative as it is, at best has to be accounted as the reflexion of it.[19]

The author of *I John* mentions our need to love God; but he deduces our love for our neighbour from something else, God's love for us.

God is love; and his love was disclosed to us in this, that he sent his only Son into the world to bring us life . . . If God thus loved us, dear friends, we in turn are bound to love one another . . . We love because he loved us first. But if a man says 'I love God', while hating his brother, he is a liar. If he does not love the brother he has seen, it cannot be that he loves God whom he has not seen.[20]

And that, too, was perhaps in Paul's mind when he appealed, with unremitting emphasis, that we should love our neighbours – that is to say, *all* other men and women. 'The only thing that counts,' he tells the Galatians, 'is faith active in love . . . the whole Law can be summed up in a single commandment: "Love your neighbour as yourself".'[21] 'Love cannot wrong a neighbour; therefore the whole Law is summed up in Love.'[22] It is the perfect link which can bind every man and woman to every other. For Paul, as Cardinal Newman suggested, 'felt all his "neighbours" to be existing in himself.'

The Gospels later attributed the same conviction to Jesus,[23] and it seems likely to have been a prominent feature in his teaching. But it was not a new doctrine in Judaism. It had been expressed long ago in *Leviticus* (at least in regard to other Israelites): 'you shall love your neighbour as a man like yourself';[24] and this was a text which a leading rabbi, like Jesus, later declared to be the greatest of all the precepts in the Torah.[25] (In some versions of *Tobit*, additional words were added: 'do not do to anyone what you yourself would hate.'[26] And this senti-ment was repeated by the great Rabbi Hillel who was Paul's older contemporary.[27])

Our fellow men and women may seem to us unlovely and unlovable: but we must love them all the same. And the old doctrine of an eye for an eye and a tooth for a tooth (which was not altogether absent from some of Paul's views of the Last Judgment) is ultimately rejected: 'never pay back evil for evil.'[28] There were Old Testament and Apocryphal precedents for offering such counsel. But Paul also goes further. He does not employ the same dramatically explicit words as the Gospels attributed to Jesus, 'love your enemies and pray for your persecutors.'[29] But what Paul says is not dissimilar: 'call down blessings on your persecutors – blessings, not curses.'[30]

The scriptural writings of the past[31] as well as the scrolls of Qumran, had been full of imprecations against enemies; for Jewish opinion usually held that it was no good asking people to love their foes, since it cannot be done.

Nowhere is the command given in the Bible [Old Testament] to *love* one's enemy. This is contrary to human nature, and as such it is impossible of fulfilment. To require men to fulfil the impossible is to bring confusion and frustration into their spiritual lives and possibly to cause them to recoil in despair even from those duties which are capable of accomplishment. 'As far as reason is concerned,' declared Saadia,* 'it demands that the All-Wise does not charge anyone with aught that does not lie within his competence or which he is unable to do.' The Torah was not given to ministering angels, but to men – mortal, fallible men.[32]

Nevertheless, *Exodus* had already offered the injunction: 'when you come upon your enemy's ox or ass straying, you shall take it back to him.'[33] And *Proverbs*, echoing this, enjoined, in a passage specifically quoted by Paul: 'If your enemy is hungry, give him bread to eat; if he is thirsty, give him water to drink; so you will heap glowing coals on his head'; and then (though Paul does not continue his quotation as far as this) 'the Lord will reward you.'[34] Later, too (at an uncertain date) the Jewish *Testaments of the Twelve Patriarchs** urged the good man to show *universal* mercy to all men, even 'though they devise with evil intent concerning him'.[35] And the idea was carried further by one of the leaders of the eighteenth-century Jewish reform movement of Hasidism* in Poland, who was said to have commanded his sons: 'pray for enemies that things go well with them.'[36] So these ideas have not been wholly absent from Judaism, ancient or modern.

And Paul, too, preferred this minority Jewish opinion that one should bless and minister to one's enemy – and it did not seem to him an impossible injunction. He was deliberately giving expression to a paradox, the same paradox ascribed by the Gospels, in even more vivid form, to Jesus. And he was doing so in order to illustrate his conviction that the Christian love which is the necessary base and inspiration of the single, unified, Christian community he so nobly envisaged must be *universal*, acknowledging no reserves or exclusions or exceptions whatsoever.

Despite the numerous, if incomplete, scriptural analogies that Paul was able to draw upon, his doctrine of this Universal Church, in which Jews and Gentiles were indissolubly bound together, ran into difficulties with the Jews. Their history, ever since the nation first embraced monotheistic beliefs, had struck an uneasy balance between the tribal and the universal. Judaism was tribal because its devotees were the Chosen People to whom God had given the task of carrying out and transmitting his will. On the other hand, since he was One, he was everyone's God, and salvation for all nations was his goal. As he was believed to have declared to Abraham, 'all the families on earth will pray to be blessed as you are blessed.'[37] And the *II Isaiah* proclaimed the mission of Israel 'to be a light to all peoples, a beacon for the nations . . . a light to the nations, to be my salvation to earth's farthest bounds.'[38]

Yet there were also Jews ready to remind each other that the Gentiles were hostile to Israel and Israel's God, and in consequence neither deserved the divine favour nor would ever be its recipients. Tragic exile, and then Greek and Roman oppression, caused this view to appear and reappear in ever more embittered forms. As E. W. Hunt observes,[39]

In Paul's day the normal attitude of the sect to which he belonged, and of most other Jews, towards Gentiles was that they would either be destroyed, or, if they were spared, be Israel's slaves. What some extremist Pharisees thought of the Gentiles in the first century AD is summed up thus: 'Thou hast said that they are nothing and that they are like spittle and thou hast likened the abundance of them to a drop in a bucket.'[40]

True, the Apocryphal work from which the last passage is quoted, *II Esdras*, contains other passages which show traces of universalist thinking – for example its writer seems to view the fated destruction of the Gentiles, however distasteful they may be, with a certain regret.[41] But nothing is said about their having a share in the Messianic Kingdom.

Nevertheless, the Dispersion of the Jews and the translation of their scriptures into the Greek Septuagint, which was used outside Palestine, had already, in days long since past, decisively moved the Bible to foreign lands. Among the Dispersed, universalism was always dreamt of as a way out of Jewish isolation. And so Gentiles were converted to Judaism, and there is literary evidence that they were many.[42] How many we cannot say, because when *Matthew* makes Jesus tell the scribes and Pharisees that they 'travel over sea and land to win one convert',[43] this seems to be an exaggeration: other Jewish opinion is more cautious and ambiguous, for there was a rival view that converts were not entirely desirable because they were liable to fall back into idolatry.[44]

Yet Judaism continued to possess a strong attraction for the outsider. This was an age in which men and women felt a fierce longing for supernatural inspiration and help. Judaism gave them what they needed. And it offered other allurements too – simple moral rules, an impressive Holy Book, a regulated way of life, a weekly day of rest and a community that was closely and tightly knit. Circumcision,* however, was a step which, although many pagan converts saw no objection to it, others – however favourably inclined towards Judaism – found that they were not prepared to take; either because of physical distaste, or owing to the fear that such a very thoroughgoing sign of conversion would draw censure from their disparaging and uncomprehending Greek neighbours. In such circumstances, the idea that circumcision could be omitted by Gentile proselytes gained ground in the Dispersion. There were also a further, larger category of God-fearers or Judaizers, who sympathized with the Jewish faith but did not actually enrol among its adherents, instead enjoying a recognized status upon its fringes. Although they often had their sons circumcised, their own obligations seem to have been generally limited to the maintenance of what were described by the Talmud as the Noachian or Noahide commandments, consisting of basic ethical principles supposedly addressed to Adam and in a complete form to Noah.[45]

Paul's innovation, however, in seeking Gentile adherents to Christianity was to shift the emphasis altogether away from this half-way type of conversion. Judaizers and even Jewish converts (especially if uncircumcised) had alike tended to be second-class Jews. Paul's Gentile converts, on the other hand, were to be first-class Christians, every bit as Christian as any Christian of Jewish origin. The point is made simply and sharply by a balanced statement in *Galatians*. The church authorities in Jerusalem, Paul said, 'acknowledged that I had been entrusted with the Gospel for Gentiles as surely as Peter had been entrusted with the Gospel for Jews.'[46] The two missions are thus set against each other and equated in novel and revolutionary fashion. True, the equation was not wholly and completely even. For it was only right that an attempt should be made to convert the Jews first. Jesus had virtually directed his ministry almost exclusively towards them; Paul, too, had initially done the same, and even after the extension of his mission to the Gentiles he still allotted priority to the conversion of Jews. 'The Gospel . . . is the saving power of God for everyone who has faith – the Jew first, but the Greek also.'[47] In that passage, the balance tilts in favour of the Jews. But it was an uneasy priority, for if they would be the first to be rewarded they would also be the first to be punished.[48] Moreover, elsewhere in the Letters, the balance tilts back in the opposite direction towards equality between the two groups. For, although the Jews have a great advantage, namely the opportunity to know right from wrong, 'God has no favourites . . . When Gentiles who do not possess the Law carry out its precepts by the light of nature, then, although they have no Law, they are their own Law, for they display the effect of the Law inscribed on their own hearts.'[49]

What is more, because the Jews have become Paul's opponents (or he has become theirs), he sees the conversion of the Gentiles as something which will, in fact, *come first*, before the conversion of the Jews, who will thus be inspired to adopt the same course afterwards. 'Because they [the Jews] offended, salvation has come to the Gentiles, to stir Israel to emulation . . . This partial blindness has come upon Israel only until the Gentiles have been admitted in full strength.'[50] This same argument was dramatized, perhaps over-dramatized, by the two passages of *Acts* in which, as we have seen, Paul was alleged to have formed the project of the Gentile mission during the course of his travels. At Pisidian Antioch Paul and Barnabas were said to have declared to their Jewish critics, quoting scriptural authority, 'it was necessary that the word of God should be declared to you first. But since you reject it and thus condemn yourself as unworthy of eternal life, we now turn to the Gentiles.'[51] And then, when the Jews at Corinth likewise opposed him, he supposedly cried out to them in similar terms: 'Your blood be on your own heads! My conscience is clear; now I shall go to the Gentiles.'[52]

The same shift in missionary priorities took root in certain sections of non-Christian Jewish thought also. Like the principle of loving one's enemies, it was echoed in eighteenth-century Hasidism, one of whose holy men, the Zaddikim, was said to have appealed to God: 'Lord of the world, I beseech you to redeem Israel. And if you will it not, redeem the Gentiles!'[53] This was the principle that Paul, too, had extended to the new religion he was creating out of Judaism; and he had extended it on a comprehensive and provocative scale. Earlier in this chapter, reference was made to the question whether other Christians had tried to convert Gentiles before him. *Acts* wishes to show that they had. For that was behind its description of the original Pentecost after the Ascension, in which the divine word was at once transformed, not merely into ecstatic utterances, as may have been the original version, but into all tongues. This miraculous event is intended to indicate that the systematic Gentile mission had been part of Christian doctrine from the beginning,[54] ever since the time before Paul started his activity at all. However, this looks like a retrospective tidying-up operation, designed to give an impression of a unified policy from the first. And, similarly, *Acts'* subsequent story of Peter's conversion of the centurion Cornelius[55] bears all the signs of an attempt to compare and equate and harmonize the one apostle with the other – Peter's branch of the Church with Paul's. Nevertheless, it does seem likely that there were certain Gentile converts before Paul: for there is plausibility in the statement that some of those who fled from the Jerusalem persecutions after Stephen's death, Jews from Cyprus and Cyrene, had undertaken Gentile conversions at Antioch.[56] As for Jesus himself, the writers of the Gospels cannot claim, and are aware they cannot claim, that he had ever launched a policy of Gentile conversion. On the contrary, the tradition does not report that he generally addressed himself to Gentiles at all, and he is even specifically stated to have regarded them with aversion.[57] Nevertheless, when the Gospels report that he converted an occasional pagan, a Phoenician woman and a man from beyond the borders of Galilee,[58] there is no reason to regard this as unlikely. Very probably, then, certain Gentiles had been converted before Paul. But their conversions had been isolated products of circumstance, and not the results of any systematic plan.

It was Paul who created the plan; he dominated it from the outset. Moreover, in assuming this role he chose deliberately to blur the very antithesis between Gentiles and Jews which he himself had announced and had seemed to stress, the balanced parallel between his own mission to the former and Peter's to the latter. For Paul now insisted that the communities he and Peter were proselytising were not two after all: *they were one*. 'Circumcision is nothing; uncircumcision is nothing; the only thing that counts is new creation!'[59]

And Paul could say these things although there was no question of his Gentile converts following the Law in every respect: towards their fellow-Christians of Jewish origin, who often did just this, they were not obliged to make any such concession. For one thing, like some of the Gentiles who took up Judaism, they did not have to be circumcised. Moreover, as for the dietetic regulations observed by the Jews, Paul advised his Gentile converts to the Christian faith to follow the minimum requirements as it would be likely to cause offence to Jewish Christians should they act otherwise. But the matter, he assured them, was anyway of secondary importance: 'you may eat anything sold in the meat-market without raising questions of conscience; for the earth is the Lord's and everything in it.'[60] *Acts* declared that the Jerusalem conference which Paul supposedly held with the Jewish Christians insisted that these food-regulations should be obeyed by non-Jews who accepted the faith.[61] But, if so, then Paul nevertheless continued to dissent in principle, and only recommended his converts to concur as a matter of voluntary tact.

As we shall see, Paul's success in converting Gentiles during his lifetime was nothing like as great as *Acts* has given us to suppose: the opposition proved too formidable. Yet as the results of his mission revealed in later times, he had played a uniquely important part in launching one of the greatest movements in the history of the world. For he had begun to set up a religion that broke down the boundaries between countries and cultures, on a massive scale that had been unimaginable before: a rival to the Roman empire, which harboured it and which would eventually succumb to it.

Some new shock had been needed to precipitate Judaism into the world at large, and Paul administered it. For he was asking Israel to sacrifice its ancient national hopes in favour of quite a different task, that of being only one favoured people among many – an apostolic nation, it was true, among other nations, yet no longer their superior but their equal, within a greater unity, 'the whole Israel of God'.[62]

Many Jews considered this watering-down of their role highly distasteful; and he found it difficult to persuade them to become Christians on such terms. Among his converts, then, there was only a very small proportion of Jews. In view of his nonchalant attitude to their Law, this was not surprising. Yet Paul makes it clear that he found it disturbing. He understood very well that his universalist attitude had made it seem that he was classifying them as foes, since although 'they are God's friends for the sake of the patriarchs . . . in the spreading of the Gospel they are treated as God's enemies.'[63] As a result, many of them responded by displaying strong hostility in their turn. Indeed, even many of the Greek converts to Judaism – the sort of people who had violently opposed the unorthodoxy of Stephen – were far from pleased with Paul's assurances that complete assimilation to the Law did not matter. These were people who had taken the pious trouble to attain it, thus becoming its enthusiastic supporters. In consequence, they hated him. And among those who had been born Jews it was inevitable that he should be held in even greater detestation.

Paul violently retaliated. Certainly, he was prepared, as long as his patience held out, to act tactfully, 'to Jews becoming like a Jew, to win Jews.'[64] But his flash-point was low, and there came a time when he accused them of being murderers, the criminals who had slain Jesus Christ. This linked up in his mind with his readiness to reject the Law. First, in the days when he had been persecuting Jesus' supporters for their breaches of the Law, he had become gradually disenchanted with the Law himself. Then, after his conversion, he loathed those whom he charged with the supreme horror of killing the Saviour.

The Jews killed the Lord Jesus and the prophets and drove us out, the Jews who are heedless of God's will and enemies of their fellow-men, hindering us from speaking to the Gentiles to lead them to salvation. All this time they have been making up the full measure of their guilt, and now retribution has overtaken them for good and all.[65]

Paul had fused his two reasons for alienating himself from the Jews into one single, burning condemnation.

Anti-semitism, in the sense of anti-Jewish sentiment, was nothing new. It had been flourishing and festering among the Greeks, especially in Alexandria, ever since the Jewish community in that city had reached a substantial size in the third century BC. But it was given an immense stimulus when the Jew Paul blamed his own people for the inadequacy of the Torah, and then for the execution of Jesus. For the relative parts played in the Crucifixion by the Romans and Jews respectively already constituted a major emotional and even political issue when the Gospels came to be written down in the forms in which we know them. This (except possibly in the case of the slightly earlier Mark), was after the First Jewish Revolt (AD 66–73), at a time when the Christian communities were extremely eager to dissociate themselves, in Roman eyes, from this rebel people, whom they consequently hastened to blame for the Crucifixion, largely exonerating Pilate. Thus *Matthew* (in spite of its generally Jewish tone) laid exceptional stress on this gravest of all crimes allegedly committed by the Jews, a crime of which, it was added, they themselves freely accepted the consequences: 'his blood be on us, and on our children!'[66] And *John* went farthest of all in blaming the Jewish people, to whom he even makes Jesus declare: 'Your father is the Devil!'[67] Meanwhile the Jews themselves, as their own traditions clearly show, were very ready not only to take the responsibility upon themselves, but even to assert that the Crucifixion had been amply justified.[68]

And indeed, according to the New Testament, their hostility to the group of disciples continued adamantly after Jesus' death. But here *Acts* was of two minds. On the one hand its author, like the Gospel writers, wanted to stress that the earliest Christians were not at all the same as the Jews, who were in such disgrace with the Romans. But on the other hand *Acts* is also eager not to be too offensive to the Pharisees*,[69] who as a result of the Revolt had succeeded the Sadducees* as leaders of Judaism (and who furthermore believed, like the christians, in bodily resurrection). Moreover, this attitude fits in well with *Acts'* other leading aim, which is to display the unity of the early church – that is the harmony between the Jerusalem church of the Jewish Christians and the churches of the non-Jewish Gentiles; so that Paul's own claim to be a Jew of irreproachable ancestry and a Pharisee[70] is not only repeated but exaggerated by the additional assertion that he had studied as a boy at Jerusalem under the great Pharisee teacher Gamaliel I, which as a Jew of the Dispersion he had almost certainly not, since he does not seem to have been in Jerusalem as a young man at all.[71]

Nevertheless, emphasis on Paul's Judaism was only intended to emphasize the ingratitude of those Jews who obstructed and rejected him: his unfortunate relations with them must now be recounted.

There were preliminaries to this story. In the same anti-Jewish spirit *Acts* already told of continual Jewish attempts, from the very first days after Jesus' death, to get the Christians into trouble with the Roman governing power; and also of the very early determination of the Jews to persecute them directly, on their own account, as severely as they could. For Paul was not, in their eyes, the first offender. Before him,

Stephen, too was held to have spoken inexcusably, when he described the Temple worship as materialistic.[72] These comments embroiled Stephen with non-Palestinian Jews at Jerusalem who were more orthodox than the orthodox, and he was stoned to death, the traditional Jewish penalty for blasphemy. It was either an official Jewish execution whereby the protagonists were taking advantage of an interregnum between Roman governors, or it was presented as an ostensibly 'spontaneous' lynching. Then King Agrippa I, who became Rome's 'client' (dependent) monarch of Judaea when for three years (41–4) the country reverted from the status of a Roman province, beheaded Jesus' disciple James the son of Zebedee; this was also the occasion of the third of three arrests to which Peter was subjected in Jerusalem.[73] The antipathy of the Jewish establishment to the new sect had at once become abundantly clear.

It was to take disciplinary action against these deviants that Paul had been sent by certain Jewish authorities to Damascus, though probably his starting point had not been Jerusalem as *Acts* reported, since from his own words it seems apparent that he had not been there. Nevertheless, the Jewish leadership requested him to stamp out the new movement in Damascus. And then, by the same token, when he had reversed his course totally and become Christian, it was he in his turn who suffered repeatedly from Jewish obstructions and menaces throughout the course of his missionary journeys. *Acts* only depicts a fairly brief section of his career. But it manages to give a very consistent picture of his relationship with the Jews, in which the same pattern continually recurs. In each new town he visits, Paul first preaches in the synagogues, addressing himself to the Jewish community; and only then, after he has invariably encountered vigorous opposition from some of its members, does he turn his attention to the Gentiles, whereupon the hostile Jews poison the minds of the Gentile community. Then they arrange to have Paul and his associates expelled by the civic authorities, and follow them from one town to the next, and subject them to judicial floggings. Twice at least there were alleged plans to have Paul murdered, on both occasions in Judaea itself; first by a party of Greek-speaking Jews and then later by a group of more than forty men who vowed not to eat or drink until they had killed him.[74]

At Corinth, the Jews charged him before the Roman governor, Gallio. *Acts* says that he was accused of 'inducing people to worship God in ways that are against the Law'. But the governor, it was added, dismissed the charge with the words, 'If the question is some bickering about words and names and your Jewish Law, you must see to it yourselves; I have no mind to be a judge of these matters.'[75] A. N. Sherwin-White analyzed these proceedings as follows:

> It is not certain that the charge made against Paul at Corinth was intended to refer primarily to the Hebraic Law, though Gallio found it convenient to take it that way. The accusers do not say that Paul is persuading *Jews* to worship contrary to the Law – but that he is persuading *men* to do so . . . The best charge for the Jews to bring was that Paul was preaching to Romans, not to Jews – contrary to the Roman Law, not the Jewish Law. And that may well be what the narrative is meant to convey . . . But the Jews, being Jews, could only make their accusation in terms of the Judaic Law. By dragging in 'the Law' in the scriptural sense they provided Gallio with his way out . . . An alternative explanation is that the Jews were invoking against Paul the edicts of Claudius which guaranteed them the quiet enjoyment of their native customs throughout the Dispersion.[76]

Later, however, according to *Acts*, Paul was captured by the Jews at Jerusalem itself, and threatened with lynching:

> The Jews from the province of Asia saw him in the Temple. They stirred up the whole crowd, and seized him, shouting 'Men of Israel, help, help! This is the fellow who spreads his doctrine all over the world, attacking our people, our Law, and this sanctuary. On top of all this he had brought Gentiles into the Temple and profaned this holy place.' For they had previously seen Trophimus the Ephesian with him in the city, and assumed that Paul had brought him into the Temple.
> The whole city was in a turmoil, and people came running from all directions. They seized Paul and dragged him out of the Temple.[77]

The commandant of the local garrison, Claudius Lysias, sent troops immediately, and they extricated Paul from these Jewish enemies. But their charges were not dropped. One accusation, *Acts* states, was that, by taking the Gentile Trophimus into the Temple, and beyond the Court of the Gentiles into the Court of Israel, he had ignored the Greek and Latin notices on the barrier warning Gentiles, on pain of death, against entering the inner quadrangle or courtyard. Although, in other respects, perhaps not permitted rights of capital punishment by the Romans, the Jewish Council or Sanhedrin* appears to have been entitled to employ such powers against Gentiles who disobeyed this particular injunction – and to enforce them by authorized or semi-authorized lynching.

Anyway, this allegation against Paul did not stick, and later had to be withdrawn. A second charge against him, however, remained. This was once again primarily religious in character, complaining of his attacks upon Judaism and its institutions. But since it was the Roman officials who had to be persuaded, and since the Jews knew that Roman official-dom was unwilling to convict on purely religious indictments, they endeavoured to give a political twist to the religious charge. When Paul was brought before the Sanhedrin on the next day, it was said that he received physical violence from the attendants of the high priest, whom he thereupon insulted, asserting afterwards that he had not known who the man was. Next, with great success according to *Acts*, he tried to drive a wedge between the Pharisee and Sadducee members of the Sanhedrin because the former believed in an ultimate general resurrec-tion, as he did, and the latter did not.[78] Then the Roman authorities rescued him once again from angry crowds and removed him from Jerusalem to their provincial capital Caesarea Maritima. The Jews sent down elders and a lawyer to put the case against him. Rome's governor Felix (a Greek freedman by origin) invited his wife Drusilla, sister of the Jewish monarch Agrippa II whose kingdom was on the northern fringes of Rome's Judaean province, to attend the hearings. But Felix took no action against Paul.

His successor Festus, however, when approached afresh by his Jewish accusers, asked him if he would be willing 'to go up to Jerusalem and stand trial on these charges before him there'.[79] No doubt Festus regarded this as convenient since Jewish witnesses would be more readily available, and members of the Sanhedrin could, if necessary, act as assessors. But Paul saw it as a Jewish attempt to get him into the Sanhedrin's hands – with ob-viously fatal results for himself. So he appealed to the Emperor Nero; and Festus, after calling in for consultation the Jewish royalties Agrippa II and his sister Berenice, accepted his appeal, and sent him to Rome.

What happened to Paul in the future, therefore, was no longer influenced by the Jews at all: when he finally arrived at the capital none of them, it was said, had sent evidence for his prosecution,[80] so their case against him lapsed. Paul was safely out of their hands; out of the hands of the people who, in spite of or rather because of his own Jewish origins, hated him, and were hated by him in return.

His relationship with the Jews, after his breakaway from their ranks, had been disastrous. Indeed, it clearly pointed the way towards a total breach between Jews and Christians. But that still lay ahead. It had not come yet because Paul, in his lifetime, did not achieve enough to bring it about. But the breach was greatly hastened on by the First Jewish Revolt (66–73), from which Christians were at great pains to dissociate themselves. These endeavours were exemplified by the extremely anti-Jewish language of *Matthew* and *John*. And the Jews, for their part, retaliated by introducing a prayer which directly attacked Christians and heretics.[81] After both parties had thus had their say in the matter, the rift, it would seem, could scarcely have been more complete, even allowing for the customary rhetorical overstatements of near-eastern writings. It is true that *Hebrews*, at the end of the first century, reverted to the idea that Jesus had united in himself all aspects of the Jewish tradition. Yet it was not long afterwards that Marcion went to the opposite extreme, and, by rejecting the Old Testament completely, cut Christianity's final link with Judaism. The Fathers restored the Old Testament to favour, but by now the Christian and Jewish faiths were separate for all time to come. This final split occurred long after Paul's death. But it had very largely been his doing. Had he not lived and thought as he did, we cannot of course guess how the relations between the two religions might have developed; but surely they would not have been so hostile, and the history of the world could have taken a different course.

2.   *The Other Christians who Objected*

If the Jewish community at the time of Paul consisted of a number of very different branches and persuasions, Paul's attacks on 'heretics' reveal that the same was already true of Christianity; a fact which it is all too easy to lose sight of since the survival of his Letters, in contrast to the disappearance of all other contemporary Christian literature, focuses our attention too exclusively upon himself and his doings. True, Paul was of enormous, overriding importance, and he stood the test of time, whereas his contemporaries did not. Yet there were many other kinds of early Christians as well. If we knew a little more about them, we should be in a better position to appreciate the true proportions and nature of his own gigantic achievement.

In the first place, of course, there was the difference between the Jewish Christians (Judaeo-Christians) of Judaea and the Gentile Christians of the Dispersion. But that is far too simple a distinction to draw, because each of these two main geographical groups within itself was exceedingly diversified and complex. With regard to this variety among the early Christians of the Dispersion, Paul wrote to Corinth in revealing terms:

> I have been told, my brothers, by Chloe's people that there are quarrels among you. What I mean is this: each of you is saying, 'I am Paul's man' or 'I am for Apollos'; 'I follow Cephas, or 'I am Christ's.'[1]

Cephas, despite suggestions to the contrary by Clement of Alexandria,[2] is Peter, a name which in Greek has the same meaning of 'rock' as *kepha* has in Aramaic.[3] As for Apollos, Paul tells us that he watered the seed which Paul himself had planted,[4] and that they were all working as one team. But this probably does not do justice to the autonomy of Apollos, described in *Acts* as an eloquent, fervent Alexandrian learned in the scriptures, who 'taught accurately the facts about Jesus, though he knew only John's baptism.'[5] Here indeed is a specific illustration of the variety that was to be found inside the Christian fold. And it reminds us, in particular, how totally ignorant we are about the vastly important Christian community at Alexandria. Was the church at this second city of the Roman world – or rather the churches, for surely there was more than one kind of church in this great centre of mixed populations – completely divergent from Paul's or Peter's Christianity, just as the allegorical, esoteric Judaism of the Alexandrian Philo* differed utterly from the Judaism of Jerusalem? And who founded the church of the Alexandrian Christians? Was it Paul's companion Mark, as the tradition maintained,[6] or someone earlier? And why does Paul tell us nothing about this? Why, too, for that matter is there no mention in the New Testament of the significant church at Damascus – where *Acts* say that Paul himself was baptized?[7] Nor do we even know who founded the church at Rome itself. It must have been established long before Peter could ever have come there. But who did this we are not told.

At all those cities – Corinth, Alexandria, Damascus, Rome – the essential dichotomy repeated itself: in each place there were not only Gentile Christians[8] but also very many Jewish Christians, people who had originated in the Jewish communities which were so important in such cities. At Corinth, for example, the group 'which followed Peter' was presumably Jewish Christian; which is to say, even during the few years before Paul's missionary activity began, a Jewish Christian missionary movement had already spread widely. It had spread to begin with, as *Acts* tells us, in the immediate environs of the homeland: through the agency of Peter on the coast and elsewhere, and through the Greek-speaking Philip in Samaria, and other Greek-speakers in Phoenicia and Antioch and Cyprus. But this Jewish Christian mission had also spread much farther afield, to other major towns including many of those which Paul subsequently visited, encountering the sharp opposition of the Jewish Christians who had arrived there before him. And it would be a mistake, all too easily prompted by the survival of Paul's Letters and *Acts* to the exclusion of the almost wholly lost Jewish Christian literature, to suppose that Paul in his lifetime succeeded in superseding their churches either in the eastern imperial provinces or in Rome itself.

Moreover, just as any supposition of a single, uniform Gentile Christianity *outside* Judaea would be misguided, so, too, it would be equally misleading to think of a monolithic, homogeneous Jewish Christianity within that country. Indeed, it needs an effort of the imagination for us to think of the Jewish Christians at all: for their permanent disappearance, almost without a trace, had already occurred before modern or even medieval times began. But in Paul's day they were immensely significant, and we must recognize that they were always in his mind, and that they often seemed to him a menacing, constricting, overpowering force.

Yet the Jewish Christians, too, even in Jerusalem itself, were extremely varied *among themselves*. For one thing, they comprised men who had come from a wide range of countries (just as the Jews of the same city too, according to the story of Pentecost, had come from many lands[9]). The differing origins of the earliest Jewish Christians at Jerusalem are revealed by the story of Stephen, who emerged, apparently, as leader of a Greek-speaking section against those who spoke Aramaic.[10] (And there were, of course, also many temporary Greek-speaking Jewish visitors, notably those who had come from the province of Asia for a festival, and launched the attacks on Paul which led to his arrest.)[11]

Yet, while these groups of Christians at Jerusalem and Judaea came from widely divergent geographical and theological backgrounds, they were all Jews by birth: Jewish Christians whose faith was described by Cardinal Jean Daniélou as 'a form of Christianity whose liturgical, theological and ascetic structure has been borrowed from the Jewish milieu in which Christianity itself appeared'.[12] These were the first followers of the crucified Jesus Christ; the term 'saints' was applied to them, and their nucleus comprised the Twelve Apostles of whom eleven (all except Matthias, successor of Judas) had been the apostles of Jesus.[13] The author of *Acts* declares of these early days, with patent propagandist intent, that 'the whole body of believers was united in heart and soul.'[14] Yet its own narrative cannot help belying this protestation – thus confirming Paul's Letters. Nevertheless, when *Acts* states that the numbers of these believers rapidly increased, even if its frequent repetition of such statements gives a somewhat exaggerated impression, there must be some measure of truth in such a claim.[15]

Owing to the dominant position of this Jewish Christian Church inside the Christian community, Paul's relations with it are a matter of the utmost importance. And these relations were disastrous. Such was the view of the Tübingen school of theologians in the nineteenth century. It was a view which subsequently became eroded since its authors had somewhat underestimated the complexity of the mid-first-century religious scene. And yet the Tübingen view was more right than wrong, because Paul's Gentile mission and his depreciation of the Jewish Law remained totally distasteful to a church which, although accepting Jesus Christ, remained thoroughly Jewish all the same. For as S. G. F. Brandon has stressed:

> To the Jewish Christians Paul's teaching outraged their deepest convictions. That the tragic death of their Master, the Messiah of Israel, at the hands of the hated Romans, should be presented as a divine act to save the Gentiles from the perdition they so richly deserved, was, in their eyes, tantamount to blasphemy. Moreover, for such an interpretation to become known to their fellow-Jews, and for themselves to be regarded as responsible for it, was obviously very dangerous for the Jerusalem Christians. From the Jewish point of view, such a presentation of the death of Jesus was not only theologically outrageous, it amounted to apostasy of a most shocking kind, involving both race and religion ...
>
> In the 'gospel' of the Jerusalem Christians it is obvious that the Gentiles could have no part. Indeed, the end which that 'gospel' had in view, namely, the vindication of Israel, implied both the overthrow of Rome and the punishment of the Gentiles. Jesus was the Messiah of Israel, who had been done to death by the Romans as a menace to their rule. His death was thus a martyrdom for Israel, witnessing to God's purpose for Israel as his holy and elect people against Roman oppression and Jewish obduracy.

Paul had been scandalized, as other Jews were, before his conversion, with this Jewish Christian doctrine of a 'crucified Messiah', and he had taken practical action to suppress it. His subsequent assertion, that his conversion was not due to the Jewish Christians and that he had received his 'gospel' directly from God, attests, together with an abundance of other evidence, that Paul recognized how profoundly his interpretation of Jesus differed from that of the original disciples of Jesus. His depreciatory references to knowledge of Christ 'according to the flesh' clearly indicate his defensive repudiation of the 'gospel' of the Jerusalem Church, which was based upon eyewitness knowledge, which Paul had not shared, of the historical Jesus, whom the Romans had crucified for sedition.[16]

This conclusion seems to be correct. But in attempting to demonstrate that this is so we first have to come to grips with a notorious difficulty, and it is one which cannot, despite numerous attempts, be explained away. It is created by the unmistakable differences between what Paul himself tells us in his Letters and what we are told in *Acts*. For one thing, *Acts* speaks of five separate visits by Paul to Jerusalem after his conversion, whereas Paul's own Letters only mention three. This, in itself, need not be a very serious divergence, since the Letters never claim to offer a complete narrative of Paul's career. But the discrepancies go much deeper than that, as Archibald Robertson points out.

The account given in the *Acts* of the relations between Paul and the Palestinian apostles is hopelessly at variance with that given in the *Epistles*, and above all in *Galatians*, 1–2. In the *Acts* Paul joins in the work of the apostles at Jerusalem soon after his conversion. He preaches to Gentiles, but only after Peter and others have set the example. Later, he revisits Jerusalem with Barnabas when bringing relief from Antioch during the famine. After their first missionary journey they again visit Jerusalem as delegates of the church of Antioch in order to submit to the apostles and elders the question whether Gentile converts should be circumcised. On this occasion it is decided by a council of the whole church, on the motion of Peter and James, that Gentile converts need not be circumcised, but must abstain from eating meat sacrificed to idols and from fornication, and observe certain Jewish dietary rules. Paul and his companions carry the decision back to Antioch; and the matter is never raised again. Paul himself conforms to the whole Jewish Law, nowhere denies its validity for Jews, and circumcises Timothy, a convert of mixed Greek and Jewish parentage, in deference to Jewish sentiment.

In *Galatians* we are told a very different story. Paul is the apostle of the Gentiles from the moment of his conversion: Peter is the apostle 'of the circumcision'. For the first three years after Paul's conversion he does not go near the other apostles. Then for the first time he visits Peter, but sees no other apostle 'save James [the Just] the Lord's brother,' and is 'still unknown by face unto the churches of Judaea.' After fourteen years' absence Paul revisits

Jerusalem with Barnabas, not as a delegate, but 'by revelation' (i.e. of his own accord), in order to communicate privately to Peter, James [the Just] and John [the son of Zebedee] (sarcastically described as 'those who were reputed to be somewhat') the gospel which he is preaching to the Gentiles. They recognize his independent mission and leave him a free hand on the sole condition that the Gentile converts contribute to the relief of the poor of Jerusalem. Nothing is said of a formal council or of the promulgation of any decree. Later at Antioch Paul has a sharp difference of opinion (unmentioned in the *Acts*) with Peter because the latter, instigated by 'certain from James [the Just],' ceases to eat with Gentile converts. Paul resents this as an attempt to impose Jewish dietary rules on the Gentiles, and attacks the Jewish law as not only useless, but pernicious. The question of meat sacrificed to idols is treated from the point of view of pure expediency, and the apostolic taboo on its use, recorded in *Acts*, is entirely ignored. Paul's claim to equal authority with 'the very chiefest apostles' is asserted with vigour and even acrimony against opponents who preach 'another Jesus.'

In short, the Paul of the *Acts* and the Paul of the *Epistles* are two different men. The Paul of the *Acts* is the missionary of a united Church, acknowledging the authority of the apostles and elders at Jerusalem, and preaching the same doctrine as they. The Paul of the *Epistles* is the hierophant of a mystery revealed to himself alone, acknowledging no authority but that of Jesus Christ, anathematizing all (and there appear to be many) who preach another gospel than his, and heaping scorn and contumely on Peter and James [the Just] when they disagree with him, as they certainly do on the validity of the Jewish Law, and apparently even on the identity of the 'Jesus' whom they preach.

Of the two pictures, that in the *Epistles* is on any showing earlier than that in the *Acts*. The latter, therefore, must be unhesitatingly dismissed as unhistorical.[17]

Others are less sceptical than Robertson about the historical reality of the Jerusalem Council, described at length by *Acts* but totally absent from the Letters. Yet in any case, even assuming that the Council ever took place, Paul evidently failed to accept its decisions. The two points at issue were whether the Gentile converts should be circumcised, and whether they should abide by Jewish food regulations. Circumcision, according to *Acts*, was the subject brought up at Antioch in Syria which had caused the Jerusalem Council to be convened; the question was discussed again privately at Jerusalem, it was said, before this supposed Council held its meetings. Yet, curiously enough, when *Acts* comes to report the Apostolic Decree which allegedly emerged from the Council's deliberations, there is no longer any mention of the subject of circumcision at all;[18] so that even this book, which is so eager to paper over disagreements, implicitly concedes that the two sides never reached an accord, and that in this significant respect Paul was allowed to go his own way.

Acts does its best to give an impression of harmony by subsequently pointing out that Paul agreed to circumcise his disciple Timothy at Lystra, 'out of consideration for the Jews'. But this was a border-line case since, although Timothy's father was a Gentile, his mother was Jewish Christian.[19] More noteworthy, then, are Paul's own indignant remarks about earlier attempts to get him to circumcise another assistant, Titus, who was purely Greek – a course 'urged only as a concession to certain sham-Christians, interlopers who had stolen in to spy upon the liberty we enjoy in the fellowship of Christ Jesus. These men wanted to bring us into bondage . . .'[20] And that continued to be Paul's view for the rest of his life.

Writing of the Jewish food regulations, he advised his Gentile converts, as we have seen, to obey these if they felt it would cause offence should they omit to do so: but only as a matter of diplomacy, for he continued to reject the idea on principle. Indeed, Paul moved even further away from the Jerusalem church on this subject. For he was opposed to the idea that even the *Jewish* Christians, at least when eating with their Gentile co-religionists, should maintain dietetic purity – whether because, as Robertson suggested, he resented such strictness on their part as an attempt to bring pressure on the Gentile converts, or because he saw no reason why, under the revolutionary New Covenant, even Jewish Christians should continue to practice these taboos any longer.

It was at Syrian Antioch that the dispute had flared out into the open.

In the struggle to maintain the separateness of Israel the Rabbinical tradition had come to demand a strict keeping apart from all possibility of defilement by contact with Gentiles at meals. It seems that at Antioch this scrupulosity had been laid aside by the Jewish Christians . . . The full importance of the matter is plain when we realize that it involved the question of whether Jewish and Gentile Christians might partake together of the Lord's Supper. Paul recounts the incident to vindicate his own consistency in face of the highest authority of the Jerusalem church and his independence of that authority.[21]

This was the background against which Paul had entered upon his historic clash with Peter at Antioch.

But when Cephas [Peter] came to Antioch, I opposed him to his face, because he was clearly in the wrong. For until certain persons came from James [the Just] he was taking his meals with Gentile Christians; but when they came he drew back and began to hold aloof, because he was afraid of the advocates of circumcision. The other Jewish Christians showed the same lack of principle; even Barnabas was carried away and played false like the rest. But when I saw that their conduct did not square with the truth of the Gospel, I said to Cephas, before the whole congregation, 'If you, a Jew born and bred, live like a Gentile, and not like a Jew, how can you insist that Gentiles must live like Jews?'[22]

There can be little doubt that this dispute, with all its much wider and deeper implications, was a lasting one. That was why Paul, although almost pathetically. eager to break down hostility in the Jerusalem mother church by amassing and bringing to the city a large collection for its poor, is at the same time so anxious to deny that he owed the slightest inspiration to that church, since *his* inspiration had come to him direct from God. For this reason, in contrast to the later account in *Acts*, he made his first visit to Jerusalem sound as insignificant as possible – and stressed his version with almost strident insistence: 'What I write is plain truth; before God I am not lying.'[23] Moreover, he mentions the twelve only once[24] – and refrains, when he does so, from calling them the twelve apostles. For he had staked his own claim against them: 'Have I in any way come short of those superlative apostles?'

Moreover, he does not hesitate to admit that there were these two contradictory interpretations of the faith. In one of them, the wrong, Jewish-Christian one, he says: 'someone comes who proclaims another Jesus, not the Jesus whom we proclaimed'[25] – with the result, declares the *Letter to Titus*, that there are many Jewish Christian converts 'who are out of all control; they talk wildly and lead men's minds astray . . . lending their ears to Jewish myths and commandments of merely human origin'.[26] Paul, though conscious of the special claims of the mother church, was perfectly prepared to classify its members in Judaea ('the saints'), and its adherents abroad, among the heretics he so often deplored. And he writes scathingly about its leaders as 'the men of high reputation – not that their importance matters to me: God does not recognize these personal distinctions.'[27]

Such were the issues which fixed a deep and permanent gulf between Peter and Paul. Peter could play the immense trump card that he had known Jesus personally, and had been close to him. And yet, apart from that, he must have found Paul very difficult to stand up to. For dialecti-cally it was surely an unequal struggle. The Galilean fisherman can by no stretch of the imagination be regarded as the intellectual equal of Paul. And indeed, before long Peter – perhaps after his arrest by Agrippa I, king of Judaea in AD 41–4 when the country temporarily ceased to be a Roman province – was replaced as the Jewish Christian leader by James the Just, the brother of Jesus, who had not been one of the apostles but owed his eminence to the family relationship. *Galatians* mentions James above Peter;[28] while *Acts*, too, records that Peter sent a report to James, evidently as his superior,[29] and indicates that it was James who had the responsibility of summing up the conclusions of the supposed Jerusalem Council. Clement of Alexandria later declared that James the Just was elected 'bishop' of Jerusalem by three of Jesus' apostles, Peter and the two sons of Zebedee, James and John.[30]

Peter's subsequent career is a matter of infinite speculation. But at Jerusalem, in any case, he was no longer the central figure. As for James the Just, *Acts* reports that he responded to Paul's conciliatory collection for the Jerusalem poor by suggesting that, since Paul's Gentile mission was still encountering hostility among the Jewish Christians in the city, he should offer a *second* demonstration of his orthodoxy by paying the expenses of four of their number who were under a vow.[31] Paul agreed. But his final visit to Jerusalem, at which this was arranged, ended in his arrest. This could not be blamed on James, but it did leave him and his Jewish Christian Church supreme: for it meant the abrupt termination and eclipse of Paul's Gentile mission which so many of the members of that church had disliked. And in his subsequent captivity, *Colossians* complained, the Jewish Christian com-munity at Rome mostly gave him no help at all.[32]

Yet this community, too, was going through serious difficulties, since James the Just himself, only some four years later, met his death at the hands of the Jews.[33] So apparently not only Paul, but his enemies in the Jewish Christian Church too – despite all its careful Judaism[34] – had by now incurred the hostility of the Jewish authorities as a dissident sect. The Jewish Christians could not be faulted on the Law. But their belief in a Messiah already come and gone was an aberration which had already aroused hostility from non-Christian Jews in the very early days after Jesus' death. Besides, there was now something more, much more – to provoke them: the anti-Jewish attitude recently displayed by Paul. It was true that the Jewish Christians dissociated themselves sharply from this. Yet when such attacks upon the Jews were being made by any one Christian, whatever the particular shading of his Christian viewpoint, there was bound to come a time when they would feel that any and every Christian was at fault; so that the execution of James the Just, whom they could catch, seemed an adequate substitute for the execution of Paul, whom they could not get their hands on. Nevertheless, Jewish Christianity continued to flourish for a time, even when deprived of the leadership of James. For after his death his relatives, the relatives of Jesus, retained control of the Jewish Christian Church at Jerusalem right on into the next century.[35]

It was in Rome, where he had been sent in pursuance of his appeal to the Emperor, that Paul must have learnt of the execution of James the Just. But this event did nothing to soften the hostility of the Jewish Christians towards him, especially if they believed that indirectly he had been its cause. Indeed, it is even quite likely, as Cullmann and Daniélou suggested, that it was these Jewish Christians who caused Paul's death at the hands of the imperial Roman authorities.[36] *Acts* is at great pains to explain how, when he arrived in Rome, the *Jewish* community there assured him that none of 'the brethren' had preceded him with any reports to his discredit.[37] But, whether *Acts* intended this term 'brethren' to apply only to the un-Christianized Jews or to the Jewish Christians as well, it can scarcely be regarded as exonerating the latter. For it was surely they whom Paul had in mind when he wrote to the Philippians from his Roman prison about how news of his imprisonment had gone around among the Christians of the imperial city:

> Some, indeed, proclaim Christ in a jealous and quarrelsome spirit; others proclaim him in true good will, and these are moved by love for me; they know that it is to defend the Gospel that I am where I am. But the others, moved by personal rivalry, present Christ from mixed motives, meaning to stir up fresh trouble for me as I lie in prison.[38]

This comment is confirmed and placed in a more sinister light by what Clement of Rome wrote to the Corinthian Christians in about AD 96. Clement has just indicated to them that sinful envy and jealousy had beset Peter during his life and had resulted in his death, and 'in this way he bore his witness', which means that he died as a martyr. And then he goes on to say of Paul, too, that 'because of jealousy and contention, he has become the very type of endurance rewarded'; who likewise, eventually, 'bore his testimony before kings and rulers' and died.[39] In other words, Paul, too, was martyred. But Clement is not attempting to assert that it was the envy and jealousy *of the same people* which caused the martyrdom of the two apostles, nor is the tradition that they died together a reliable one.[40] The identities of the envious and jealous persons who, according to Clement, brought about the death of Peter we cannot determine. But his observation that men of the same qualities were responsible for the death of Paul does harmonize very readily with Paul's reference, in *Philippians*, to Christians who made trouble for him at Rome. Since, therefore, his worst Christian foes, as we know, were Christians of Jewish origin, and since, also, there were many of them at the imperial capital (where the Jewish community from which they originated was so large), these Jewish Christians cannot be exonerated from the suspicion of complicity in Paul's death. It may well have been they who put up the prosecutors in the Roman court, though we could not expect *Acts*, eager to uphold the unity of the early church, to say so. Of these legal proceedings, more will be said when we come to consider Paul's relationship with the Romans.

After the two apostles were dead, the apparent victory of the Jewish Christian Church over Paul's Gentile mission, a victory which had become manifestly clear from the time of his arrest, was shortlived. For almost immediately after Paul had perished, this Jewish Christian community in its turn, already weakened by the execution of James the Just, soon suffered a further disastrous loss of authority and influence. That is to say, the events leading up to and arising from the Jewish Revolt against Rome which broke out in AD 66 – only four years after James' execution and perhaps less than half that duration after Paul's – exercised a catastrophic effect on its relations both with the Jews and with the Romans. As to the latter, the Jewish Christians had attempted to take precautionary measures. Seeing how fatal it would be for their reputation with the occupying power if it classified them along with the rebels, they had already (apart perhaps from some national extremists) sought to dissociate themselves from the national Jewish cause. For already before the war began, when pressure from the extreme anti-Roman wing of the Jews was becoming intolerable, they had departed from Jerusalem. According to tradition, they left in a single party and settled at Pella (Fahl) across the Judaean frontier and the Jordan River;[41] although, in fact, the process may have been more piecemeal and gradual, involving migrations not only to Pella but also to a number of other centres beyond the borders of Judaea.

After the revolt had been crushed, some of these Jewish Christians returned to Jerusalem. But at this juncture they found themselves under cross-fire. For on the one hand the Jews, whose cause they had earlier deserted, now rejected them in their turn – and when they placed the Christians under a curse, it was these deserters whom they had in mind. But at the same time, the attempt of the Jewish Christians (or most of them) to dissociate themselves from the Jews had evidently failed to persuade the Romans not to lump them together with the defeated rebels.

This was a matter of profound concern to the writers of the Gospels, who, as spokesmen for Gentile Christianity, felt it imperative to show the Romans and the world that they were quite different from the Jerusalem Christians.[42] That is why in these Gospels the latter come under such vigorous attack. It is also why (apart from other reasons, including Judas' act of betrayal) the original apostles are presented, to the reader's surprise, as spiritually insensitive, ambitious, greedy and cowardly (before long, the *Letter of Barnabas** is even calling them 'ruffians of the deepest dye'.[43]). Moreover, *Mark's* assertion that Jesus deliberately rejected the claims of blood-relationship – 'Who is my mother? Who are my brothers? Whoever does the will of God, he is my brother, my sister, my mother.'[44] – might well be intended, in part, as another attack on the Jewish Christian Church, which was still led by a member of Jesus' own family.

Paul's conversion of the Gentiles, on the other hand, was made by the Jewish Revolt to look much more respectable than it had appeared before that disaster,[45] since his mission so laudably flouted and by-passed the Jewish Christians. This was the spirit in which *Acts*, although offering no convincing picture of Paul's teaching as described in his Letters, nevertheless displays the full retrospective glorification of this Gentile mission. For, recovering from its severe set-back in his lifetime, it had now come into the ascendancy – at the expense of Jewish Christianity.

From these traumatic experiences the Jewish Christians never completely recovered. Nevertheless, they maintained their supremacy in the Church of Jerusalem and Judaea until the Second Jewish Revolt broke out and was crushed by Hadrian in AD 135. Then, after Hadrian had forcibly converted Jerusalem into a non-Jewish city, its church was at last Jewish Christian no more, and it was governed by Greeks. Elsewhere in the country, however, particularly at Nazareth and Hebron, groups of Jewish Christians still survived in an astonishing diversity of sects. One of these congregations, whose members called themselves the Ebionites, excommunicated the Gentile Christians altogether, and utterly repudiated Paul as an apostate. But like the other surviving Jewish Christian sects, these Ebionites remained relatively uninfluential, being absorbed in esoteric ritual and symbolism and apocalyptic and angelology. In the fourth century, some of the Jewish Christian communities still remained in existence, but eventually, cut off from the main stream of Christianity and condemned as Judaizers, they died out.[46] The attempt to retain Christianity as a branch of the Jewish faith had failed – and it has never again widely or deeply influenced any Semitic civilization.

So by an astonishing series of vicissitudes, Paul's mission to the Gentiles, which during his lifetime the adamant opposition of Jews and Jewish Christians alike seemed to have doomed, had triumphed after his death. Thus Christianity, instead of remaining a limited offshoot of Palestinian Judaism, began to fulfil Paul's intention by approximating to a world religion.

3. *Paul and Rome*

Paul's mission to the Gentiles not only angered the Jews and Jewish Christians, but inevitably, with their encouragement, aroused the hostile interest and suspicion of the Roman officials in those provinces where Gentiles were converted. Later, long after his death, his efforts resulted in the total transformation of Rome's Empire. But already in his own day awkward questions about his relationship with the Roman power were being raised.

True, the Roman authorities must have found his attitude to their social system, based on slavery, reassuring. For, while Paul urged slave masters to be just and fair to their slaves, *Ephesians* and *Colossians* presumably reflect his sentiments by recommending that slaves should continue to obey their masters implicitly, as a duty of their religion.

Slaves, obey your earthly masters with fear and trembling, single-mindedly, as serving Christ. Do not offer merely the outward show of service, to curry favour with men, but, as slaves of Christ, do whole-heartedly the will of God. Give the cheerful service of those who serve the Lord, not men. For you know that whatever good each man may do, slave or free, will be repaid him by the Lord.[1]

Paul also advised any of his Corinthian readers who happened to be of slave status to 'remain in the condition in which they were called'.[2] Joachim Kahl accuses him of 'monstrous cynicism'.[3] But what Paul was trying to tell the Corinthian Christians was that things like slavery do not really matter: what matters is religion – especially as the Second Coming, even if not exactly imminent, will not be too long delayed (and he had relegated marriage and sex to an unimportant place for much the same reason). With this apocalyptic prospect in mind, his brief *Letter to Philemon* does not trouble to display the fundamental disapproval of slavery which his modern admirers would like to have found in it. Philemon's slave Onesimus has run away, apparently after stealing some money, and has come to join Paul in Rome. Paul is not freeing him, but sends him back to his master. Yet in doing so, and offering to repay anything that Onesimus has stolen, he expresses the tactful hope that Philemon will treat his returning slave decently. Paul does not, in so many words, ask his correspondent to liberate the slave, but to treat him 'no longer as a slave, but as more than a slave – as a dear brother, very dear indeed to me and how much dearer to you, both as man and as Christian'.[4]

In the strictest sense, this can be described as reactionary, since Paul's words do not condemn the institution of slavery outright. In this respect the Essenes* (according to the literary tradition) and Paul's Roman contemporary Seneca (with whom he was wrongly believed to have corresponded) were more progressive. But instead Paul lifts the whole problem to another plane altogether, and, in a sense, becomes more radical than any abolitionist.

As Paul sends the slave back to his master we see Christianity in contact with the institution of slavery, accepting its outer form but undermining it with a new understanding of master and slave as brothers in Christ. And we can discern here the pattern for the movement of Christianity in the social order.[5]

Nevertheless, for the time being slavery, like matrimony, seems to Paul more or less irrelevant. And the same sort of feeling of comparative irrelevance colours Paul's attitude not only to these aspects of the Roman Empire's social structure, but also to its specific administrative organs like the lawcourts. Paul does not propose that they should be abolished; that would be unrealistic, and in any case undesirable. Moreover the Crucifixion had been, after all, the supreme and sublime mockery of all earthly courts of law, cutting them right down to size. As for himself, therefore, he does not in the least mind being called to account by any human court; the prospect leaves him indifferent.[6] Nevertheless, he advises the Christians of Corinth never, if they can help it, to refer their disputes to pagan justice. For what was the point? And he had felt exactly the same about marriage and the freeing of slaves. Instead of getting mixed up with such worldly matters at all, they had much better concentrate on their religious concerns. 'Do not unite yourselves with unbelievers; they are no fit mates for you.'[7] And so do not, if you can help it, have recourse to non-Jewish courts. Centuries later this injunction, which had appeared in Jewish writings as well,[8] was to have an important effect in strengthening episcopal authority. After Constantine had declared Christianity the official religion, he recognized the authority of bishops in AD 318, and fifteen years later placed them on an equal footing with magistrates appointed by the state. Within a century, bishops like Ambrose were browbeating emperors.

In all this, then, Paul's teaching was nowhere near as conformist with Roman imperial social patterns as on the surface it looked, at least if one considers its explosive ultimate effects. Indeed, his attitude, that these secular institutions were really of altogether secondary importance, was potentially subversive in the highest degree, for it was destined to change Roman society from top to bottom. It is therefore ironical that the many modern writings emphasizing the revolutionary character of early Christianity can find nothing whatever to say about Paul. And yet his Letters, beneath their quietist surface, were potentially incendiary.

Another and somewhat more obviously radical aspect of his thinking becomes apparent in his references to the poor. 'Do not be haughty', said Paul, 'but go about with humble folk.'[9] Such doctrines had already been pronounced by Jesus (not so much from motives of compassion or sentiment as because the Kingdom of God was open to everybody). It was perhaps Paul who wrote them down first, and their possible implications were socially dangerous. Later, in the same vein, the *Letter of James* declared to its recipients, 'You have insulted the poor man. Moreover, are not the rich your oppressors? Is it not they who drag you into court and pour contempt on the honoured name by which God has claimed you?'[10]

Paul had not gone as far as that. But he was arousing hazardous expectations. True, the Jewish Law had already insisted that underprivileged persons and groups are especially cherished by God; and it was within that framework that Paul and Barnabas raised money to assist them, readily agreeing with the suggestion of the Jewish Christian leadership that 'they should keep the poor in mind, which was the very thing I made it my business to do'.[11] But Paul also went further along the path of social reform when he maintained that God was favourable to the sinner even without his repentance. This was a doctrine which not only, as we have seen, shocked the Jews very much, but might well have been understood by the Roman authorities as providing undue encouragement to the underprivileged: Adolf Hitler remarked that Paul had used Christ's teaching to mobilize the riff-raff, and it was only to be expected that Roman provincial governors might likewise feel that Christianity was cutting across patterns of society more deeply than any religion had done before. However, it was some time before such functionaries seriously appreciated this particular threat. If they had been able to discern what vast amendments Paul's teaching and mission would eventually impose upon the whole imperial system, they would indeed have had reason for dismay. But, until the time of Celsus in the second century AD, nobody seemed to realize the power of Christianity to transform the entire Roman Empire.

Moreover, Paul went to a great deal of trouble to assuage any such anxieties. For example 'the Kingdom of God' was a formula that raised somewhat sensitive issues. As we have seen elsewhere, the Jewish Dispersion, which provided Christianity with so many of its converts, had already been allowed by the Romans to enjoy, within each city-state, a sort of autonomy comprising, semi-political, almost statelike, features only too easily capable of stirring up suspicions of disloyalty; references to the Kingdom of God seemed disquietingly to envisage an alternative regime to the emperor's.[12] In consequence, we note a falling-off of the frequency with which Paul makes use of this conception in his later Letters. Another phrase, however, which was much more frequently on his lips and which did evidently worry at least one Roman governor, Felix, was the 'Last Judgment', since this likewise appeared to appeal to a power beyond and above Caesar.[13] But on the whole Paul was careful. Indeed, it has been argued that his injunctions to avoid *zelos*, though the term is generally translated 'jealousy' or 'envy', are specific warnings against supporting the Zealots, the Jewish national extremists who led the resistance against the Romans.[14] And this has some plausibility, though the question whether nationalists in Paul's time already bore the name of Zealots is disputed.[15]

What is quite certain, in any case, is that he deliberately and directly preached obedience to the imperial government. Thus in *Romans* he declared:

> Every person must submit to the supreme authorities. There is no authority but by act of God, and the existing authorities are instituted by him; consequently anyone who rebels against authority is resisting a divine institution, and those who so resist have themselves to thank for the punishment they will receive. For government, a terror to crime, has no terrors for good behaviour.
>
> You wish to have no fear of the authorities? Then continue to do right and you will have their approval, for they are God's agents working for your good. But if you are doing wrong, then you will have cause to fear them; it is not for nothing that they hold the power of the sword, for they are God's agents of punishment, for retribution on the offender. That is why you are obliged to submit. It is an obligation imposed not merely by fear of retribution but by conscience. That is also why you pay taxes.[16]

Certainly, Paul had to urge such obedience, in this particular Letter, all the more strongly, not only since the crucified Jesus could be regarded as a dissident, but also because the recipients of his words on the present occasion were the Christians at Rome itself, who apparently had already been in trouble under Claudius and were soon destined to be brutally exploited by the current Emperor Nero, who held them responsible for the Great Fire of Rome.[17]

Nevertheless, this expression of Paul's views was not merely motivated by the peculiar metropolitan situation of the church he was addressing, for these were counsels which he regarded as universally applicable. Thus in a striking passage of *II Thessalonians* he speaks of 'the Restrainer' whose eventual disappearance from the scene will precipitate the temporary triumph of the Enemy preceding the Second Coming.[18] Some have thought that the Restrainer is some supernatural, angelic authority which is at present staving off the total victory of Evil. On the other hand, J. Munck believed that the Restrainer is Paul himself.[19] But Paul was not as conceited as all that; and in fact, this mysterious personification is evidently the Roman Empire, which Paul believed to exercise a restraining power over the forces of Evil. Nor does he even attempt to distinguish between the divine authority of the *institution* of government and the authority of the individual ruler (Nero!) at any given moment. That is another reason why the numerous modern books arguing that early Christianity preached political revolution feel they must relegate

Paul to resounding silence. But once again this implied condemnation of Paul as a reactionary is, taking the long view, misguided; for the transforming power of what he wrote eventually proved revolutionary in the highest degree, so that matters like political revolution paled to insignificance before the magnitude of the changes he achieved.

He was also profoundly stimulated by the Roman Empire's possibilities of unity and solidarity which foreshadowed his own visions of a united Christendom mirroring the Jerusalem 'that is above' in contrast to the Jerusalem that exists now.[20] Besides, as Paul was thoroughly well aware, it was only by means of the roads and sea-ways of the Roman Peace that he himself could carry out his mission; moreover, in the last resort his only safeguards against hostile Jews and Jewish Christians were the Roman provincial officials. In consequence, he deliberately brushed aside and rejected any thoughts of violent political reversals. Conform promptly, he told the Christian inhabitants of the imperial city, in order to avoid entanglement: then you will be able to concentrate on what is infinitely more significant – your faith. And there was all the more need to concentrate on this and not to waste time interfering in less important matters such as politics, because the Second Coming would not be indefinitely delayed, and all energies must be devoted to preparing for that.

Paul's counsel of obedience to the earthly authorities, echoed in the pastoral *Letters to Timothy and Titus*[21] that bear his name but were not by his hand, is in accordance with scriptural tradition. 'It is the Lord who gave you your authority,' declared the *Wisdom of Solomon* to the monarchs of the world; 'your power comes from the Most High.'[22] Rabbis, too, later declared that 'the Law of the state is binding on us.'[23] Among the Christians this doctrine, it was asserted by the Gospels, went back to the teaching of Jesus himself, who was believed to have said: 'Pay Caesar what is due to Caesar, and pay God what is due to God.'[24] Even if Jesus' words had originally been two-edged, placing at least as much emphasis on the second of the two injunctions as on the first, the writers of the Gospels seized on the first of them, since they were eager to erase any possible suspicions that Jesus' aims or sayings contained seditious implications. Later, the writer of *I Peter* echoes Paul's plea for obedience, though he describes secular governments as 'human institutions', toning down the Pauline suggestion that they were divinely appointed.[25]

Augustine followed up Paul's thinking on this subject in two major respects. First, the distinction in the Letters between the 'Jerusalem that is now' and the 'Jerusalem that is above' became one of the major inspirations prompting the contrast between the Two Cities, Earthly and Heavenly, in the *City of God*.[26] Yet at the same time Augustine agreed with Paul's contention that the earthly governments are of divine origin and must be obeyed. His mentor, Ambrose, had taught and shown that acts of secular power should in certain circumstances be resisted. But Augustine dismissed such reservations, and even gave explicit utterance, with scriptural backing, to Paul's implied belief that the duty of obedience still holds good even if the ruler is a bad one, such as Nero: 'Even to men like this the power of domination is not given except by the providence of God, when he decides that man's condition deserves such matters.'[27]

Thereafter, as David Knowles wrote:

St Gregory the Great went far towards teaching that the established powers must be obeyed, right or wrong, and the history in Europe of the theory and practice of the Divine Right of the monarch is evidence of the permanence of the appeal of this teaching. In our own age we have seen and see at the present moment the extreme of opinion: first, the reign of the totalitarian state under a dictator, and then the denial of all authority in presence of the individual 'conscience', which may in practice denote no more than unreflective emotion or self-interest. Between these extremes must lie the truth . . .[28]

Paul might seem, at first sight, nearer to the former of these two modern attitudes, the totalitarian viewpoint, owing to his conviction that secular governments deserve obedience and even enjoy divine authority. Yet his quietism was not due to any feeling of submissiveness. In spite of what he said he was always willing to run the gauntlet of any political authority for the sake of his beliefs, although in order to retain for as long as possible the opportunity of spreading the Gospel, he continued to handle the Roman functionaries as tactfully as he could. The passivity he advocated was advocated for a very special purpose. It was because he regarded the whole question of politics as entirely subordinate to what was truly significant: belief in the redemptive Crucifixion of Jesus Christ.

For the practical working out of Paul's relations with the Roman authorities during the course of his career, we have to turn to *Acts*. As often, this proves for the student of history not entirely satisfactory. It is true that the book devotes careful attention to Paul's dealings with the Roman officials. However, in order to ingratiate the Christians of his own day with the imperial power, the author goes to great lengths to stress the amicable outcome of each of these successive confrontations. Indeed the very last word of the work, in that most surprising of endings, is a Greek adverb meaning 'without hindrance'.[29] It was without hindrance from the Romans, according to this writer, and quite openly, that Paul spent two whole years in the capital after he had been taken there in response to his appeal to the Emperor. That, then, is the keynote of *Acts* which is, in consequence, tendentiously selective in its presentation of material. Indeed, this is proved to be the case in Paul's relations with the Romans by his own statement in *II Corinthians* that he had been three times subjected to beatings with rods – a Roman penalty, of which more will be said shortly – whereas *Acts* only mentions a single one of these occasions.

And yet Paul, although suffering these punishments, possessed a remarkable advantage in being a Roman citizen, apparently by birth.[30] It was for this reason that he bore the Roman name of Paulus. He did not, it is true, have to assert his Roman citizenship very frequently. Perhaps it was a little awkward to do so on provincial territory where the population were mostly non-citizens, and for this reason he tended to present himself first and foremost as a Jew from the free (Greek) city of Tarsus. But when on occasion he did find it necessary to invoke his citizenship of Rome, the results tended to be effective; and it is arguable that, had he lacked this privileged status, he could never have been so active in the spreading of Christianity – which might, therefore, never have spread at all.

As was to be expected, he encountered Roman functionaries on a number of occasions, and each of these encounters, in so far as we can reconstruct what happened, raised interesting questions. During his travels, even in the East, he entered into a Roman sphere whenever he visited a Roman colony. These were more or less autonomous towns which, instead of consisting of non-Roman inhabitants under native Greek control, comprised Roman citizen settlers, many of them army veterans, under a Roman-type government headed by two annually-elected officials whose posts were analogous to those of the consuls in the imperial capital. Such Roman colonies, while abundant in the West, were somewhat sparse in the eastern provinces; but Paul stayed for a time at a number of them.

At the first two Roman colonies he is recorded to have visited, Pisidian Antioch (Yalvaç) and Lystra (Hatunsaray) – both in central Asia Minor – he attracted the unfavourable attention of the colonial authorities. They expelled him and his companion Barnabas from the first of these towns, after the Jews had agitated for such action, and from Lystra also the two missionaries were forcibly ejected, though this was probably the act of a Jewish mob rather than of the colonial administration.[31] Then, at another colony, Philippi in Macedonia, there was an attempt by the population to persuade the Roman city functionaries that Paul and his new companion Silas (and perhaps Luke was with them too) were presenting a threat to Roman interests and institutions. The plaintiffs, this time, were not apparently Jews but pagans, the owners of a slave-girl whose gifts of oracular speech, a source of extensive financial profit to themselves, had been suppressed or exorcised by Paul.

When the girl's owners saw that their hope of gain had gone, they seized Paul and Silas and dragged them to the city authorities in the main square; and bringing them before the magistrates, they said, 'these men are causing a disturbance in our city; they are Jews; they are advocating customs which it is illegal for us Romans to adopt and follow.' The mob joined in the attack; and the magistrates tore off the prisoners' clothes and ordered them to be flogged. After giving them a severe beating they flung them into prison and ordered the jailer to keep them under close guard. In view of these orders, he put them in the inner prison and secured their feet in the stocks.[32]

There are two separate, though not unconnected, accusations against Paul and Silas here – the causing of riots and the advocacy of an alien religion. 'Officially', observes A. N. Sherwin-White,

. . . the Roman citizen may not practice any alien cult that has not received the public sanction of the state, but customarily he might do so as long as his cult did not otherwise offend against the laws and usages of Roman life, i.e. so long as it did not involve political or social crimes. The Julio-Claudian period was characterized by general laxity towards foreign cults, which spread freely in Italy and Rome. But this laxity is occasionally interrupted by a sharp reversal of policy when the extravagances of a particular sect call down a temporary and ill-enforced ban upon its activities . . .

The grounds of such bans, however, are found, not in the general principle of excluding alien cults as such, but in the criminal by-products of the cults . . . What is remarkable in the charges against Paul at Philippi is that the dormant principle of *incompatibility* is revived against an alien sect.[33]

This idea that his religious proceedings were depraved because they were un-Roman had not, as far as we know, been voiced in the Empire for two hundred years past; or at least it had not been used as a principal argument for the suppression of such rituals. For this reason it seems doubtful whether *Acts* has understood the objections to Paul's preaching correctly.

But another legal issue, too, was raised by this incident, for Paul was subjected to a flogging. This was a normal preliminary to the judicial examination of non-Romans. But Roman citizens, although not exempt from such treatment after they had been convicted on a charge, were protected by law against arbitrary beating without a prior trial.[34] Now Paul himself, as was recalled above, refers to three occasions when he was beaten by rods. The other two occasions are unidentifiable, but this is the third, as he suggests in another Letter.[35] It caused subsequent embarrassment to the Roman officials. *Acts* spoils the story, for rationalists at least, by recording that an earthquake, ascribed miraculous origin, broke the doors of the prison open. But then, after the authorities had sent men to interview him and Silas, his companion on this journey, the account returns to the juridical aspect.

Paul said to the officers:

'They gave us a public flogging, though we are Roman citizens and have not been found guilty; they threw us into prison, and are they now to smuggle us out privately? No indeed. Let them come in person and escort us out!' The officers reported his words. The magistrates were alarmed to hear that they were Roman citizens, and came and apologized to them. Then they escorted them out and requested them to go away from the city.[36]

This is a probable enough situation; and it is one of the occasions when Paul's Roman citizenship stood him in good stead. True, it had operated somewhat belatedly, for it had not saved him from physical mishandling. But it had at least extricated him and Silas from the further and graver dangers which threatened them in the colony.

They moved on to Thessalonica (Salonica), which was not a Roman colony but a large 'free' Greek city enjoying considerable autonomy under its traditional Hellenic constitution and officials. Here, the Jews attacked the house of their host, Jason, and dragged him and others before the leading municipal office-holders, once again on the pretext that the visitors were infringing *Roman* legality and security. 'The men,' they shouted, 'who have made trouble all over the world have now come here; and Jason has harboured them. They all flout the Emperor's laws, and assert that there is a rival king, Jesus.'[37] The accusation is obscure, and again *Acts* is likely to have garbled its terms. But if we can believe, as is reasonable enough, that it included the charge of acting against the decrees of the Emperor, the first and natural reaction of any Greek city authorities such as those of Thessalonica would have been to drop such a perilous case like a hot brick. And that is what they did, binding over Jason and his friends, and allowing or encouraging Paul and Silas to depart for another Greek town, Beroea.

For the security arrangements of the Roman Empire were, to our eyes, inadequate. The eastern provinces for the most part were made up of the territories of a number of self-governing cities – normally Greek in the east, except for the occasional Roman colony. Each of these cities had some sort of a not very strong police force of its own. But these local forces rarely cooperated with those of any other city. Moreover, the commanders of the Roman garrisons – legionaries, where these existed, or auxiliary troops of various kinds – were rarely asked to intervene, and except in extreme crises hardly ever volunteered to do so. Paul, by rapidly flitting from one place to another, frequently exploited this situation to the uttermost – although by these sudden departures he sometimes had to abandon his little Christian communities to persecution.[38] And not only did the regional police chiefs never act in concert, but the city governments which employed them were always eager to move him and his companions on, so that the next town, instead, could be harnessed with the troubles which their presence invariably involved.

The next attempt to embroil Paul with the Roman ruling power was at Corinth, a Roman colony like Philippi, and the capital of the Roman province of Achaea (Greece). Here Paul is brought before a recognizable historical figure,[39] Seneca's brother Gallio, who is known from independent sources to have been governor (proconsul) of the province in *c.* AD 52.

When Gallio was proconsul of Achaea, the Jews set upon Paul in a body and brought him into court. 'This man,' they said, 'is inducing people to worship God in ways that are against the Law.' Paul was just about to speak when Gallio said to them, 'If it had been a question of crime or grave misdemeanour, I should, of course, have given you Jews a patient hearing, but if it is some bickering about words and names and your Jewish Law, you may see to it yourselves; I have no mind to be a judge of these matters.' And he had them ejected from court.

Then there was a general attack on Sosthenes, who held office in the synagogue, and they gave him a beating in full view of the bench. But all this left Gallio quite unconcerned.[40]

What the Jews were probably attempting here was to repeat the sort of charge which had been brought at Philippi – an accusation that Paul was preaching to Romans (not Jews) against the Roman (not the Jewish) Law. But Gallio, an imperial official quite as unwilling as any municipal authority to get involved, chose to interpret the complaint as relating not to Roman but to Jewish matters, and consequently dismissed the case. Thereupon the Jews seized the synagogue elder Sosthenes, presumably a Christian sympathizer, and beat him up. 'But all this left Gallio quite unconcerned' – or, in the famous rendering of the Authorized Version, 'Gallio cared for none of these things.'

Later, at the immensely distinguished metropolis of Ephesus (which, like Thessalonica, was not a Roman colony but a self-governing Greek city), Paul and his current companions, two Macedonians named Gaius and Aristarchus, ran into serious trouble over a matter specifically affecting, this time, the *Greek* population: as in all parts of the east, they intensely disliked Judaism, and were therefore ill-disposed to Christianity which was its offshoot (and about Paul's differences with the Jewish Christians they presumably neither knew nor bothered). The protest was raised by 'a man named Demetrius, a silversmith who made silver shrines of Diana (Artemis) and provided a great deal of employment for the craftsmen.'[41] His complaint was that Paul, by teaching that gods and goddesses made by human hands are not divine at all, was ruining the livelihood of everyone engaged in this important local industry. There seems to have been no specific charge of impiety, but it was felt that the prestige of the city was undermined by his mission. Shouting furiously 'Great is Diana of the Ephesians!', the crowd which had been listening to the angry silversmith hustled Paul and his friends to the local theatre (which is still to be seen). But after a good deal of turbulence the Greek town-clerk managed to calm the demonstrators, and the speech which he is plausibly reported to have made illustrates the problems raised for local administrations everywhere when Paul came to their cities.

'These men whom you have brought here as culprits have committed no sacrilege and uttered no blasphemy against our goddess. If therefore Demetrius and his craftsmen have a case against anyone, assizes are held and there are such people as proconsuls; let the parties bring their charges and counter-charges. If, on the other hand, you have some further question to raise, it will be dealt with in the statutory assembly.

We certainly run the risk of being charged with riot for this day's work. There is no justification for it, and if the issue is raised we shall be unable to give any explanation of this uproar.' With that he dismissed the assembly.[42]

These cautious, nervous words by the Ephesian town-clerk show how Paul's preaching, although potentially inflammatory in so many and various ways, managed to escape final retribution for so long. Neverthe-less, although *Acts* credits him with an orderly departure from the city, it seems probable that he ran into far more serious trouble than this writer suggests during the two years he spent at Ephesus. For in *I Corinthians* he remarked: 'If, as the saying is, "I fought wild beasts at Ephesus", what have I gained by it?'[43] – and he goes on to explain that his gain will be resurrection after he is dead. Paul is not suggesting that he was literally forced into the Ephesian arena to fight wild animals: as Ignatius realized,[44] he is declaring in metaphorical terms that he had to contend with frightening opposition. What its nature was we cannot say. But probably the Greek rulers of the city were among his enemies, since it has been surmised that 'fighting with wild beasts' may have been a colloquial way of indicating that he had been arrested by the local authorities. Here, then, is an early example of a pagan reaction to Paul's teaching; and perhaps, despite *Acts*, it was an official reaction by the city functionaries of Ephesus.

Nor can we always suppose that he himself spoke with great sweetness about the pagans. At Athens, admittedly, he was reported to have mobilized all the tact he possessed in addressing his heathen listeners, though even there he allegedly failed to conceal that 'he was exaspe-rated to see how the city was full of idols.'[45] But to the Ephesian com-munity itself he was later said to have written:

Give up living like pagans with their good-for-nothing notions. Their wits are beclouded, they are strangers to the life that is in God, because ignorance prevails among them and their minds have grown hard as stone. Dead to all feeling, they have abandoned themselves to vice, and stop at nothing to satisfy their foul desires.[46]

Whether Paul, while he was previously at Ephesus in person, had already been attacking pagans in such terms we cannot tell. But even if his words, as they have come down to us, appear in a slightly elaborated form, that is, no doubt, approximately how he wrote to the Christian community of the place; and his abuse will not have failed to reach the ears of the Greek administrators of the city. If so, language of this kind will hardly have endeared him to their hearts.

Subsequently, however, after he had nearly been lynched by Jews at Jerusalem, it was with Roman, not Greek, functionaries that he once again had to deal. This time they were not the leaders of Roman towns, but the military and civil powers of a Roman province. *Acts* evidently considers the whole sequence of events profoundly important, as if Paul were repeating the ordeals of Jesus Christ himself. When the crowds in the Jewish capital started man-handling him and demanded his life, he was saved by Claudius Lysias, a Roman citizen (of Greek or other eastern birth) who commanded the military garrison of the city.

As soon as they saw the commandant and his troops, they stopped beating Paul. The commandant stepped forward, arrested him, and ordered him to be shackled with two chains; he then asked who the man was and what he had been doing. Some in the crowd shouted one thing, some another. As he could not get at the truth because of the hubbub, he ordered him to be taken into barracks. When Paul reached the steps, he had to be carried by the soldiers because of the violence of the mob. For the whole crowd were at their heels yelling, 'Kill him!'

Just before Paul was taken into the barracks he said to the commandant, 'May I have a word with you?' The commandant said, 'So you speak Greek, do you? Then you are not the Egyptian who started a revolt some time ago and led a force of four thousand terrorists out into the wilds?' Paul replied, 'I am a Jew, a Tarsian from Cilicia, a citizen of no mean city. I ask your permission to speak to the people.'[47]

That this request, as *Acts* next records, was granted, and that Paul was allowed to deliver such an oration to the assembled throng, must be regarded as much less likely.

At all events, although he had cleared up the misapprehension that he was a Jewish guerrilla fighter from Egypt (who had evaded a Roman military operation in Judaea a short time previously), Lysias planned to have him flogged as a preliminary to examination. But Paul, once again, claimed the immunity which was his entitlement as a Roman citizen. When this point had been made, the commander felt that the Jewish Council (Sanhedrin) ought to see his detainee, 'wishing to be quite sure what charge the Jews were bringing against Paul'.[48] That is to say the officer shared the usual Roman hope of shelving the possible charge of sedition, so that the whole business could be transferred to the religious field and thus to Jewish jurisdiction. When, however, the Council, or the crowds surrounding its chamber, broke into an uproar, Lysias, fearing that Paul would be torn to pieces, once again had him rescued, and escorted to the Roman barracks. But then he learnt of a plot by more than forty Jews to murder the prisoner, and in consequence, not wanting to take risks with a Roman citizen, he sent him down to the provincial capital Caesarea Maritima with an escort of four hundred infantry and seventy cavalry.

On arrival at Caesarea, Paul was taken into custody by the provincial governor Felix – a freedman who possessed extremely powerful Roman and Jewish connections. Undeterred by the possible technical difficulty that Paul came from another province, Syria-Cilicia (and from one of its 'free' cities too), Felix decided he had better not refuse to conduct the investigation required by the Jews. And so he requested the attendance of the high priest, who arrived from Jerusalem and argued, through his lawyer Tertullus, that Paul had not only caused disturbances in Jewish communities throughout the world but was also guilty of the *Roman* offence of causing a riot, that is to say of treasonable, subversive activity.

After this preliminary hearing, Felix decided that he must have the evidence of Lysias, the essential Roman eyewitness, in person. But after interviewing Paul he broke off the session once again. This was apparently because he regarded Paul's talk of the coming Judgment as susceptible of anti-imperial interpretations. In any case Felix was quite content not to come to a decision. For he knew he was going to be recalled quite soon to Rome, where changes at the imperial court had weakened his position. At this juncture, therefore, any verdict on Paul seemed likely to cause trouble: condemnation because of the Christian turbulence it might provoke, and acquittal because this could impel the disappointed plaintiffs to write a letter of complaint to the Emperor. So he decided to defer his verdict altogether. The charge against Paul remained on the books, so that his accusers could not say he had been let off; and he seems to have been kept in prison at Caesarea for two years.[49]

By that time Felix had been succeeded by Festus. In the intervals between grappling with Jewish nationalist guerrillas, he found time to consider further the problem of Paul. The high priest and his party were pressing the new governor to send him back to Jerusalem to undergo a

Jewish trial for his alleged religious offences, and according to *Acts* there was a plot to assassinate him on the way. But Festus said that these Jewish functionaries could themselves come to Caesarea instead, to bring any accusations they wished; and when they came he himself presided, thus implicitly if reluctantly admitting that the issue was concerned with Roman law and order. At the hearing, Paul declared not only that he was innocent of all offences against the Jews, but that he had also infringed in no way whatever upon imperial Roman legality. But when Festus suggested moving the whole case to Jerusalem so that he might preside over it there with easier access to Jewish witnesses, Paul strongly resisted because he was afraid that in any proceedings held in that city Jewish influence would predominate, with fatal results to himself.

It was at this juncture that he appealed to the Emperor Nero. The term 'appeal' may seem confusing since there was not yet any sentence to appeal against. Paul was, in effect, requesting that his case should be transferred to the imperial court at Rome. For a Roman citizen was protected by law, not only against arrest and flogging, but also against trial or summary punishment by any Roman officials outside Italy; that is to say, he was entitled to appeal from a provincial governor's jurisdiction. But the governor's own agreement had first to be obtained. On this occasion Festus, after conferring with advisers, granted the request, declaring: 'You have appealed to Caesar: to Caesar you shall go.'[50] In order to cover himself from future Jewish attacks or misinterpretations, he arranged for Paul to be interviewed, in his presence, by the Jewish monarchs Agrippa II and Berenice. During this further session, if *Acts* is to be believed, the governor lost patience and told Paul that he was raving – 'too much learning is driving you mad!' Nevertheless, he confirmed his decision to grant the appeal. Agrippa, feeling all the fuss was unnecessary, observed to him, 'the fellow could have been discharged, if he had not appealed to the Emperor.' Festus, however, like Felix before him, was only too glad to avoid the responsibility.

And so Paul went to Italy instead. *Acts* lays great emphasis upon this historic journey, since the bringing of Paul to the imperial capital was a vital stage in the triumph of the Gentile mission. Indeed, the main reason for his appeal may have been that he wanted transportation to Rome. When, after an adventurous voyage, he finally arrived at his destination, he was, initially at least, allowed to lodge by himself under the charge of a soldier, with full access to the synagogues and the Christian community, and with complete liberty of speech. We are told that 'he stayed there two full years at his own expense.'[51] But at this point *Acts* tantalizingly stops, without indicating whether Paul's trial in the imperial court, if it ever took place, resulted in his condemnation or acquittal.

Clement of Rome (*c.* AD 96) asserted that he subsequently travelled to 'the furthest limit of the west',[52] which perhaps means Spain. But this report may only be an inspired deduction from Paul's own statement in *Romans* that Spain was a country he eventually hoped to visit after he had finished his visit to Rome.[53] If, then, we are entitled to discount Clement's statement, it may well be that Paul never got away from Rome at all. And the Letters he wrote, apparently, from that city indicate that after his period of house arrest he was put into prison.[54]

Some further light on the last period of his life is cast by *II Timothy*. This Letter was not in its present form itself written by Paul, but it contains Pauline material. It was ostensibly one of the epistles written by Paul while he was a prisoner; and its concluding passages contain these words:

As for me, already my life is being poured out on the altar, and the hour for my departure is upon me. I have run the great race, I have finished the course, I have kept faith. And now the prize awaits me . . .

Do your best to join me soon; for Demas has deserted me because his heart was set on this world . . . Alexander the coppersmith did me a great deal of harm. Retribution will fall upon him from the Lord. You had better be on your guard against him too, for he violently opposed everything I said. At the first hearing of my case no one came into court to support me; they all left me in the lurch; I pray that it may not be held against them.[55]

Nevertheless, *II Timothy* continues, Paul on this occasion 'was rescued out of the lion's jaws'. But the reference to a 'first hearing' implies that a second hearing was also to take place. Whether or not it formed part of Nero's persecution of the Roman Christians in AD 64, it appears to have been fatal to Paul. If, as we have seen, there is some reason to believe that the prosecutors were Jewish Christians, *Acts*, in the interests of church unity, avoids admitting any such fact. Yet the same work is equally eager to distract attention from the ultimate responsibility of the Roman government for Paul's death. For to stress this would have destroyed the whole pattern and bias of the book, which emphasized on all occasions that Rome's officials had tried to behave justly to the Christian Church – or had at the very least refrained from adverse decisions – since they fully realized that the Christians were not their natural enemies: with the obvious corollary, implied by the Gospel writers as well as *Acts*, that it was only proper for this state of affairs to continue in the future. That, then, is probably why *Acts* terminates so abruptly and unsatisfactorily with the picture of Paul, though under house arrest at Rome, continuing his teaching there 'quite openly and without hindrance'. For to have carried the story on further, to his execution by the Romans, would have negated and contradicted one of the main purposes of the book.

VI

Summing Up

The vicissitudes of Paul's renown after his death form a curious story, inspiring reflections about the strange and devious ways in which great reputations come into being. At first, his career seemed to have been an almost total failure. His churches among the Dispersion do not seem to have prospered or even in most cases to have survived, at least in the forms that he ordained for them. Instead, the Christian communities of all those cities gave their allegiance to the apostles – the leaders and figureheads of that Jewish Christian Church which he had so strongly opposed. Likewise, Paul's extremely daring views, for example his radical rejection of the Law, failed almost completely to gain acceptance; because the Jewish Christian doctrine was manifestly so different, being based on that very code he had rejected. No doubt a number of his Gentile converts remained loyal to his memory, but they lived on in an atmosphere which, initially, was unfavourable to the concept of any Christianity that was not Jewish. True, the head of the Jewish Christian Church, James the Just, the brother of Jesus, succumbed to the Jews in AD 62, even before the martyrdom of Paul at Rome. Nevertheless, throughout the small Christian churches of the Dispersion it was still the Jewish Christian doctrines that prevailed, and Paul's reputation, by the time of his death, was at a very low ebb.

Then, in AD 66–73, the course of events was changed by the Jewish Revolt. When the Jews fell into total discredit with the Roman ruling power, it seemed imperative to the Christians, as we saw above, that they should dissociate themselves from any taint of Judaism. This, however, they could not do by maintaining their Jewish Christian character, for the Jewish Christians, despite endeavours to avoid ill-repute among the Romans, became discredited in their eyes along with the Jews. In consequence, Paul's Gentile mission became the dominant theme and force once again. The Gentile-born churches provided, apparently (though some have argued that *Matthew* is an exception), all four Gospels: they, and especially *Matthew*, preach a sharp dissociation from the Jews. They also display the Jewish Christian apostles as somewhat inferior creatures; moreover, they retrospectively transform Jesus' possible conversion of an occasional, individual, Gentile into a significant and systematic feature of his activity – with Roman centurions among the first to come under his spell.[1] At the same time *Acts* attempts a cautious rehabilitation of Paul as the continuator of this Gentile mission. The endeavour is cautious in so far as his strife with the Jewish Christians, though it cannot be completely erased from the tradition, is minimized and played down; accordingly, his soaring, provocative teaching is totally avoided and ignored. What was left? Not that he was the initiator of anything much at all, for this he was not allowed to be, but that he was an indefatigable missionary: in the words of Clement of Rome (before AD 100), Paul was the 'divine apostle' because he was 'the greatest example of endurance'.[2] And such was the label that he retained. His Gentile churches rose to the surface again, but without claiming him as their founder or inspirer. *Revelation*, addressed to seven churches of Asia Minor,[3] the country on which he had lavished such laborious efforts, had nothing to say about him at all.

Nevertheless, the recovery of his reputation, even in this imperfect guise of the tireless worker in the field, was enough to ensure that his Letters survived. Clement knew and used *Romans, Corinthians* and *Ephesians:* already by his time, that is to say, some sort of corpus of Paul's writings had evidently been collected. True, *II Peter*, written early in the second century, found them puzzling and potentially misleading, and therefore, despite their 'inspired wisdom', suspect.[4] At about the same time, however, Ignatius recognized Paul as a figure to whom obedience was due, speaking of him to the Ephesians in profoundly respectful terms, and writing to the Roman community: 'I do not command you as if I were a Peter or a Paul.'[5]

But meanwhile the gulf between Christianity and Judaism had widened, so that Ignatius could declare it to be impossible to talk of

Jesus Christ and practise Judaism.[6] One outcome of this growing breach was the extraordinary figure of Marcion, who, although denounced subsequently as a heretic, was among the most powerful Christian personalities of the second century AD. Pursuing the dismissal of the Jews to its logical conclusion, Marcion entirely rejected the pre-Christian, Jewish part of the Bible, the Old Testament, and in contrast raised Paul to startling eminence; because he too had rejected the Law. Indeed, the Marcionites saw him sitting in heaven on the right hand of Christ, with Marcion, as the one true interpreter of them both, seated on the Saviour's left.[7] These views were associated with interpretations and exaggerations of Paul's derogatory remarks about worldly, fleshly things, while stress was also laid upon his lack of interest in Jesus' mortal life: so that the universe of Marcion emerged as a scene of the dualist struggle between good and evil powers, and his Jesus as 'docetic',* lacking a truly human body.[8]

Such developments, in the very substantial Marcionic church, led to two important and partly contradictory consequences. First, Marcion had raised Paul to a new eminence, where henceforward he permanently remained. For it was very likely he who first collected Paul's ten Letters into a single volume, the *Apostolicon* (*c.* AD 150).[9] That these epistles of Paul, therefore, occupy no less than one-fifth of the entire New Testament is to a great extent Marcion's doing. But if the first result of the latter's attempted religious revolution operated in favour of the prestige of Paul, its second effect was the distortion and suppression of his message by those who vigorously, and in due course successfully, reacted against what Marcion had been saying. Already in earlier years *Acts* had found it desirable to tone down Paul's bold teaching. And now his views on the dualist universe and the nature of Christ, as presented by Marcion, seemed so shocking and so entirely contrary to what had become orthodox thinking that they demanded thorough eradication. Since, however, Paul's reputation, partly due to Marcion's own efforts, had by this time attained massive stature which could no longer be effectively diminished or ignored, the demolition of Marcion somehow had to be accomplished without any overt anti-Pauline attitudes. But how was this to be done? The answer was clear: Paul the missionary could be praised, but the awkward, radical, thoughts in his Letters – the thoughts which, daring but ambiguous, had inspired Marcion to such embarrassing deductions – must be reinterpreted into something much more sober, even if it meant ironing them almost out of existence.

This process is clearly seen in Polycarp, just after the middle of the second century AD. While stressing Paul's importance and citing him side by side with the apostles, Polycarp presents opinions about the nature of Jesus Christ and the significance of baptism that are far less vivid and imaginative than Paul's, soothingly keeping away from those hazardous Pauline contrasts between flesh and spirit, with their insidious suggestion that the evil power in the universe might be comparable in potency to the good. Moreover, Paul's rejections of the Law are carefully explained away by these second-century Fathers; because the growing Church, like any growing institution, felt it needed to have discipline and a moral system, and therefore found the Law very necessary. It could not possibly afford these breath-taking, dazzling speculations which seemed to strike at the very roots of order and ethics.

And so the Paul who emerges from this careful process of reinterpretation was only a shadow of his real former self. He had been snatched rather late in the day from the heretics, 'as the decisive interpreter, to the Gentile future, of that Gospel which the Jewish Christian church of the Apostolic Age had taught'.[10] But in the process he had undergone transformation into respectability! Thus neutralized, there was no harm in granting full recognition to his Letters; the fact that the deplorable Marcion had also done so was no longer a disadvantage. By AD 200, therefore, these works were safely enrolled in the New Testament canon and it was possible to regard them as inspired by God. By this time Peter and Paul, though they had been at variance in their lives, were constantly bracketed together (as they had been by Ignatius) by the two million or so Christians who now existed in the world[11]; though the Roman Church, despite Paul's eloquent Letter to its earlier members, subordinated him to Peter, who, unlike him, had been an original apostle.[12] Criticisms of Paul's theories did not cease to be put forward, since the *Clementine Homilies**,[13] for example (perhaps of the fourth century, but possibly reflecting much earlier views) felt that his doctrine of Original Sin had unduly calumniated Adam.[14]

When Augustine's intense spiritual struggles eventually led him to a burning Christian faith, he owed a very great deal of it to the Letters of Paul. More than a millennium afterwards, Martin Luther passionately rediscovered the 'divine apostle's' teaching about faith and grace, and the Reformation came into being. Two hundred years later still, it was while Luther's *Preface to the Epistle to the Romans* was being read aloud that one of the members of the congregation, John Wesley, felt his intellectually-held Christian beliefs transfigured into profound personal experience: he, like Paul, suddenly knew that he could proclaim universal redemption by faith alone.

In our own century, the publication of Karl Barth's *Römerbrief (Commentary on the Romans)*, and particularly its second edition in 1922, created an upheaval that seemed like a new Reformation. Barth's own part in this process was described strikingly by himself. As a contributor to what had now happened, he said, he could compare himself with a man stumbling up a ruined tower staircase in the dark, who, putting out his hand to save himself from falling, found he had grasped a bell rope and had unexpectedly sounded a peal that was now reverberating far and wide.[15]

Paul's reverberations, for nearly two thousand years, whenever they have not been softened and muffled by deliberate intention, have always been explosively loud. Rarely, the saying is, has there ever been anyone at the same time hated with such fiery hatred and loved with such strong passion.

Within the Christian Church, he has been the greatest single source of all its spiritual revivals. Whenever the faith has been in danger of flagging, he has come back time and time again to give it new life. Could anyone else have done this but him? James Stalker suggested that Paul was one of the men 'expressly sent into the world to do the work required by the juncture of history on which they fell'.[16] This recalls the divergence between Thomas Carlyle's assertion that history is the work of Great Men, and the opposing view of Engels and Plekhanov that if Napoleon had not been there, nevertheless the exigencies of the age would have produced someone else who would have done much the same job. Stalker, with his mind chiefly on God's purpose, was not exactly taking sides in this dispute, but he was suggesting that Paul was precisely the man for his time. This, however, underestimates the *surprising* quality of Paul. It was very surprising indeed that the infant Church, with its mainly humble and uneducated adherents, should have suddenly acquired an apostle and prophet who breathed the terrific intellectual and imaginative power and exaltation of Paul.

He was also startlingly original, with an originality which was ready to distort all traditional forms out of recognition. The question has been continually raised of the relationship of his thought to the thought of Jesus Christ; indeed, Paul has variously been named the greatest of his followers and interpreters, or the total destroyer of all that he had stood for. But the question has been misconceived. Certainly it is possible to compare – and contrast – the detailed ethical injunctions of Paul, known from his Letters, with what is believed to be the teaching of Jesus. And indeed this is a revealing procedure. Yet such ethical comparisons can only be of limited significance. For in the first place, it is not always easy to say what portions of the Gospels accurately reflect the actual words of Jesus himself. Secondly, Christianity's code of behaviour is not, for the most part, very original, being generally a reproduction of Jewish moral precepts. Thirdly, the whole field of ethics was only of subsidiary significance to Paul, being subordinated in his mind to the pre-eminence of faith.

Faith in what? And the answer gives a fourth reason why comparisons between the instruction ascribed to Jesus and to Paul scarcely even touch on the most vital difference between them. Because the faith which Paul himself came to hold, and desired others to hold with him, was faith in the Crucifixion and Resurrection of Jesus Christ, and in the consequences of those events for mankind. This was by far the most important part of his beliefs and his preachings and teachings, and it means that they can scarcely be compared at all with those of Jesus. For, even if Jesus in his last days came to foresee his own violent death as in some way redemptive, this idea had manifestly *not* stood in the forefront of his ministry – which, throughout his career, had centred instead upon the dawning and shortly to be consummated Kingdom of God. It was scarcely surprising, then, that Paul showed so little interest in Jesus' life. For what the two men preached was quite different, and the Christianity that we have today is largely Paul's creation.

Clearly, then, Paul's transformation of the course of religious history was incalculably great. Besides, the breakaway from the Jewish Law which opened the way to his total concentration on the redemptive Crucifixion had, eventually, a second enormous result as well: the extension of Christianity to the Gentiles. In time, it spread to thousands and millions. Already before the end of the third century AD there were more Christians than Jews: and the process, begun by Paul, has never been reversed.

Yet to regard him as a figure whose significance applies *only* to the religious branch of history is a mistake – a mistake frequently made, which is largely encouraged by the willingness of historians to relinquish his study to theologians. It is part of a much more far-reaching mistake: the widespread reluctance to regard religious history as part of secular history, and one of its most important parts at that, affecting it repeatedly at countless points. 'The dynamic of religion,' wrote C. H. Dodd, 'remains, for good or ill, the strongest of human motives.'[17] So the events of millennia have shown. 'For good or ill': the good is manifest, but the ill includes innumerable wars of religion which still continue.

For such strife, a good deal of the responsibility can be traced back to Paul, whose sponsorship, sometimes fairly, sometimes unfairly, religious militants on all sides have always hastened to claim. But his noble words and deeds have also made millions of people behave better. That is to say, for good and for ill, he has impinged, one way or another, on secular as well as religious history almost continually, and to an extent beyond measurement. Scarcely anyone has ever changed the course of history more than Paul. By means of his life and his Letters, he has left a greater imprint on the human race than almost any other man. Lord Birkenhead had some reason to declare that, beside Paul, the doings of Alexander the Great and Napoleon pale into insignificance.

But the epoch-making figures of the world have been of two kinds. There are those who played a great and deeply significant part in the history of their own time, and perhaps later times as well, but are no longer of vital and essential concern to *our* lives. And there are also those, far fewer in number, whose impact on the events and thoughts of their own epoch does not ever cease to be felt throughout subsequent epochs as well; so that they still exercise, or can exercise, a transforming force on ourselves, here and now. Those who study Paul have generally agreed that Paul belongs to that second and very small group: that he is one of those exceptional, strange personages who, although they lived a very long time ago, are still valid and relevant today. In the words of Karl Barth, 'Paul veritably speaks to all men of every age ... if we rightly understand ourselves, our problems are the problems of Paul.' And according to Malcolm Muggeridge, Paul is 'desperately needed today, in the world of the 1970's'.[18]

Both these writers are writing as Christians, and from that point of view, what they say is beyond question. For if Christianity is ever to be revived to anything approaching its earlier strength, then it will first be necessary that Paul's burning belief and his elevation of faith should reappear as an inspiring, awakening force in the Christian community; in other words, someone of the calibre of Paul will be needed to accomplish the immense revival.

But the assertions of Barth and Muggeridge would be misleading if we deduced from them that Paul's career and his thought are of concern today to no one but practising Christians. They are the people to whom books with titles such as *The Meaning of Paul for Today* and *Paul through Modern Eyes* are habitually addressed; and this is considered right by theologians such as Dr William Barclay, who declares: 'No man can enjoy Paul's experience of Christ unless he has made Paul's surrender to Christ'.[19] Such a restriction of his readership, however, reduces Paul to an esoteric personage whom none but sharers in his own rare experience can understand or derive benefit from.

But on the contrary, he is, and should be, of overwhelming significance to a vastly wider circle. This includes Jews: who, having once regarded him as the arch-apostate, now write about him with an insight equal to that of the foremost Christian Pauline scholars. But Paul is also profoundly relevant to the men and women who have no religion whatever. This is, simply, because he felt a massive urge to break down the barriers between one human being and another, as countless people wish to do today.

He pursued this universalist aim in two ways: through his Letters and through his missionary work. True, his Letters are difficult, and this difficulty has been recognized since the first century AD. Inevitably also, after so long a passage of years, they are 'encumbered with references to feelings and beliefs which are now dead to the interest of mankind'.[20] Yet to leave it at that, and present an 'easy' Paul of the *Acts* whose Letters, on the other hand, need not be studied seriously, is to incur a grievous and unnecessary loss. For once the required adjustments to unfamiliar formulations have been made, the Letters emerge among the most potent, argument-provoking and inspiring contributions to the world's literature that have ever been written.

As for Paul's missionary journeys, one can but echo Clement's conclusion that never had such an example of endurance been seen in the world before. This, too, is of permanent and modern value. When Paul demonstrated that a human being is capable of enduring the unimaginable and almost unendurable, by his own life and purpose he was confirming what Sophocles had said in the *Antigone:* that men and women can rise to fantastic heights.[21] To read of Paul's scarcely credible fortitude and perseverance strikes a note of challenge in the exacting world of today and kindles our hearts. So does the power which kept his endurance going: his faith. For although faith has gained such an equivocal reputation in our own century when millions have shown unquestioning faith in what is inhumane and misguided, there have also been innumerable contrary examples. Karl Barth's faith, for instance, encouraged by Paul's emphasis on the individual conscience, caused him to stand up against oppression with a steadfast courage that he could not have mustered otherwise.[22]

But what, in 1976, may seem to many the most fascinating and topical aspect of Paul is his recognition of *total change*. Not for him the easy assumption, prevalent in the rest of the Greco-Roman world, that all is a matter of historical traditions and backgrounds and age-old developments. Nor was this sort of fatalistic pessimism altogether lacking in Jewish thought, leading some, even, to the conclusion of *Ecclesiastes*, that 'what has happened will happen again, and what has been done will be done again, and there is nothing new under the sun. Is there anything of which one can say, "Look, this is new"? No, it has already existed, long ago before our time.'[23] Paul might have been prepared to accept this as a general description of the world, oppressed by evil as it utterly was, up to the time of the Crucifixion of Jesus Christ. But that event seemed to him to have changed everything, and it was a change which he believed to be total and irrevocable. Paul, that is to say, possessed in an exceptionally high degree the receptive attitude which is prepared to envisage that the world has been transformed out of all recognition, and will never be the same again. This quality of his would indeed have been useful – quite outside religious affairs – in our own time, where there was and is such great reluctance to admit that certain events and developments happening now, like the energy crisis which began in 1974, have radically altered the world, and are likely to alter it still further.

Indeed, Paul's capacity to recognize change was uniquely strong. The historian's characteristic view that everything which happens has evolved from existing historical tendencies and trends would have seemed to him to be disproved by what, in fact, had happened: the redemptive death of Jesus Christ. Whether one agrees with him or not – Jews, for example, do not – that Christ's death was this total reversal of everything that had taken place hitherto, at all events Paul's general attitude, insisting that such totally world-changing occurrences *can* take place, seems plausible, defensible and right in our own day; the years which lie immediately ahead of us are likely to confirm the cogency of Paul's viewpoint even more insistently.

Notes

The following abbreviations are used in the notes:

B.	Babylonian Talmud
Clem. Alex.	Clement of Alexandria
I Clem. (Rom.)	First Epistle of Clement of Rome
Col.	Letter of Paul to the Colossians
I, II Cor.	Letters of Paul to the Corinthians
Dan.	Daniel
Deut.	Deuteronomy
Eccl.	Ecclesiastes
Ecclus.	Ecclesiasticus
I Enoch	The Ethiopic Enoch
Eph.	Letter of Paul to the Ephesians
II Esdras	The Second Book of Esdras, or Ezra Apocalypse (IV Ezra in the Vulgate)
Ex.	Exodus
Ezek.	Ezekiel
Gal.	Letter of Paul to the Galatians
Hab.	Habakkuk
Heb.	Letter to Hebrews
Is.	Isaiah (II Isaiah – Deutero-Isaiah or Second Isaiah is the author of chapters 40–66 of this book).
J.	Jerusalem (or Palestinian) Talmud
James	Letter of James

Jer.	Jeremiah
John	Gospel According to John
I, II John	Letters of John
M.	Mishnah
I, II Macc.	Books of the Maccabees
Num.	Numbers
Phil.	Letter of Paul to the Philippians
Prov.	Proverbs
Psalms	The Psalms of David
Rev.	Revelation of John the Divine
Rom.	Letter of Paul to the Romans
I, II Sam.	Books of Samuel
I, II Thess.	Letters of Paul to the Thessalonians
I, II Tim.	Letters of Paul to Timothy
Wisdom	The Wisdom of Solomon
Zech.	Zechariah

CHAPTER I   THE LIFE AND WORK AND CHARACTER OF PAUL

1   *Acts of Paul and Thecla*, 3.

2   John Malalas, *Chronographia*, 10.

3   Nicephorus Callistus, *Ecclesiastical History*, 2.37.

4   Sources in G. Ricciotti, *Paul the Apostle*, pp. 157f.

5   Cf. R. M. Grant, *A Historical Introduction to the New Testament*, p. 173. His tentative chronology of the Letters is followed here.

6   R. P. C. Hanson, *The Second Epistle to the Corinthians*, pp. 5f.

7   K. Barth, *Der Römerbrief*, 1918, translation of 6th ed. as *The Epistle to the Romans*, 1933.

8   E.g. I Thess. 4.1, I Cor. 15.3; The 'hymn' in Phil. 2.5–11 is often regarded as pre-Pauline. For this primitive, original *kerygma* or proclamation of the Gospel, see C. H. Dodd, *According to the Scriptures*; R. R. Williams, *Acts of the Apostles*, pp. 46ff., etc.

9   I Cor. 1.26.

10 Augustine, *Confessions*, 7.21.

11 Gal. 6.11: 'you see these big letters? I am now writing to you in my own hand.'

12 For his metaphors from pagan foot-races, etc., see E. W. Hunt, *Portrait of Paul*, pp. 288ff.

13 Acts 17.32–34. Paul had quoted Aratus, *Phaenomena*, 5; and also, possibly, Epimenides, *Cretica*.

14 II Peter, 3.16.

15 Eusebius, *Church History*, 2.22.
16 Acts 1.1.
17 For these see C. S. C. Williams, *Commentary on the Acts of the Apostles*, pp. 1ff.
18 G. Bornkamm, *Paul*, pp. xvff.
19 E.g. Acts 5.36 (wrong date), 4.4. It has been argued, however, that there are useful early sources behind, e.g., the speeches of Peter in the early chapters.
20 Acts 27.20, 27–28.6, 11. The reference to the Sea of Adria or Adriatic Sea has caused some to suppose that Paul was cast ashore not on Malta but at Mljet near Dubrovnik. But 'sea of Adria' is used loosely, e.g. by the geographer Ptolemy, to signify the whole expanse of water between Crete and Sicily.
21 H. Musurillo, *The Acts of the Pagan Martyrs: Acta Alexandrinorum*, (1954).
22 For these see C. S. C. Williams, op. cit. pp. 7ff.
23 For varying estimates see G. Bornkamm, op. cit., pp. 4f., M. Grant, *The Jews in the Roman World*, p. xi.
24 Phil. 3.5.
25 Gal. 1.22 against Acts 22.3.
26 Acts 18.3.
27 Phil. 4.10, 16.
28 M. Aboth 2.2.
29 I Cor. 4.12, I Thess. 2.9, II Thess. 3.8, Acts 20.34, 28.30.
30 Discussions in A. N. Sherwin-White, *Roman Society and Roman Law in the New Testament*, pp. 151ff.
31 Acts 7.58.
32 Acts 9.1–9, 22.6–11, 26.12–18.
33 Acts 11.26 (at Syrian Antioch).
34 II Cor. 11.32, against Acts 9.23.
35 Later Paul and Barnabas split over the circumcision issue and over their companion Mark; Paul took Silas instead on his second journey, Gal. 2.13, Acts 15.37–40. Subsequently he employed other assistants, including Luke: Col. 4.14, II Tim. 4.11, Philemon 24.
36 A. H. McNeile, *St Paul: His Life, Letters and Christian Doctrine*, pp. xiii–xix.
37 Rom. 15.19 ambiguously states that he went 'as far round as Illyricum' (Yugoslavia).
38 Acts 25.12.
39 I Cor. 9.16.
40 II Tim. 4.2.

41 Quoted by S. Perowne, *The Journeys of St Paul*, p. 72.
42 II Cor. 10.1, 10.11. It would be unfair (as any teacher would agree) to count it against Paul that one member of his audience, Eutychus at Alexandria Troas, fell asleep: Acts 20.9.
43 I Cor. 2.3.
44 II Cor. 11.5.
45 II Thess. 2.13.
46 I Cor. 4.18, II Cor. 11.13–14.
47 Rom. 15.1–5, Gal. 5.26–6.5, Col. 4.6; I Cor. 9.20–2, 10.33, 3.2.
48 Eph. 5.4 warns against flippancy.
49 E.g. II Cor. 10–13 (19 times).
50 Phil. 3.12.
51 Psalms 143.2, Job 35.2, 36.3, etc.
52 Rom. 3.27, I Cor. 9.16, Phil. 3.9.
53 Gal. 2.19; cf. II Cor. 4.10.
54 Phil. 1.23, 3.11. His admirer Martin Luther was criticized for excessive concern with his own salvation.
55 II Cor. 10.15, Rom. 15.20.
56 Rom. 7.15, 18, 24.
57 Discussion in A. M. Hunter, *Romans*, pp. 73ff.
58 II Cor. 12.7–9.
59 A. D. Nock, *St Paul*, p. 71.
60 Eph. 5.25, 28, Col. 3.19; I Cor. 6.18–19, I Thess. 4.3–8, Eph. 5.32.
61 I Cor. 14.34–35 (contradicted by 11.5?).
62 Gen. 2.21–22.
63 Gal. 3.28.
64 Phil. 4.2 (Euodia and Syntyche).
65 Rom. 16.3, cf. Acts 18.26 (reversed in I Cor. 16.19).
66 Sources in A. H. Silver, *Where Judaism Differed*, pp. 232f.
67 Sources in G. Vermes, *Jesus the Jew*, pp. 99ff.
68 I Cor. 7.1–2, 8–9.
69 I Cor. 5.5, 15.51, etc.
70 Sources in J. Kahl, *The Misery of Christianity*, pp. 73ff. Col. 2.18 had tried to guard against such exaggerations. In the second century, Tatian declared marriage to be corruption and fornication. Literally applying Matt. 19.12, Origen had himself castrated. Augustine, *City of God*, 14.16, advocated the avoidance of enjoyment in procreating children.
71 For a more modern study of Paul in psychoanalytical terms, see R. L. Rubinstein, *My Brother Paul*, vividly analyzing his religious consciousness.

72 Gal. 4.13–14.
73 The argument for ophthalmia is based on the passage in n. 11
above. The argument for epilepsy is developed by J. Klausner,
From Jesus to Paul, pp. 328f. It is often supposed that Luke 'the
beloved physician' (Col. 4.14) treated Paul's illness.
74 II Cor. 6.4–5, cf. 9, and 4.8–9.
75 II Cor. 11.21–27. See Deut. 25.3 for the 40 strokes.
76 I Cor. 15.32.
77 I Clem. (Rom.), *Corinthians*, 5.
78 Gal. 6.17: i.e. in Jesus' service; such brands indicated ownership,
but were also supposed to protect the bearer against assault. Cf.
I Cor. 9.27 on his bruises.
79 II Cor. 4.8–10, cf. Col. 1.24.
80 I Cor. 4.13.
81 Rom. 5.2–3.
82 I Cor. 15.31.
83 Rom. 8.17.
84 Phil. 2.17, cf. 1.24.
85 E.g. Ignatius, *Romans*, 1.4–8, I Peter 4.12–13.

CHAPTER II   OUR DISASTROUS PAST HISTORY

1. The Age-long Rule of Evil

1 D. E. Nineham, *St Mark*, p. 58.
2 Matt. 3.7, 7.17 etc.
3 Rom. 5.12–14. Paul here adopts a widespread view that Adam
caused not only human sin but death and mortality, though in
Rom. 8.20 he attributes the flux of birth and decay not to Adam
but vaguely to the will of God.
4 W. D. Davies, *Paul and Rabbinic Judaism*, pp. 34–4.
5 Rom. 7.15, cf. 21.
6 E.g. II Sam. 24.10–25. For contradictions about posterity Ex.
7–9 (quoted by Rom. 9.17), Deut. 5.9, 24.16, 30.19, etc.
7 Rom. 8.29.
8 II Esdras 7.118; but 7.127–9, 8.56 partially qualify this.
9 II Baruch 54.17–19.
10 A. H. Silver, *Where Judaism Differed*, pp. 189–90. Cf. the Pharisaic
Psalms of Solomon, 9.7, 'our works are in the choice and power of
our souls'. This was also the Sadducee view.
11 M. Grant, *The Climax of Rome* (Cardinal ed.), p. 268. Cf. Eph. 1.11
(note 41 below).

12 G. Ebeling, *Luther*, p. 220.
13 Psalms 119. 4–5, 97.
14 Sources in A. T. Hanson, *Studies in Paul's Technique and Theology*, pp. 204, 235, 250, etc.
15 Eph. 6.12.
16 II Cor. 12.7.
17 I Cor. 11.10.
18 Eph. 2.2, Gal. 4.4.
19 Plato, *Symposium*, 202E.
20 E. R. Dodds, *Pagan and Christian in an Age of Anxiety*, p. 38. He adds that these daemons sometimes stood for aeons (epochs of time).
21 G. A. Wells, *The Jesus of the Early Christians*, p. 288.
22 *War Rule*, 1.12.
23 M. R. James, *The Lost Apocrypha of the Old Testament*, pp. 36–7.
24 Rev. 12.9 ('thrown down to the earth'), 20.2, 7–10. But the Bible is fragmentary and ambiguous about the circumstances of their fall, cf. below note 34 for those who see references to it as predictive or figurative.
25 C. H. Dodd, *The Meaning of Paul for Today*, pp. 62–3.
26 Acts 16.18–19.
27 Acts 19.12.
28 J. Shabbath 14 D.
29 II Cor. 11.14.
30 II Cor. 12.7.
31 I Cor. 5.5.
32 II Thess. 2.3–9
33 Luke 10.18 (cf. Is. 14.12).
34 G. B. Caird, *St Luke*. p. 143, G. E. Ladd, *Jesus and the Kingdom*, p. 153; see also note 24 above.
35 John 14.30, I Peter 5.8, I John 5.19.
36 James 1.13.
37 I John 1.5.
38 Origen, *Against Celsus*, 6.55.
39 J. James, *Why Evil?* pp. 24, 31–2.
40 I Cor. 3.7.
41 Eph. 1.11.
42 Rom. 11.33, 9.21.
43 Gal. 5.17.
44 Rom. 7.18; I Cor. 9.27, II Cor. 5.2, 5.6, 4.7.
45 II Cor. 1.18.
46 Acts 8.9–13.

47 Clem. Alex., *Stromateis*, 7.17. Or Clement may have called him Theodorus or Theodotus.

48 Augustine, *Against the Manichaeans*, 24, 26; cf. *Confessions*, 5.10, 6.5.

49 G. B. Caird, *St Luke*, p. 79 lists five moral truths conveyed by belief in the devil.

2. The Need for Total Change

1 E.g. Philo regarded the Law of Moses as secondary to the Law of Nature.

2 Eccl. (e.g. 1.9, 15, etc.) is the only Old Testament book which questions human progress.

3 S. Sandmel, *The Genius of Paul*, pp. 28–9; cf. C. G. Montefiore, *Judaism and St Paul*, p. 69.

4 Gal. 3.19, I Tim. 1.8: the Law is excellent provided we recognize it is not aimed at good citizens!

5 Rom. 7.7.

6 Rom. 4.15.

7 Augustine, *Confessions*, 2.6.

8 Rom. 7.7.

9 Gen. 15.6.

10 Rom. 4.9–17, Gal. 3.6–9. The same argument was later used by Mohammed.

11 Gal. 3.10; cf. James 2.10.

12 Deut. 27.26.

13 Rom. 8.3. But the question was also being asked whether Jesus, too, had not demanded the impossible: cf. below, chapter V, section 1 (n. 31).

14 Rom. 3.21.

15 I Cor. 14.21.

16 Gal. 3.19–20.

17 Deut. 33.2.

18 II Cor. 3.6.

19 Psalms 143.2.

20 Rom. 3.20.

CHAPTER III   THE FIRST ACT OF RESCUE

1. The Coming of the Messiah

1 Dan. 9.25; cf. Ezek. 34. 23–4.

2 Dan. 7.13–14.

3 I Enoch 46.1, 3, 48.4, 62.6–7, 27–9
4 *Hymn Scroll*, 3.9.
5 *Habakkuk Commentary*, 1, 2, 4, 7–8, etc.
6 G. Vermes, *The Dead Sea Scrolls in English*, 1975 ed., pp. 67f.
7 *Community Rule*, 9; cf. *Damascus Document*, 6. W. S. LaSor, *The Dead Sea Scrolls*, Moody Press, 1962 ed., p. 154, is not satisfied that two separate Messiahs are intended.
8 II Sam. 7.14.
9 Sources in G. Vermes, *Jesus the Jew*, pp. 69–79, etc.
10 Mark 6.14, *Clementine Recognitions*, 1.60.
11 John 3.28.
12 Deut. 6.4.
13 The uses of the titles Son of Man and Son of God in Jesus' lifetime are discussed further in my forthcoming book on Jesus.
14 Rom. 8.3, Gal. 1.16.
15 Rom. 1.3.
16 Rom. 8.29.
17 Gal. 4.4.
18 Is. 63.16, Jer. 3.4.
19 Psalms 2.7.
20 *Psalms of Solomon*, 17.
21 Philo, *On Cherubim*, 40.7.
22 Agadath Bereshith (ed. S. Buber), 31.
23 And even: 'no one knows the Son but the Father, and no one knows the Father but the Son' (Matt. 11.27, Luke 10.22).
24 Phil. 2.6.
25 I Thess. 3.11. The meaning of Rom. 9.5 is disputable.
26 Phil. 2.10.
27 I Cor. 8.6; cf. 3.23, 11.23.
28 Phil. 2.6.
29 II Cor. 4.4.
30 Col. 1.15, 19, 2.9.
31 Rom. 1.3, 8.3.
32 Rom. 1.4.
33 Mark 1.11.
34 Gal. 4.5.
35 Rom. 1.3.
36 I Cor. 7.10. On Jesus' much disputed teaching on this subject see R. V. G. Tasker, *Matthew*, pp. 179ff., etc.
37 For indirect echoes see J. N. D. Anderson, *Christianity: the Witness of History*, pp. 29–30, etc. But the absence of more direct references remains striking: G. Bornkamm, *Jesus of Nazareth*, pp. 16f., cf.

C. K. Barrett, D. E. Nineham, L. E. Keck, M. Dibelius, S. G. F. Brandon, R. Bultmann, K. Barth, G. A. Wells.

38 II Cor. 5.16.
39 A. E. J. Rawlinson, *The New Testament Doctrine of the Christ*, p. 90, n. 5.
40 Augustine, *Confessions*, 5, 10.
41 I Cor. 12.3.
42 Phil. 2.7.
43 Is. 53.12.
44 W. Barclay, *The Mind of Paul*, pp. 48f.
45 Phil. 2.6, cf. above at note 28. Perhaps pre-Pauline; cf. chapter 1, note 8.
46 Col. 1.16–17.
47 J. L. Houlden, *Paul's Letters from Prison*, pp. 75f.; cf. M. Wiles, *The Remaking of Christian Doctrine*, p. 53.
48 John 1.1–14.
49 Heb. 4.12–14.
50 I Cor. 1.24.
51 Prov. 8.22, 30.
52 Ecclus. 24.3, 12, 23.
53 Wisdom 7.25.
54 Col. 3.16.
55 S. Sandmel, *The Genius of Paul*, pp. 68f.

2. The Relevance of Jesus' Death

1 I Cor. 1.23.
2 Cf. Mark 15.28 (absent from most texts).
3 Luke 24.21.
4 *Psalms of Solomon*, 13.10, 18.4–5.
5 II Macc. 7.38–40, etc.
6 Zech. 12.10–12.
7 Is. 53.5.
8 *Hymn Scroll*, 3.9–10.
9 Acts 3.18
10 Acts 17.3; cf. 26.23.
11 Rom. 15.8.
12 Phil. 2.7.
13 A. T. Hanson, *Studies in Paul's Technique and Theology*, p. 211.
14 M. Muggeridge, *Jesus Rediscovered*, p. 188.
15 Deut. 21.22.
16 W. D. Davies, *Paul and Rabbinic Judaism*, pp. 227f.

17 Gal. 3.13.
18 A. Cole, *Galatians*, p. 100.
19 A. M. Hunter, *Galatians to Colossians*, pp. 28f.
20 I Cor. 2.1–2, 1.18.
21 I Thess. 5.10.
22 Rom. 6.5.
23 II Cor. 5, 14.
24 Gal. 3.1.
25 I Cor. 15.55; echoing Hosea 13.14.
26 I Cor. 2.8.
27 Col. 2.15.
28 Col. 2.8.
29 I Cor. 15.22.
30 Rom. 5.14–15.
31 J. H. Newman, *Praise to the Holiest*.
32 I Cor. 5.7–8.
33 Rom. 5.9, 3.25, 12.1.
34 Rev. 17.11.
35 Ex. 12.21–27.
36 Mark 14.24.
37 John 1.29.
38 But the concept appears in Acts 20–28.
39 C. A. Anderson Scott, *St Paul: the Man and the Teacher*, p. 103.
40 Rom. 3.25; cf. I Cor. 15.3. But the Authorized Version translated *hilasterion* as 'propitiation'.
41 Is. 53.11.
42 Cf. above, note 5.
43 Sources in G. Vermes, *Scripture and Tradition in Judaism*, pp. 195–225.
44 J. James, *Why Evil?*, pp. 100f.
45 Rom. 6.2, 15; cf. 7.7.
46 Gal. 5.15.
47 Rom. 5.11.
48 II Cor. 5.18–19.
49 Col. 1.21–23.
50 S. Sandmel, *The Genius of Paul*, p. 92.
51 II Cor. 8.9.
52 John 17.22–3.
53 I Cor. 7.23, 6.20; cf. Mark 10.45.
54 Psalms 130.8.
55 I Peter 1.18. The idea that Christ's death was 'an example' (2.21) is much weaker.

56 Rom. 9.4.
57 Gal. 4.5, Eph. 1.5.
58 W. Barclay, *The Mind of St Paul*, pp. 71f.
59 Eph. 4.9 (probable interpretation); cf. I Peter 3.19. For this 'underworld' concept, cf. M. Buber, *Two Types of Faith*, pp. 99f. After death, the soul existed like a shade in Sheol as long as the bones at least remained; R. de Vaux, *Ancient Israel*, p. 56.
60 I Cor. 15.1, 3–8. The passage contains Semitisms of Palestinian origin; cf. J. Jeremias, *Eucharistic Words*, pp. 187ff.
61 Mark 16.3–4, Luke 24.22, John 20.2. It is sometimes argued that the Marcan account goes back to earlier origins than Paul's.
62 Dan. 12.2.
63 Acts 17.18.
64 Matt. 22.23, Acts 23.8.
65 Is. 26.19, etc.
66 I Cor. 15.4.
67 Hosea 6.2.
68 II Kings 20.5.
69 Matt. 12.40.
70 Mark 6.14.
71 Rom. 1.4.
72 I Cor. 15.17.
73 Ibid.
74 Col. 1.18, 27.
75 Augustine, *City of God*, 22.3.
76 I Cor. 15.35, 42–44, 45.
77 John 11.39.
78 Jubilees 23.30–1.
79 II Esdras 7.75.
80 J. L. Houlden, *Paul's Letters from Prison*, p. 63.
81 Luke 24.39. But Luke 20.30ff. suggests a more spiritual interpretation.
82 John 20.27.
83 Augustine, *City of God*, 13.22.
84 Phil. 2.9.
85 Eph. 4.10.
86 II Cor. 5.8, Phil. 1.23–4.
87 Gen. 5.24, II Kings 2.11.
88 Acts 1.3. 'Forty days' was a round number; but for O.T. links, cf. K. Barth, *Church Dogmatics* (1960), III, 2, p. 452.
89 *Letter of Barnabas*, 15.
90 I Cor. 15.8–9.

91 Rom. 6.4.
92 Acts 2.33; cf. 1.9.
93 John 20.17.
94 Eph. 1.21; cf. I Peter 3.22.
95 Col. 1.13–20.
96 II Cor. 5.17 (various readings); cf. Gal. 6.15.
97 Rom. 6.4.
98 Phil. 2.10.
99 A. Schweitzer, *The Mysticism of Paul the Apostle*, p. 98.

3.   Belief in the Unbelievable

1 Rom. 10.4 (one reading).
2 Rom. 1.16–17.
3 Eph. 6.16.
4 Heb. 11 is devoted to this task.
5 Gal. 3.11.
6 Hab. 2.4.
7 Gen. 15.6.
8 Rom. 5.18.
9 I Cor. 6.11.
10 M. Burrows, *The Dead Sea Scrolls*, p. 335.
11 Augustine, *City of God*, 21.5.
12 Rom. 1.20. Cf. St Thomas Aquinas: the Order of Nature seemed the expression of divine reason. The Argument from Design maintains the existence of God by pointing to the adaptation of means to ends in the universe.
13 I Cor. 13.8, 3.18–19, 1.21.
14 Rom. 1.22.
15 Col. 2.8; cf. I Tim. 6.20.
16 Psalms 94.11, etc.; cf. Job 5.12–14.
17 Sources in A. H. Silver, *Where Judaism Differed*, pp. 26f.
18 Acts 17.32.
19 Clem. Alex., *Stromateis*, 6.8.
20 Origen, *Against Celsus*, 1, 13.
21 Eph. 2.10 (Pauline?).
22 Matt. 6.33.
23 Rom. 2.6, Gal. 6.6–7.
24 Psalms 2.12, 118.22 (the 'stone' they fell over).
25 Rom. 9.32.
26 Titus 3.5 (modified by 3.8).
27 *Hymn Scroll*, 1.1, 7.11, etc.
28 *Community Rule*, 11.

29 II Esdras 8.36; cf. I. Abrahams, *Studies in Pharisaism and the Gospels*, I, chapters 19 and 20.
30 Sources in A. H. Silver, op. cit. pp. 206f.
31 Acts 13.39.
32 Acts 26.20.
33 James 2.14–17, 1.27.
34 The Council of Trent in the sixteenth century maintained that human beings cannot merit initial grace of justification by their works, but can earn increase of grace and eternal life.
35 Gal. 3.24.
36 Rom. 3.21.
37 Cf. Rom. 11.28: the Jews are God's enemies *and* friends.
38 Deut. 27.26, Gal. 3.10.
39 Gal. 3.13.
40 Deut. 21.23.
41 Rom. 10.4.
42 Gal. 2.21, 5.2.
43 Col. 2.14.
44 Gal. 6.2.
45 I Cor. 9.20.
46 Rom. 8.2.
47 Phil. 3.8–9.
48 II Cor. 3.6, 14.
49 I Cor. 11.25.
50 Jer. 31.31; cf. 7.21–22, Amos 5.21–22.
51 *Community Rule*, 1–3, 5; cf. *Damascus Document*, 6–8.
52 M. Sanhedrin 10.1.
53 I Cor. 11.1.
54 A. Schweitzer, *The Mysticism of Paul the Apostle*, p. 225.
55 Rom. 3.24, 16.20.
56 Eph. 2.5.
57 II Cor. 6.1.
58 Ex. 23.7. *Poenitentia* in the Vulgate is misleading.
59 Cf. M. Grant, *Jesus*, forthcoming.
60 Acts 2.38.
61 Rom. 2.4.
62 According to the Jesuits, the Dominican approach to this problem left doubt as to how a human being was really free under the influence of grace.
63 Gal. 5.1.
64 Rom. 3.24.
65 Eph. 3.12.

66 II Cor. 3.17.
67 II Cor. 2.14.
68 I Cor. 9.19.
69 Rom. 2.14–15. The Franciscans maintained that the root of conscience lay in the affections, St Thomas Aquinas and the Dominicans in the will.
70 I Cor. 4.4, II Cor. 1.12.
71 Rom. 15.1.
72 Rom. 7.7.
73 Clem. Alex., *Stromateis*, 3.10.
74 Gal. 5.13.
75 I Cor. 6.12.
76 See Clem. Alex., op. cit.; chapter III, section 2, notes 44–5.
77 Rom. 3.8.
78 Matt. 5.17; cf. 24.12. One Jewish tradition claimed that Jesus had eventually revoked his attack on the Law.
79 *Letter of Barnabas*, 10.9; cf. *Letter to Diognetus* 3–4.

4.   Direct Contact with the Deity

1   I Cor. 9.1, 15.8.
2   Gal. 1.13–17.
3   Acts 9.1–9. For 'Saul' see p. 14.
4   Acts 22.6–11.
5   Acts 26.11–20.
6   Acts 22.15.
7   S. Perowne, *The Journeys of St Paul*, p. 24.
8   II Cor. 4.6.
9   W. James, *The Varieties of Religious Experience*, p. 251.
10 Laura A. Huxley, *This Timeless Moment*, pp. 22f.
11 F. von Hügel, *The Mystical Element in Religion*, II, pp. 90f.
12 Rom. 7.16, 21, 24.
13 Acts 22.7–8, cf. 8.1.
14 Acts 7.47–50.
15 Acts 7.60.
16 Luke 23.34.
17 Acts 7.58, 8.1.
18 Gal. 1.22, cf. p. 155.
19 Acts 7.56.
20 Gal. 1.15.
21 Is. 49.1, Jer. 1.5.
22 E. W. Hunt, *Portrait of Paul*, p. 31.

23 J. Stalker, *The Life of St Paul*, p. 12. Bernard Shaw, however, regarded Paul's conversion as no conversion at all, but a monstrous imposition on Jesus; and Bishop Joseph Butler said to John Wesley, 'Sir, the pretending to extraordinary revelations and gifts of the Holy Spirit is a horrid thing, a very horrid thing.'

24 II Cor. 12.1–4.

25 Acts 22.17.

26 Gal. 2.20.

27 I Cor. 15.10.

28 A. Lalande, *Vocabulaire de la philosophie*, 5th ed., p. 644.

29 C. H. Dodd, *The Meaning of Paul for Today*, pp. 140f.

30 II Cor. 3.18 (various interpretations).

31 E. R. Dodds, *Pagan and Christian in an Age of Anxiety*, pp. 96f.

32 II Tim. 2.11.

33 S. Spencer, *Mysticism in World Religion*, p. 173. But he wishes, all the same, to classify Paul's experiences as mystical, unlike, e.g. W. L. Knox, *St Paul*, p. 52, who regards him as a visionary rather than a mystic.

34 W. E. Hocking, *The Meaning of God in Human Experience*, p. 511.

35 Ezek. 3.15.

36 I Cor. 2.9; cf. Is. 64.4.

37 Gal. 1.15–16; cf. Is. 49.1, Jer. 1.5.

38 I Macc. 14.41; Josephus, *Jewish Antiquities*, 13.1.

39 Mark 6.16, Luke 24.19. Cf. Matt. 17.3–4 and Mark 9.4–5 on the Transfiguration.

40 Sources in G. Vermes, *Jesus the Jew*, p. 98.

41 J. Sanhedrin, 11.6, 8.

42 I Cor. 14.4.

43 I Cor. 12.28.

44 Matt. 19.28, Luke 22.30.

45 I Cor. 9.1; cf. 15.8.

46 Gal. 1.1.

47 Gal. 2.6–8.

48 II Cor. 11.5, 10.7.

49 Gal. 2.6.

50 I Cor. 15.5.

51 I Cor. 2.7.

52 Eph. 3.3; cf. 1.9.

53 Rom. 16.25.

54 Col. 2.2–3; cf. 1.26.

55 *War Rule*, 10; cf. *Habakkuk Commentary*, 7.

56 C. F. A. Pfeiffer, *The Dead Sea Scrolls and the Bible*, p. 139.

57 I Cor. 8.1.
58 I Cor. 14.5, 11.
59 Jer. 23.16–18.
60 I Cor. 12.28.
61 I Cor. 14.18.
62 Acts 2.4.
63 C. S. C. Williams, *The Acts of the Apostles*, p. 63.
64 Acts 16.18.
65 I John 4.1.
66 Rom. 8.14, 26.
67 Num. 27.18, etc.
68 W. Barclay, *The Mind of St Paul*, pp. 135ff., quoting Rom. 8 and
    15 and II Thess. 2.
69 A. D. Nock, *Conversion*, p. 189.
70 II Cor. 13.14.
71 Phil. 1.19.
72 Eph. 2.18.
73 II Cor. 3.17.
74 Acts 19.2.
75 I John 4.1–3.
76 Matt. 28.19.
77 Gal. 3.27.
78 Rom. 6.3–4; cf. Col. 2.12.
79 Titus 3.5 speaks of rebirth.
80 Acts 18.25, 19.3.
81 Mark 1.4; Josephus, *Jewish Antiquities*, 18, 117, was wrong to
    deny that John's baptism was for the remission of sins.
82 *Community Rule*, 3, etc. It is disputed whether, elsewhere at this
    date, Jewish proselytes were baptized.
83 I Cor. 1.17.
84 E. W. Hunt, *Portrait of Paul*, p. 123.
85 I Cor. 10.2, 5.
86 I Cor. 1.13–16.
87 Acts 9.19; cf. 21.16.
88 John 3.22, 4.2; cf. J. Marsh, *St John*, pp. 195, 203.
89 Acts 2.38.
90 I Cor. 11.23–6, 10.14–17.
91 I Cor. 5.7.
92 I Cor. 10.3–4.
93 Cf. Ex. 16.4ff., 17.5ff.
94 I Cor. 10.5.
95 I Cor. 11.27, 34.

96   Augustine, *Sermons*, 272.
97   E. Rolfe, *The Intelligent Agnostic's Introduction to Christianity*, p. 207.
98   I Cor. 10.17; cf. 12.12.
99   Eph. 4.25.
100 E. Rolfe, op. cit., p. 209.

CHAPTER IV   WHAT THE WORLD STILL HAS TO WAIT FOR

1   Luke 24.21.
2   II Thess. 2.2.ff.; cf. II Tim. 2.18 (the general resurrection).
3   Acts 6.14.
4   W. D. Davies, *Paul and Rabbinic Judaism*, pp. 287f. According to the *Damascus Document*, 8, the Apocalypse will come about forty years after the Teacher of Righteousness (cf. Deut. 2.14). For 'forty', see chapter III, section 2, note 88.
5   I Cor. 16.22 (more probably than *maran atha*, 'the Lord has come'). It has been suggested that this formula had already been established by Christ's earliest disciples.
6   I Thess. 4.15–5.8; cf. perhaps Rom. 16.20, 'the God of Peace will *soon* crush Satan beneath your feet'.
7   II Thess. 2.1–5.
8   I Cor. 7.29.
9   Acts 2.40, I Cor. 7.26, II Tim. 3.1.
10   Rom. 8.22; cf. John 16.21f.
11   I Peter 2.11.
12   John 5.24, 28.
13   II Peter 3.3–12.
14   E.g. Mark 13.30, Luke 19.11: authenticity disputed, e.g. by G. E. Ladd, *Jesus and the Kingdom*, pp. 307ff.
15   Rev. 20.7.
16   I Cor. 15.12–15; cf. I Thess. 4.14.
17   Eph. 5.14; cf. Is. 26.19, 60.1.
18   I Cor. 15.22–4.
19   Dan. 12.2.
20   Phil. 3.20.
21   II Thess. 2.16.
22   I Thess. 5.8; cf. I Cor. 15.19.
23   Col. 1.27.
24   Rom. 8.18.
25   I Cor. 15.55; cf. Hosea 13, 14.
26   I Thess. 1.10.
27   II Cor. 4.3.

28 *Community Rule*, 3.
29 II Thess. 1.9.
30 Rom. 2.5, 8; 9.22 (*orgé*).
31 Rom. 11.29, 8.29. Cf. chapter II, section 1, n. 7.
32 Augustine, *On the Gift of Perseverance*, 35.
33 Gal. 6.7.
34 II Cor. 5.10; cf. Rom. 2.6.
35 Rom. 12.19; cf. Deut. 32.35.
36 *Hymn Scroll*, 15; *Community Rule*, 5.
37 K. Schubert, *The Dead Sea Community*, p. 61.
38 Rom. 9.11.
39 Rom. 11.5, 9.27; cf. Is. 10.22.
40 I Cor. 15.22.
41 E. W. Hunt, *Portrait of Paul*, pp. 159f.
42 Matt. 25.41.
43 Heb. 10.31.
44 Augustine, *City of God*, 21.9.
45 Mishnah: 12 months' duration. Rabbi Johanan ben Nuri: 7 weeks (and no one under 20). The Catholic doctrine of Purgatory is based on I Cor. 3.10–15 and Old Testament and Apocryphal texts.

CHAPTER V   WHILE WE WAIT

1. The Unification of All Human Beings

1 Eph. 3.9.
2 Gal. 1.16.
3 Acts 13.46, 18.6.
4 Rom. 3.29–30, 10.12, 15.16.
5 Eph. 2.14–16.
6 I Cor. 12.27, 26.
7 Eph. 4.16.
8 J. G. Davies, *The Early Christian Church*, p. 54.
9 Deut. 23.2.
10 Bishops, elders, deacons, priests – the terms seem to be used untechnically.
11 E.g. I Cor. 1.2.
12 I Cor. 1.13.
13 Rom. 16.17–19, Gal. 1.9.
14 Phil. 2.3; cf. 14.
15 II Cor. 11.12–14.

16   Tertullian, *Against Marcion*, 3.5.
17   I Cor. 13.1–13. For the meaning of *agape* see W. Barclay, *New Testament Words*, pp. 17–30.
18   Deut. 10.12.
19   M. Buber, *Two Types of Faith*, p. 135.
20   I John 4.9–20.
21   Gal. 5. 6, 14.
22   Rom. 13.10.
23   Mark 12.31, etc.
24   Lev. 19.18.
25   J. Nedarim 9.3 (Rabbi Meir).
26   Tobit 4.15.
27   B. Shabbath 31A.
28   Rom. 12.17.
29   Matt. 5.44.
30   Rom. 12.14.
31   Cf. Matt. 5.43.
32   A. H. Silver, *Where Judaism Differed*, p. 159.
33   Ex. 23.4.
34   Prov. 25.21–2; cf. Rom. 12.20.
35   *Testament of Benjamin*, 4.2,3.
36   M. Buber, *Two Types of Faith*, p. 77.
37   Gen. 12.3.
38   Is. 42.6, 49.6.
39   E. W. Hunt, *Portrait of Paul*, p. 20.
40   II Esdras 6.56.
41   II Esdras 7.72–73.
42   *Sibylline Oracles* 3.271f., etc.; cf. M. Grant, *The Jews in the Roman World*, p. 36.
43   Matt. 23.15.
44   Sources in W. D. Davies, *Paul and Rabbinic Judaism*, p. 63.
45   Ibid., pp. 114f. (Gen. 2.16, 9.4).
46   Gal. 2.7.
47   Rom. 1.16.
48   Rom. 2.9.
49   Rom. 2.11, 14–15.
50   Rom. 11.11, 25.
51   Acts 13.46, quoting Is. 49.6.
52   Acts 18.6.
53   M. Buber, *Two Types of Faith*, p. 77.
54   Acts 2.1.
55   Acts 10.1–48.

56 Acts 11.20.
57 Mark 7.27. J. V. Bartlet, *St Mark*, p. 234, and others attempt to explain this away. The matter is discussed further in my forthcoming book *Jesus*.
58 Mark 7.25–30, Luke 8.26–39.
59 Gal. 6.15.
60 I Cor. 10.25–6; cf. Rom. 14.2–3. Jesus' teaching on this question is hard to reconstruct.
61 Acts 15.29.
62 Gal. 6.16.
63 Rom. 11.28.
64 I Cor. 9.20.
65 I Thess. 2.14–16. The genuineness of the passage cannot be questioned (as it is by S. G. F. Brandon, *Jesus and the Zealots*, p. 11) – except perhaps for the second sentence.
66 Matt. 27.25; cf. passage referred to in n. 52 above.
67 John 8.44.
68 *Toledoth Yeshu*; cf. B. Sanhedrin 43A.
69 Acts 5.34–9, 23.6–9.
70 Phil. 3.5; cf. Acts 26.5.
71 Cf. above, pp. 14, 110.
72 Acts 7.47–50.
73 Acts 4.3, 5.18, 12.3.
74 Acts 9.29, 23.12.
75 Acts 18.15.
76 A. N. Sherwin-White, *Roman Society and Roman Law in the New Testament*, pp. 101f.
77 Acts 21.27–30.
78 Acts 23.6–9.
79 Acts 25–9.
80 Acts 28.21.
81 After the eleventh petition: quoted by W. Förster, *Palestinian Judaism in New Testament Times*, p. 157. Those denounced were the *nosrim* (Jewish Christians) and *minim* (other Jewish heretics). After the Revolt, the Jewish leaders also declared the Septuagint unacceptable, thus cutting themselves off from the Hellenistic world.

2. The Other Christians who Objected

1 I Cor. 11–12.
2 Clem. Alex., *Hypotyposes*, V, in Eusebius, *History of the Church*, 1.12.
3 In a Qumran fragment of I Enoch 89, *kepha* is the rock on which

Moses received his revelation for Israel; cf. Peter as the rock on which the church will be built, Matt. 16.18.

4 I Cor. 3.6.

5 Acts 18.25. Apollos has been suggested as a possible author of *Hebrews*.

6 Eusebius, op. cit. 2.16.

7 Acts 9.19, 22.16.

8 To add complexity to the picture, some of these Gentile Christians (like Greek converts to Judaism) became very strongly Jewish in sentiment; cf. note 11 below.

9 Acts 2.5.

10 Acts 6.1, 5.

11 Acts 21.27.

12 J. Daniélou, *The Crucible of Christianity* (ed. A. Toynbee), p. 280.

13 Acts 1.26: Matthias replaced Judas Iscariot.

14 Acts 4.32.

15 Acts 6.7 refers mysteriously to the conversion of priests.

16 S. G. F. Brandon, *Jesus and the Zealots*, pp. 4f., 182f.

17 A. Robertson, *The Bible and its Background*, pp. 42ff. But see also n. 25.

18 Acts 15.23–9.

19 Acts 16.1.

20 Gal. 2.4–5. The text is too uncertain to show whether Paul finally agreed to have Titus circumcised or not. For a crude attack by Paul on circumcision see Phil. 3.2.

21 J. A. Allan, *Galatians*, p. 42.

22 Gal. 2.11–14.

23 Gal. 1.20.

24 I Cor. 15.5.

25 II Cor. 11.4; i.e. probably 'another interpretation' of Jesus, not another Jesus altogether as A. Robertson suggested in the passage referred to in n. 17 above.

26 Titus 1.10, 14.

27 Gal. 2.6.

28 Gal. 2.9.

29 Acts 12.17.

30 Clem. Alex., *Hypotyposes*, VI; cf. Eusebius, op. cit. 2.1. A modern theory, not generally accepted, is that the Jewish Christian leader was neither James nor Peter, but someone unknown.

31 Acts 21.23–4.

32 Col. 4.11.

33 Josephus, *Jewish Antiquities*, 20.9.1ff.; Eusebius, op. cit. 2.23ff.

34 There was a tradition that he had a meeting with Rabbi Eliezer ben Hyrcanus at Sepphoris in Galilee.

35 Hegesippus in Eusebius, op. cit. 3.32.

36 O. Cullmann, *Peter: Disciple, Apostle, Martyr*, 2nd ed., p. 107.

37 Acts 28.21 (*tōn adelphōn*).

38 Phil. 1.15–17.

39 I Clem. (Rom.) *Cor.* 5.

40 Dionysius of Corinth in Eusebius, op. cit. 2.25.

41 Eusebius, op. cit. 5.3.

42 This was even true of *Matthew*, whose Gospel may partly have been written for Jews by birth.

43 *Letter of Barnabas*, 5. *Matthew*, too, had attacked the apostles, though he felt reverence for Peter.

44 Mark 3.33–5.

45 The Gentile Christians ascribed the failure of the First Jewish Revolt to merited retribution for the killing of Jesus.

46 Mosaics of *c.* AD 410 at the church of S. Sabina at Rome showing personifications of the Gentile and Jewish Churches, equally balanced, were anachronistic.

3.   Paul and Rome

1 Eph. 6.5–8; cf. Col. 3.22, I Tim. 6.1–2, Titus 2.9–10.

2 I Cor. 7.20. In the passage immediately following, the condition of the text does not allow us to decide whether Paul is advising them to gain their liberty if they can, or not to bother.

3 J. Kahl, *The Misery of Christianity*, p. 29. He accuses Paul of playing a verbal trick by giving double meanings to 'slave' and 'freedman'.

4 Philemon 16.

5 H. Rolston, *Thessalonians to Philemon*, p. 126.

6 I Cor. 4.3.

7 II Cor. 6.14. A basic text of the Exclusive Plymouth Brethren.

8 Including a warning in *Damascus Document*, 9.

9 Rom. 12.16.

10 James 2.6–7.

11 Gal. 2.10.

12 Justin Martyr 1, 11 seeks to discount such suspicions.

13 Acts 24.25.

14 E.g. Rom. 13.13; cf. B. Reicke, *The New Testament Era*, pp. 222f.

15 Sources in M. Grant, *The Jews in the Roman World*, pp. 90, 109, 299f. H. Maccoby, *Revolution in Judaea*, argues on the basis of Gal.

1.14 that Paul may originally have been a Zealot himself, but the reference is rather to a strict form of Pharisaic piety.

16 Rom. 13.1–6.
17 Suetonius, *Claudius*, 25.4; Tacitus, *Annals*, XV, 44, 3–8.
18 II Thess. 2.7.
19 J. Munck, *Paul and the Salvation of Mankind*, p. 38.
20 Gal. 4.25–26. Melito of Sardes, in the second century, linked the Christian world religion to Rome's world empire.
21 I Tim. 2.2., Titus 3.1.
22 Wisdom 6.3.
23 Rabbi Samuel in B. Baba Kamma 113A; cf. M. Aboth 3.2.
24 Matt. 22.21. John the Baptist likewise advised soldiers to be satisfied with their pay, Luke 3.14.
25 I Peter 2.13.
26 Augustine, *City of God*, 15.2.
27 Augustine, *City of God*, 5.19; cf. Prov. 8.15, Job 34.30.
28 D. Knowles, *Augustine: City of God*, p. xx.
29 Acts 28.31.
30 Acts 22.28.
31 Acts 13.50, 14.19.
32 Acts 16.19–24.
33 A. N. Sherwin-White, *Roman Society and Roman Law in the New Testament*, pp. 79f.
34 Ibid., pp. 74, 76.
35 I Thess. 2.2.
36 Acts 16.37–9.
37 Acts 17.6–7.
38 II Thess. 1.4.
39 The account in Acts 13.7–12 of the earlier 'conversion' of Sergius Paulus, a governor (proconsul) of Cyprus, is clearly legendary.
40 Acts 18.12–17.
41 Acts 19.24.
42 Acts 19.37–41.
43 I Cor. 15.32. Some of the hardships in II Cor. 11.23–7 no doubt occurred at Ephesus; cf. above, chapter 1, the passages referred to in notes 75, 76.
44 Ignatius; Rom. 5.1.
45 Acts 17.16. John Chrysostom was surprised that he spoke so mildly.
46 Eph. 4.18–21.
47 Acts 21.32–40.
48 Acts 22.30.

49 Acts 24.27 (most probable interpretation).
50 Acts 25.12.
51 Acts 28.30.
52 I Clem. (Rom.), *Corinthians*, 5.
53 Rom. 15.23, 28.
54 There was a tradition that he was imprisoned with Peter in Rome's Mamertine prison.
55 II Tim. 4.6–16.

CHAPTER VI SUMMING UP

1 Matt. 8.5–13, 27.54, etc.
2 I Clem. (Rom.), *Corinthians*, 5.
3 Rev. 1.4.
4 II Peter 3.16.
5 Ignatius, *Ephesians*, 12; *Romans*, 4.
6 Ignatius, *Philadelphians*, 6.
7 Origen, *Homilies*; *On Luke*, 25.
8 The link between the dualists and Paul is symbolized by the tradition that one of them, Valentinus, received his esoteric doctrines from Theudas (?), a supposed pupil of Paul; see above, Chapter 2, Section 1, note 47.
9 Marcion's *Apostolicon* included *Col.* and *Eph.* but excluded the Pastoral Letters (*I, II Tim., Titus*).
10 G. Dix, *Jew and Greek*, p. 58; cf. M. Wiles, *The Divine Apostle*, passim.
11 E.g. by Dionysius, Bishop of Corinth; in Eusebius, *Church History*, 2.25; and by early artists. For divergent views on their joint shrine on the Appian Way outside Rome, see H. Chadwick, *The Early Church*, pp. 162f.
12 The calendar of Pope Liberius (AD 354), unlike previous (eastern) lists, omits Paul, stressing Peter as bishop of Rome.
13 *Clementine Homilies*, 3.
14 Discussion in W. D. Davies, *Paul and Rabbinic Judaism*, p. 51.
15 C. H. Powell, *Paul through Modern Eyes*, pp. 96f.
16 J. Stalker, *Life of St Paul*, p. 11.
17 C. H. Dodd, *The Meaning of Paul for Today*, p. 18.
18 M. Muggeridge and A. Vidler, *Paul: Envoy Extraordinary*, p. 30.
19 W. Barclay, *The Mind of St Paul*, p. 100.
20 J. Stalker, op. cit. p. 54.
21 Sophocles, *Antigone*, 332–68.
22 J. Bowden, *Karl Barth*, pp. 38ff.
23 Eccl. 1.9–10.

Table of approximate dates

† For the itineraries of Paul's journeys, see the Maps, pp. 17–20.

Ancient Writings and Terms

ABOTH (The Fathers) or PIRKE ABOTH. A collection of ethical maxims. One of the tractates of the fourth division (*Nezikin*, 'Damages') of the Mishnah (q.v.).

ACTS OF PAUL AND THECLA. See Paul and Thecla.

ACTS OF THE APOSTLES. Book of the New Testament, traditionally attributed to Luke, describing the story of the early Church and the career of Paul.

ACTS OF THE PAGAN MARTYRS. Fragments of Alexandrian nationalist literature preserved on papyri, mostly of second or early third centuries AD.

AGADATH BERESHITH. Hebrew commentary on *Genesis (Bereshith)*.

ALCIBIADES. Athenian statesman, fifth century BC, after whom are named two dialogues wrongly attributed to Plato.

AMBROSE (SAINT), *c.* AD 337–97. Bishop of Mediolanum (Milan); his works include ninety-one letters and hymns.

AMOS. Eighth century BC. Prophet of Israel, after whom the earliest prophetic book of the Old Testament is named.

ANSELM (SAINT). 1033–1109. Archbishop of Canterbury. His works included *Cur Deus Homo?*, the classic treatment of the Redemption.

APOCALYPSE. Revelation; prophetic description of the end of the world. There were many writings of this kind in Jewish and Christian literature. For the *Apocalypses of Paul, Peter* and *John*, see Paul, Peter, Revelation.

APOCRYPHA, NEW TESTAMENT (Greek, meaning 'hidden away' from public use). Early Christian or semi-Christian writings that resemble New Testament books in form but were not finally admitted to the Bible.

APOCRYPHA, OLD TESTAMENT. Certain religious books, in Greek and Hebrew (some probably first composed in Aramaic), which were highly regarded by the Jews but never admitted to the Hebrew canon of Scripture. A number of these works were included in the Vulgate (q.v.), and twelve books appear in the standard Apocrypha of the English Bible.

APOLOGISTS, EARLY CHRISTIAN (Greek, meaning 'defenders'). A group of writers, mainly of the second century AD, who attempted to provide, first in Greek and later in Latin, semi-philosophical defences of Christianity.

APOSTLES (Greek, meaning 'messengers'). The Twelve, whom, according to the New Testament, Jesus sent out to preach the Gospel. (After the death of Judas Iscariot he was replaced by Matthias). Paul also claimed the status of apostle for himself, and the term was used for other missionaries and leaders.

APOSTOLIC FATHERS. See Fathers.

AQUINAS, (SAINT) THOMAS, 1226–1274. The outstanding Christian theologian, philosopher and writer of the Middle Ages.

ARAMAIC. A Semitic language which, in Paul's time, was the current speech of the people of Judaea. The two Talmuds (q.v.) are written in its western and eastern dialects.

ARATUS of Soli in Cilicia, *c.* 316–239 BC. Greek philosophical poet, quoted by Paul to the Athenians according to *Acts*.

ARIANS. Followers of Arius of Alexandria (died *c.* AD 355), who was denounced for maintaining that Christ is not divine but a created being. The forerunners of modern Unitarianism.

ASSIDAEANS. See Hasidim.

ASSUMPTION OF MOSES. See Moses.

AUGUSTINE (SAINT), AD 354–430. Bishop of Hippo Regius (Annaba in Algeria). Writer of many works including the *Confessions* and *City of God* and *On the Trinity*.

BABA KAMMA (The First Gate). One of the tractates of the fourth division, (*Nezikin*, 'Damages'), of the Mishnah and Talmud (q.q.v.).

BABYLONIAN TALMUD. See Talmud.

BARDESANES (Bar Daisan), AD 154–222. Christian writer of Edessa (Urfa) in Mesopotamia.

BARNABAS (SAINT). The most important Christian apostle to the Gentiles next to Paul. His authorship is wrongly ascribed to the *Letter (Epistle) of Barnabas*, which dates from *c.* AD 130.

BARUCH. The secretary of the Prophet Jeremiah. His name was chosen as a pseudonym for a number of Jewish writings, including the Book of Baruch in the Old Testament Apocrypha (containing material of various dates) and the Syriac Apocalypse of Baruch (*II Baruch, c.* AD 100–130).

BENEDICTIONS, EIGHTEEN. The central prayer of the Jewish synagogue liturgy.

BERESHITH (Genesis), AGADAH. See Agadah.

BUNYAN, JOHN, 1628–88. English Puritan minister and preacher. Author of *The Pilgrim's Progress.*

CALLISTUS, NICEPHORUS. See Nicephorus.

CALVIN, JOHN, 1509–64. Genevan theologian and reformer. Founder of the Calvinist Reformed Churches (including the Presbyterians).

CELSUS, later second century AD. Writer of the first comprehensive philosophical attack against Christianity, preserved to a large extent in Origen's book *Against Celsus.*

CENTURION. Roman military rank: the principal professional officers of the Roman army. The term is also used for the corresponding ranks in the armies of the Jewish 'client' states of Herod Antipas, etc.

CHRONICLES, BOOKS OF THE. Two narrative books of the Old Testament, first divided in the Septuagint (q.v.).

CHRYSOSTOM (SAINT) JOHN. See John.

CIRCUMCISION. The operation of cutting away the whole or part of the foreskin of the penis: a rite which to the Jews represents the fulfilment of the Covenant between God and Abraham. The major issue in Paul's dispute with the Jewish Christian Church.

CITIZEN. The privilege of Roman citizenship (*civitas*) depended upon birth or upon a grant made by the state. The autonomous Greek cities of the Roman Empire had citizen bodies of their own.

CLEMENT OF ALEXANDRIA, *c.* AD 150–215. Head of philosophical Christian school of Alexandria. His numerous works included *Stromateis* (Miscellanies) and *Hypotyposes* or *Adumbrationes* (Outlines).

CLEMENT OF ROME (SAINT). Bishop of Rome (Pope), *c.* AD 88/92–7/101. One of the Apostolic Fathers (q.v.). Author of a Letter to the church at Corinth (*I Clement*).

CLEMENTINE HOMILIES and RECOGNITIONS. Two works of the 'Clementine Literature' which, although of later and various authorship, was associated with the name of Clement of Rome (q.v.). The *Homilies* (preserved in the Greek original) and the *Recognitions* (translated into Latin and Syriac), were composed towards the end of the fourth century AD to glorify the eastern churches at the expense of Rome; but they contain material of two or even three centuries earlier.

COLONY. Cities in the Roman Empire consisting of Roman citizens (q.v.), and governed by officials bearing Latin titles, were known as *coloniae civium Romanorum*, colonies of Roman citizens (or *municipia civium Romanorum*, chiefly found in Italy).

COLOSSIANS, LETTER TO THE. Addressed to the Christian community at Colossae in Phrygia (Asia Minor), and reputedly written in prison by Paul. The text, as we have it, probably includes later rewritings of Paul's original words.

226

COMMUNITY RULE, or *Manual of Discipline*. One of the oldest writings of the Jewish community at Qumran (q.v.), preserved on one of the 'Dead Sea Scrolls.' Perhaps of the later second century BC.

CORINTHIANS, LETTERS TO THE. Two Letters addressed by Paul to the Christian community at the Roman colony (q.v.) of Corinth in Achaea (Greece), the first written from Ephesus between 52 and 55, and the second probably from Macedonia in the same period. The second Letter may be a combination of two originally separate epistles.

DAMASCUS DOCUMENT (or RULE or ZADOKITE WORK). A Hebrew exhortation and list of statutes, preserved on the 'Dead Sea Scrolls' found at Qumran (q.v.) and in medieval copies from Cairo. Probably *c.* 100 BC. The phrase that it contains, 'land of Damascus', may refer to a branch of the sect located there, or may be a symbolical name for Qumran, or may refer to the kingdom of Nabataean Arabia (which at times exercised a protectorate over Damascus).

DANIEL. The name of this Jew of the sixth century BC was given to an Old Testament Book written in *c.* 167–4 BC, in which the Messiah is forecast.

DAVID, PSALMS OF. See Psalms.

DEAD SEA SCROLLS. Manuscripts found in caves, illustrating the history of the Jewish community at Qumran (q.v.).

DEUTERO–ISAIAH. See ISAIAH.

DEUTERONOMY ('the second Law', a Greek mistranslation of the Hebrew term 'copy of the Law'), the fifth and last book of the Pentateuch (q.v.) in the Old Testament (Devarim in Hebrew). The nucleus of the book probably dates from the seventh century BC.

DIASPORA. See Dispersion.

DIOGNETUS, LETTER TO. A treatise about Christian beliefs and customs, author and recipient unknown; *c.* AD 124.

DIONYSIUS, *c.* AD 170. Bishop of Corinth, quoted by Eusebius (q.v.).

DISCIPLINE, MANUAL OF. See Community Rule.

DISPERSION (Greek *Diaspora*). The term applied to the dispersion of the Jews after the Babylonian captivity and then, in general, to Jewish communities living outside Palestine.

DOCETISM (from the Greek 'to seem'). Christian sect based on the theory that Jesus, during his life, did not possess a real or natural but only an apparent or phantom body.

DUALISM. The belief of Gnostics and Manichaeans (qq.v.) that there are two supreme principles or deities in the universe, the one good and the other evil.

EBIONITES (from the Hebrew *ebionim*, poor). Ultra-Jewish sect of the Christian Church in the second and subsequent centuries AD: one of the heirs of the

Jewish Christianity (q.v.) of the time of Paul, whom they rejected as an apostate.

ECCLESIASTES. One of the wisdom books (q.v.) of the Old Testament. The writer uses the pseudonym of 'the Preacher' (*koheleth*). Third or perhaps second century BC.

ECCLESIASTICUS. Book of the Old Testament Apocrypha (q.v.), written by Ben Sira (Sirach) in the early second century BC.

ENOCH. The grandson of Adam (or seventh in descent from him), who was believed to have ascended to heaven. Three Jewish books have been preserved under his name. *I Enoch*, or the *Ethiopian Enoch*, was a favourite work at Qumran (q.v.) where Aramaic MSS, bearing a complex relation to the known Greek and Ethiopic renderings, have been found. *I Enoch* (in these but not the Qumran versions) includes the *Similitudes* or *Parables of Enoch*, in which the 'Messianic' passages, referring to the Son of Man, have been claimed, with some plausibility, to be Christian interpolations, partly because they do not occur at Qumran and partly because they speak of the preexistence, concealment and revelation of the Messiah. *III Enoch* (or the *Slavonic Enoch*) contains a nucleus of the later first century AD modified by Christian influence. *III Enoch* or the *Hebrew Enoch* is a rabbinic compilation of the second half of the third century AD or later.

EPHESIANS, LETTER TO THE. Addressed to the Christian community at Ephesus (Selçuk) in Ionia (W. Asia Minor) and reputedly written in prison by Paul. The text as we have it probably includes rewritings of Paul's words.

EPIMENIDES, *c.* 600 or 500 BC. Cretan religious teacher, poet and wonder-worker, possibly quoted by Paul in his speech to the Athenians (according to *Acts*).

ESCHATOLOGY (from the Greek *eschatos*, last). The study of the 'last things': death, judgment, heaven and hell.

ESDRAS (the Greek equivalent of Ezra, q.v.). The name given to two books of the Old Testament Apocrypha (q.v.). *I Esdras* or *Greek Ezra* or *Apocryphal Ezra*) is a Greek translation, perhaps of the early second century BC, of non-extant versions of *Ezra* and *Nehemiah* (qq.v.). *II Esdras* (*IV Esdras* in the Vulgate, q.v., also known as the Ezra Apocalypse), of the late first century AD, has not survived in its Semitic (probably Aramaic) original or (except for a few verses) in the Greek translation, but only in Latin and other derived versions. It describes the revelation claimed by Ezra.

ESSENES. An ascetic Jewish sect or brotherhood founded in the second century BC, living in monastic communities in the Dead Sea region and elsewhere, under strict rule. See also Qumran.

EUCHARIST (from the Greek for, 'thanksgiving'). The central rite of Christian worship, also called the Lord's Supper, the Mass, Holy Communion, the Divine Liturgy, the Blessed Sacrament (q.v.).

EUSEBIUS, *c*. AD 260–340. Bishop of Caesarea Maritima (Sdot Yam) in Syria Palaestina (Judaea). Writer of *History of the Church*.

EXODUS (Shemoth). The second book of the Old Testament. The title refers to the escape of the Israelites from their slavery in Egypt.

EZEKIEL. A Jewish priest and prophet (q.v.) who was taken into exile by the Babylonians in 597 BC. The book of the Old Testament bearing his name and containing his prophecies was perhaps completed in the fifth century BC.

EZRA. A Babylonian Jew who led a party of Jews to Palestine in the fifth (or early fourth) century BC and refounded Judaism there. The historical book of the Old Testament bearing his name was written in *c*. 330 BC by an unknown author.

EZRA, APOCRYPHAL (Greek) and EZRA APOCALYPSE. See Esdras.

FATHERS OF THE CHURCH. A term used for eminent Christian teachers and writers from the first until the seventh or eighth centuries AD. A group of early Apostolic Fathers, Greek authors who belonged to the second and third generation after the Apostles (with whom tradition associates them), included Clement of Rome, Ignatius and Polycarp (qq.v.).

GALATIANS. Letter addressed by Paul to the Christian communities in the cities of southern (more probably than northern) Galatia, in central Asia Minor. Probably written in *c*. AD 54, though an alternative theory dates the Letter to *c*. 49 and regards it as the earliest of Paul's Letters. The exponents of the north Galatian view tend to prefer a dating to *c*. 57–8.

GEMARA. See Talmud.

GENESIS (Bereshith). The first book of the Old Testament; traditionally ascribed by traditional legend to Moses. A number of independent sources have been distinguished.

GENTILES (from the Latin *gentes*, races or nations). Persons who are not Jews (Hebrew *goyyim*).

GNOSTICS. Sects blending Christian and Jewish characteristics, dating from the second or possibly first centuries AD, which laid claim to special knowledge (Greek *gnosis*) and propounded dualism (q.v.).

GOD-FEARERS. A designation sometimes applied to Judaizers (q.v.).

HABAKKUK. Jewish prophet (q.v.) at the end of the seventh century BC. Whether the Old Testament book which bears his name dates, in whole or part, from that or a later period is disputed.

HABAKKUK COMMENTARY. One of the writings of the sect at Qumran (q.v.) preserved on the Dead Sea Scrolls.

HASIDIM ('the pious', in Greek *Assidaeans*). A Jewish sect of the third and second centuries BC which resisted Hellenization and contributed to the emergence of the Pharisees (q.v.). Hasidism was also a mystic movement in twelfth and thirteenth century Germany, and its modern variety began in eighteenth century Poland, under leaders named Zaddikim (righteous).

HEBREWS, LETTER TO THE. A New Testament book of uncertain authorship, not by Paul as was sometimes supposed; probably written at about the end of the first century AD. It may have originated in Italy; and Rome, Judaea and Egypt each have been suggested as the place to which the Letter was addressed. It strongly stresses the role of Jesus Christ as Jewish high priest (q.v.).

HEGESIPPUS, *c.* AD 160. A Christian writer quoted by Eusebius (q.v.).

HIGH PRIEST. The head of the Jewish community at Jerusalem, recognized as its representative by the Roman governor. He presided over the priesthood of the Temple and depended on the support of the Sadducees (q.v.). The post was abolished after the suppression of the first Jewish Revolt (q.v.).

HORACE, 65–8 BC. Roman poet: author of *Epodes, Odes, Satires, Epistles*.

HOSEA. Jewish prophet in the eighth century BC. The book of the Old Testament bearing his name includes additions and changes of later dates.

HYMN SCROLL. One of the 'Dead Sea Scrolls' preserving documents of the Jewish community of Qumran (q.v.). It comprises more than two dozen hymns or psalms of thanksgiving (Hodayeth).

IGNATIUS (SAINT), died as a martyr, *c.* 110. Bishop of Antioch in Syria, and one of the Apostolic Fathers (q.v.). Author of epistles to churches in the province of Asia (W. Asia Minor) and at Rome. Ignatius was familiar with *I Corinthians* and probably with *Ephesians*, and perhaps with other Pauline Letters as well.

IRENAEUS (SAINT), *c.* AD 130/140–200. Bishop of Lugdunum (Lyon in France). Author of numerous works restating Biblical attitudes in opposition to the Gnostics (q.v.), with an evolutionary emphasis.

ISAIAH. Jewish prophet (q.v.) of the eighth century BC. The book of the Old Testament named after him contains the work of at least two principal authors. The second, *II Isaiah* (Deutero-Isaiah or the Second Isaiah), who perhaps lived in *c.* 400 BC and wrote Chapters 40–66, dwelt on the Suffering Servant, who provided a partial prototype of the Messiahship of Jesus.

JAMES THE GREAT (SAINT), son of Zebedee, was one of Jesus' two apostles (q.v.) of that name (distinct from Jesus' brother James the Just who became the head of the Jewish Christian (q.v.) Church. The New Testament *Letter of James*, in which the author names himself, has often been attributed to James the Just, though this has been disputed from early times).

JEREMIAH. Jewish prophet before and after 600 BC. The Old Testament book bearing his name consists of a document dictated by Jeremiah himself with many additions over a period of several centuries.

JEROME (SAINT), *c.* AD 347–420. Founder of a monastery at Bethlehem and the most learned of the Latin Fathers. The numerous works ascribed to his hand include the Vulgate (q.v.).

JERUSALEM TALMUD. See Talmud.

JEWISH CHRISTIANS (Judaeo-Christians). Christians of Jewish origin whose beliefs and liturgical institutions were derived from the Jewish milieu and centred upon the church at Jerusalem. Jewish Christianity, with which Paul came into collision, outlasted him but suffered in the Jewish Revolts (q.v.) and did not survive ancient times. See also Ebionites.

JEWISH REVOLTS against the Romans. The first (known by the Jews as the First Roman War) started in AD 66 under Nero and terminated, early in the reign of Vespasian, with the capture of Jerusalem by his son Titus in AD 70 and the fall of Masada in AD 73 (or 74?). The Second Revolt, led by Bar Kochba, took place in AD 132–5 under Hadrian. In the previous reign, that of Trajan, there had been serious rebellions in the Dispersion (q.v.), AD 115–18.

JOB. A book of the Old Testament describing the sufferings of the Edomite folk-hero Job. It comprises material of various dates from the sixth (or eighth?) century BC onwards.

JOHN CHRYSOSTOM (SAINT), *c.* AD 354–430. Greek Father of the Church, writer and bishop (patriarch) of Constantinople.

JOHN, GOSPEL OF. The fourth New Testament Gospel. Traditionally the work of Jesus' apostle John, the son of Zebedee, but in fact of subsequent composition (*c.* AD 90–120, though earlier sources have been postulated). Probably written at Ephesus in W. Asia Minor.

JOHN, LETTERS OF. These three New Testament letters were attributed to Jesus' apostle John, the son of Zebedee, but like the Gospel bearing his name (see above), with which the first Letter is closely related, they seem to belong to a date around AD 100. The second and third letters purport to have been written by 'the elder': he might be John the Elder who lived in Asia Minor at about that time.

JOHN MALALAS, *c.* AD 491–578. Byzantine historian. His *Chronicle* includes biblical history.

JOHN, REVELATION OF. See Revelation.

JOHN THE APOSTLE, APOCALYPSE OF. See Revelation.

JOHN THE BAPTIST, son of Zacharias and Elisabeth. Preacher from the Judaean hill-country from *c.* AD 28/9; executed by the Tetrarch Herod Antipas at his frontier fortress Machaerus. The Gospels stress his role as the forerunner of Jesus, but an independent sect of his followers continued for a long time.

JOHN THE ELDER. See John, Letters of.

JONAH. Supposedly a Jewish prophet of the early eighth century BC. The Old

Testament book named after him and claiming to describe his experiences may have been written in the later years of the fifth century BC.

JOSEPHUS, *c.* AD 37 – after 94/5. Jewish historian who fought in the First Jewish Revolt (q.v.) and was captured and released. Author of the *Jewish War, Jewish Antiquities, Against Apion* and his own *Life.* These works are in Greek, but in some cases at least were translated into that language from the original Aramaic.

JUBILEES, second century BC or later. A book of the Old Testament Apocrypha (q.v.) retelling Genesis and parts of Exodus with apocalyptic variations (see Apocalypse). The only known version of the full work is the Ethiopic, translated from the original Hebrew.

JUDAEO-CHRISTIANS. See Jewish Christians.

JUDAIZERS. People who sympathized with the Jewish religion but did not become full members of it, enjoying a recognized half-way status. See also proselytes.

JUSTIN MARTYR (SAINT), *c.* AD 100–165. The greatest of the early Christian apologists (q.v.). His works include a *Dialogue* with the Hellenistic Jew Trypho.

KIDDUSHIN. See Qiddushin.

KINGS (Melakhim). Two historical books of the Old Testament recounting the history of Solomon and of the two Israelite kingdoms, Israel and Judah. The work, originally a single book, was probably completed in *c.* 600 BC and re-edited about half a century later.

LAW, JEWISH. See Torah.

LEVITICUS (Wayigra). The third book of the Old Testament, mainly comprising legal and religious regulations. Parts of this material date back to Moses, but additions were still being made in *c.* 400 BC.

LIBERIAN CALENDAR. An ecclesiastical calendar of the Roman Church drawn up in AD 354 for Pope Liberius.

LUKE, GOSPEL OF. The third New Testament Gospel. Traditionally the work of Luke the physician, an associate of Paul, to whom the *Acts of the Apostles* (q.v.) was also ascribed, but these attributions are uncertain. The Gospel was written, in part from earlier sources, between *c.* AD 80 and 100.

LUTHER, MARTIN, *c.* 1483–1546. The German religious leader who began the Protestant Reformation. Founder of the Lutheran (Evangelical) Church.

MACCABEES. A name given to the house (and later to the adherents) of the family of the Hasmonaeans (i.e. descended from Hasmon), who led the successful Jewish rebellion against the Greek Seleucids (q.v.) in 168–142 BC. Of the four Greek *Books of the Maccabees* only the first two, historical in character, are canonical Catholic scripture and included in the Protestant Apocrypha (q.v.). *I Maccabees* is translated from a Hebrew or Aramaic original, now lost.

MALALAS, JOHN. See John Malalas.

MANI, *c.* AD 215–74. The Iranian founder of the Manichaean religion which, incorporating certain Christian features, propounded dualist (q.v.) doctrines. See also Gnostics.

MANUAL OF DISCIPLINE. See Community Rule.

MARCION, of Smyrna, second century AD. Author of *Martyrdom of Polycarp* (q.v.).

MARCION, second century AD. The founder of a powerful Christian church which was subsequently denounced and is known mainly from these denunciations. He favoured docetism and dualism (qq.v.), rejected the Hebrew scriptures and regarded Paul as the only true apostle.

MARK, GOSPEL OF. The second New Testament Gospel in position, but apparently the earliest in date. Traditionally the work of John Mark, 'the interpreter of Peter' and companion of Paul; but this, although possible, is not certain. The most likely period of final composition (partially from earlier sources of information) is AD 70–75, though some favour a slightly earlier date. It has been conjectured that the book was written at Rome.

MATTHEW. The first of the New Testament Gospels. Tradition identified the author with Matthew the tax-gatherer, one of Jesus' apostles; but this is improbable since an apostle, having known Jesus personally, would not have needed to use *Mark* (q.v.), as this author does. The Gospel seems to have been written (in part from earlier sources) between AD 80 and 100.

MELITO, died before AD 190. Bishop of Sardes (Sart), capital of Lydia, in the province of Asia (W. Asia Minor). Author of a number of books in Greek, of which one survives almost complete.

MESSIAH (from the Hebrew *Mashiah*, 'the anointed one'). In later Judaism, the ultimate redeemer of David's line who would deliver Israel. The Greek translation, *Christos*, became the accepted designation of Jesus.

MISHNAH (from *Shanah*, 'repeat', i.e. 'to teach by means of repetition'). A collection of Jewish traditional laws, completed early in the third century AD and forming one of the two main parts of the Talmud (q.v.).

MONOPHYSITES. A Christian sect of the fourth to sixth centuries AD, denounced as heretics, who taught (or were accused of teaching) that in the person of Jesus Christ there was only one nature rather than two natures, divine and human.

MONOTHELITES. Christians of the seventh century AD, denounced as heretics, who although not denying that Jesus Christ had two natures (see Monophysites), maintained that he had only one will.

MONTANISTS. See Tertullian.

MOSES, ASSUMPTION OF. An apocalyptic book not included in the Old Testament, containing a brief history of Israel put into the mouth of Moses. Probably composed during the first three decades of the first

233

century AD (though a date after the fall of Jerusalem in AD 70 has also been suggested).

MOSES, LAW OF. See Torah.

MYSTERY RELIGIONS. Pagan cults involving secret rites of initiation (*mysteria*), the most famous being those of the goddess Demeter (Ceres) the deity of the Eleusinian Mysteries, and of Dionysus (or Bacchus), Isis, Cybele and Mithras.

NEDARIM ('vows'). One of the tractates of the third division, called *Nashim* meaning 'Women', of the Mishnah and Talmud (qq.v.).

NEHEMIAH. Governor of Israel under the Persian King Artaxerxes I or more probably Artaxerxes II (404-359 BC). The Old Testament Book of *Nehemiah*, or *II Esdras* in the Vulgate (qq.vv.) (in which the initial chapters are his own memoir) formed the concluding portion of a history of Israel in the fourth century BC in which the previous books were *Chronicles* and *Ezra*.

NESTORIANS. The followers of Nestorius (died *c.* AD 451) who was denounced as a heretic for teaching that Christ's two natures, divine and human, were not inseparably united but only loosely joined, indeed virtually independent.

NEW TESTAMENT (Latin *Testamentum*, a mistranslation of the Greek *Diatheke*, covenant). The 'canon' comprising the works that now appear in Bibles as the New Testament was gaining general, though still not quite universal, acceptance by the later fourth century AD. The Letters of Paul had become generally accepted by AD 200. For rejected books see Apocrypha (New Testament).

NICEPHORUS CALLISTUS. Byzantine ecclesiastical historian of the early fourteenth century.

NUMBERS (Bemidbar, 'In the Wilderness'). The fourth book of the Old Testament. A predominantly priestly work containing earlier material but principally composed after the Exile, in about the fifth century BC.

OLD TESTAMENT. The name (meaning 'covenant', see New Testament) given by Christians to the Hebrew scriptures. The Pentateuch and Prophets (qq.v.) were standardized by about the fourth century BC, and the canon was nearly complete by AD 100, when the Old Testament Apocrypha (q.v.) was excluded.

ORACLES, SIBYLLINE. See Oracles.

ORIGEN, *c.* AD 185-254. The outstanding theologian of the Greek and Alexandrian Church, although frequently denounced for adulterating the Gospel with pagan philosophy. His works, however, include the treatise *Against Celsus* (q.v.) vindicating Christianity against pagan attack.

PALESTINIAN TALMUD. See Talmud.

PASCAL, BLAISE, 1623-62. French scientist and religious writer.

PASSOVER (Pesach). Feast celebrating the most momentous event in Jewish history, the Exodus (q.v.). Specifically, it commemorates the night when Jewish homes in Egypt were spared by the destroying angel. The feast extends for seven days, in March or April.

PASTORAL LETTERS. Three Letters claiming to be written by Paul to give pastoral advice for the oversight of churches. See Timothy, Titus, Letters to.

PATRIARCHS (meaning 'fathers' and 'rulers', of family or tribe). The twelve sons of Jacob, after whom the tribes of Israel took their names (see Twelve Patriarchs, Testaments of the); the term was also applied to Abraham, Isaac and Jacob. From the second to the fifth centuries AD the leader of the Jewish community at Jerusalem was recognized by the Romans by this designation. The Greek Christian communities used it for some of their principal bishops, especially at Constantinople, Alexandria and Antioch.

PAUL AND THECLA, ACTS OF, second century AD. One of three parts (although this is reckoned variously) of the *Acts of Paul*, in the New Testament Apocrypha (q.v.).

PAUL, APOCALYPSE OF. One of numerous Apocalypses (q.v.) of second and later centuries AD attributed to early Christian personages, and classified as part of the New Testament Apocrypha (q.v.).

PELAGIUS, early fifth century AD. British (or Irish) theologian and critic of the Arians and Manichaeans (qq.vv.), and of Augustine's doctrine of grace.

PENTATEUCH (Greek, meaning 'book of five volumes'). The first five books of the Old Testament embodying the Law of Moses. See Torah.

PENTECOST (Greek, meaning 'fiftieth'). The Jewish Feast of Weeks (Shabuoth), on the fiftieth day after Passover (q.v.). The name is also given to the Christian Whitsunday Feast, celebrated on the fiftieth day after Easter to commemorate the descent of the Holy Spirit upon the apostles.

PETER, APOCALYPSE OF. One of the earliest, and the most important, of the Apocalypses (q.v.) attributed to early Christian personages. The work, classified among the New Testament Apocrypha (q.v.), stresses the ferocious punishments of the damned.

PETER, GOSPEL OF, second century AD. A book of the New Testament Apocrypha (q.v.); attribution to Peter was already rejected before AD 200.

PETER, LETTERS OF. These two New Testament letters, addressed to Christian communities of Asia Minor, were ostensibly written by Peter, but are more probably of early second-century date.

PHARISEES (from the Hebrew *perushim*, separated). A great and on the whole progressive Jewish religious movement which originated in the second century BC, largely inspired the creation of the synagogues (q.v.), developed the oral interpretation of the scriptures, produced the greatest Jewish religious thinkers of the early Roman imperial period, and dominated Jewish life and thought (disappearing as a distinct movement) after the downfall of their Sadducee (q.v.) rivals following the collapse of the First Jewish Revolt (q.v.).

PHILEMON, LETTER TO. The shortest of Paul's Letters in the New Testament, written from prison to persuade Philemon to forgive and take back his slave Onesimus.

PHILIPPIANS. Letter addressed by Paul from prison to the Christian community in the Roman colony (q.v.) of Philippi in Macedonia.

PHILO (JUDAEUS), *c.* 30 BC–AD 40. The outstanding philosopher of the Dispersion (q.v.) and of the large Jewish community of Alexandria in Egypt, whose numerous works, written in Greek and strongly influenced by Greek philosophy, reflect a Hellenized form of Judaism far removed from that of Jerusalem.

PIRKE ABOTH. See Aboth.

PLATO, *c.* 428–348 BC, Athenian philosopher. A passage in his *Symposium* records a belief in intermediaries between God and man not unlike the doctrines found in the thought of the Jews and of Paul.

POLYCARP (SAINT), AD 70/82–156/168. Bishop of Smyrna (W. Asia Minor). *The Martyrdom of Polycarp* is a letter in Greek commissioned by the Smyrna community, in which Marcion (q.v. [1]) describes his death.

PROCONSUL. The title of Roman governors of those provinces described as 'senatorial' (under the ostensible control of the senate, as opposed to the imperial provinces: see Procurators). The proconsuls of Achaea (Greece) and Cyprus resided at Corinth and New Paphos respectively.

PROCURATOR. The title of Roman governors in the less important of the 'imperial' provinces, i.e. those under the direct control of the Emperor (the more important of these imperial provinces were governed by legates). The procurator (earlier, 'prefect') of Judaea (subsequently known as Syria Palaestina) resided at Caesarea Maritima (Sdot Yam).

PROPHETS (from the Greek *prophetes*, one who conveys a divine utterance). The term used to render the Hebrew *nabi*. Moses was traditionally regarded as the greatest of the prophets, and the Old Testament incorporates books devoted, and to some extent attributable, to fifteen subsequent individual prophets, dating from the eighth century BC to the fifth century, at which time prophecy was believed to have become extinct. John the Baptist (q.v.), Jesus and Paul stood (like other Jews of their time) for its revival.

PROSELYTE (from the Greek *proselutos*, one who has come, rendering of Hebrew 'to dis-estrange'). A convert to Judaism (partial converts were 'proselytes of the gate'). The term was later extended to include converts to any religious faith.

PROSPER OF AQUITAINE (or Prosper Tiro) *c.* AD 390–*c.* 465. Christian writer; disciple of St Augustine and secretary to Pope Leo I.

PROVERBS (OF SOLOMON), BOOK OF (Mishle Shelomoh). Old Testament book, perhaps completed in the sixth century BC. Probably the oldest extant document of the Jewish Wisdom Literature (q.v.).

PSALMS, BOOK OF, or PSALTER. Long ascribed by Jews and Christians to King David (tenth century BC), this Old Testament collection of 'songs of praise' (*Tehillim*) seems to reflect all periods of Israel's history from the thirteenth to the sixth or fifth centuries BC.

PSALMS OF SOLOMON. A collection of eighteen Jewish poems, extant in Greek and Syriac versions, including references to the capture of Jerusalem by Pompey in 63 BC and to his death in 48 BC. (Two of the Old Testament *Psalms* (q.v.) have also been described as 'Psalms of Solomon').

PSALMS, THANKSGIVING. See Hymn Scroll.

PURGATORY. The Catholic doctrine of a condition or state of suffering in which the souls of those who have died as friends of God pay the debt of temporal punishment and are purified from the stains of sin.

QIDDUSHIN ('betrothals'). One of the tractates of the third division, called *Nashim* meaning 'Women', of the Mishnah and Talmud (qq.v.).

QUMRAN. Exclusive, semi-monastic Jewish sect, apparently dating from *c.* 140–130 BC, related to the Essenes (q.v.), and continuing until the First Jewish Revolt (q.v.); located at Khirbet Qumran near the Dead Sea, where many of their documents have been found since 1947, inscribed on the 'Dead Sea Scrolls'. See Community Rule, Damascus Document, Habakkuk Commentary, Hymn Scroll, War Rule.

RABBI, RABBAN (-ENU) (Hebrew 'my', 'our', *Rab* meaning 'master') are designations applied to Jewish scholars or teachers. The title 'rabbi' first came into formal use towards the end of the first century AD, although the heads of the Sanhedrin (q.v.) had already borne the title 'rabban' more than fifty years earlier.

REVELATION, BOOK OF (Revelation of St John the Divine, Apocalypse of St John the Apostle). The last book of the New Testament, written to churches of the province of Asia (W. Asia Minor), prophesying the end of the world. The author names himself as John, but the traditional attribution to Jesus' apostle John, the son of Zebedee (q.v.) is unacceptable (nor is the latter the man who wrote the Gospel and Letters of John, q.v.). The work was probably written in *c.* AD 95 during persecutions by the Emperor Domitian.

ROMAN WARS. The Jewish designation for the First and Second Jewish Revolts (q.v.).

ROMANS. Letter addressed by Paul to the Christian community at Rome. Probably written in *c.* AD 57, at Corinth or Ephesus.

SAADIA BEN JOSEPH, AD 882–942. Born in the Fayum, Egypt, he became head of the Jewish community in Babylonia. The greatest personage in the literary and political history of medieval Judaism.

SADDUCEES. The conservative Jewish sect which centred round the High

Priest and the Temple (qq.v.) and rejected the Pharisees' oral interpretation of the scriptures as well as their belief in the general resurrection. Their
designation is likely to come from Zadok, the high priest of King David.
The suppression of the First Jewish Revolt (q.v.) and destruction of the
Temple abolished their influence.

SAMUEL. Two historical books (originally one) of the Old Testament, named
after Samuel, the national and religious leader who brought monarchy to
Israel in the eleventh century BC. The work tells the stories of Samuel and
of Kings Saul and David, and is based on an extensive nucleus which goes
back to the time, if not of David, at least of Solomon (tenth century BC),
and is therefore the earliest historical writing to have survived in any
language.

SANHEDRIN (Hebraization of the Greek *Synedrion*, 'assembly'). The supreme
court and council of the Jewish authorities at Jerusalem, going back to the
Council of Elders of Persian and Seleucid (q.v.) times. Relegated to
insignificance by Herod the Great (37–4 BC), it was revived in AD 6 with
the support of the governor (prefect) of the new province of Judaea to
assist him and the High Priest (q.v.). The Sanhedrin was abolished after
the suppression of the First Jewish Revolt (q.v.).

SCROLLS, DEAD SEA. See Qumran.

SECOND ISAIAH (*II Isaiah*). See Isaiah.

SELEUCIDS. A dynasty of Greek monarchs going back to Seleucus, one of
Alexander the Great's generals. Their empire, comprising Syria and
Mesopotamia and, for a time, territories farther to the west and east,
included Palestine from 200 BC until the successful revolt of the Maccabees
(q.v.) in 168–142 BC.

SENECA (THE YOUNGER), *c.* 4/1 BC–AD 65. Stoic philosopher, scientist,
dramatist; minister of Nero. His supposed correspondence with St Paul is
a forgery of the fourth century AD.

SEPTUAGINT (from the Latin word meaning 'seventy'). The earliest extant
Greek translation of the Old Testament, made during the third and second
centuries BC for the use of the Jewish community in Egypt. The name is
derived from the legend that there were seventy (or seventy-two) trans-
lators.

SEXTUS. Originator of a Greek collection of maxims, the *Sentences*. The Syriac
translation bears the name of Xystus (Sixtus) II, Bishop of Rome 257–8,
but Jerome (q.v.) named the author as Sextus Pythagoreus. The original
collection was probably non-Christian, of the second century AD.

SHABBATH (The Sabbath). One of the tractates of the second division, called
Moed meaning 'Set Feasts', of the Mishnah and Talmud (qq.v.).

SHEMA (from the Hebrew word meaning 'hear'). The initial word of a verse
of *Deuteronomy* (q.v.). 'Hear, O Israel: the Lord our God is one God,' which

is chanted in the Hebrew liturgy and has been proclaimed by Jewish martyrs throughout the ages.

SIBYLLINE ORACLES. Greek prophecies in verse named after mythical prophetesses, the Sibyls. The fourteen books of oracles still extant include many poems exhibiting Jewish and Christian influences.

SIMILITUDES OF ENOCH. See Enoch.

SOLOMON, PROVERBS, PSALMS, WISDOM OF. See Proverbs, Psalms of Solomon, Wisdom of Solomon.

SOPHOCLES. Athenian tragic dramatist (*c*. 496–406 BC). Writer of *Antigone*, *Oedipus the King*, etc.

STOICS. Greek philosophy postulating the Divine Providence, founded by Zeno of Citium in Cyprus (*c*. 300 BC).

STRABO, *c*. 65 BC – after *c*. 18 or *c*. 25. Greek geographer from Amaseia (Samsun) in Pontus (N. Asia Minor).

SYNAGOGUE (from the Greek *synagogue*, assembly and later the place where the assembly gathered; translating the Hebrew *keneset* and *bet ha-keneset*). From about the fifth century BC synagogues at many cities developed side by side with the Temple cult centred at Jerusalem, and flourished in the Dispersion, the Pharisees playing a prominent part (See Dispersion, Pharisees, Temple).

TACITUS, *c*. AD 55 – after 115. Roman historian. The surviving part of his *Histories* contains part of his account of the Jews, and his *Annals* describe the Great Fire of Rome in AD 64 for which Nero's government blamed the Christians.

TALMUD (from Hebrew word for 'learning'). A mine of information for Jewish and near-eastern and middle-eastern history, law, theology, folklore and ethics, the Talmud, long revered by the Jews as a sacred book, comprises two main sections, the Mishnah (q.v.) and the Gemara ('completion'). The latter, to which the designation of 'Talmud' is generally applied, comprises a commentary on, and interpretation of, the Mishnah. There are two Gemaras, the Palestinian or Jerusalem Talmud in Western Aramaic (q.v.), of which compilation ceased in the fourth century AD, and the Babylonian Talmud in Eastern Aramaic, which was drawn up in the fifth century AD.

TATIAN, second century AD. Christian missionary and Greek writer, born in Mesopotamia of Syrian parentage.

TEMPLE, THE. The national shrine of ancient Judaism at Jerusalem, built in the tenth century BC by Solomon, destroyed by the Babylonians early in the sixth century BC, reconstructed later in the same century (the Second Temple) and again by Herod the Great in 20 BC, and finally destroyed by the Romans in AD 70 during their suppression of the First Jewish Revolt (q.v.). (There was also a Temple at Leontopolis in Egypt and an earlier sanctuary at Elephantine [Yeb] in the same country.)

TERTULLIAN, *c.* AD 155–after 220. Born at Carthage in N. Africa. Converted from paganism to Christianity and later to the extreme, ascetic, Montanist sect. Wrote numerous religious works in Latin.

TESTAMENT. See New Testament, Twelve Patriarchs, Old Testament.

THANKSGIVING PSALMS. See Hymn Scroll.

THECLA. See Paul and Thecla, Acts of.

THESSALONIANS. Two Letters by Paul, supposedly for the Christian community at Thessalonica (Salonica) in Macedonia (though the second may originally have been addressed to Philippi in the same province). Perhaps written from Corinth in Achaea (Greece) in *c.* AD 50. If, as seems probable, *Galatians* (q.v.) is later, *I Thessalonians* is the earliest extant Christian document.

THOMAS AQUINAS (SAINT). See Aquinas.

TIMOTHY, LETTERS TO. Two New Testament Letters forming, with the *Letter to Titus* (q.v.), what are known as the Pastoral Letters or Epistles. They claim to have been written by Paul to his associate Timothy, but appear on linguistic and historical grounds to be of early second-century date.

TITUS, LETTER TO. See Timothy.

TOBIT. A book of the Old Testament Apocrypha (q.v.) about Tobit and his son Tobias, devout Jewish captives in Assyria in the eighth or seventh centuries BC. The book is of uncertain date between the fourth century BC and second century AD. It is written in Aramaic, but there were early translations into Hebrew and then Greek.

TOLEDOTH YESHU. A Jewish book completed or re-edited in about the third century AD denouncing Jesus as a sorcerer and describing his trial and execution. The work is preserved in Aramaic and Hebrew versions.

TORAH. A Hebrew word which, in Jewish tradition, especially signifies the Law of Moses or Pentateuch (q.v.), but also sometimes denotes the entire Hebrew scriptures (including, subsequently, oral interpretations). It is derived from a root which conveys the meaning of instruction or revelation, but was somewhat misleadingly translated in the Septuagint (q.v.) as *nomos*, Law.

TRIBES. See Patriarchs.

TWELVE PATRIARCHS, TESTAMENTS OF THE. A work, surviving in whole or part in several languages, which purports to contain the last words of the twelve sons of Jacob (see Patriarchs). These Testaments, from which portions of the Aramaic *Testament of Levi* and Hebrew *Testament of Naphthali* have been found at Qumran (q.v.), contain evident references to Jesus Christ as the Messiah, which are regarded by some as Christian interpolations in an earlier Jewish text; others believe (a) that the whole work was written by the Essenes, (b) that it all dates from the second century AD.

TYPOLOGY (from Greek *typos*, 'model', 'pattern'). The Jewish and subsequently Christian interpretations of the Old Testament as predicting and prefiguring subsequent events.

VALENTINUS, born AD 100. Gnostic (q.v.) Christian teacher educated in Alexandria; founder of a large sect.

VULGATE. The standard version (*editio vulgata*) of the Latin Bible, traditionally ascribed to Jerome (q.v.).

WAR RULE or SCROLL (*The War of the Sons of Light against the Sons of Darkness*). One of the writings of the Jewish community at Qumran (q.v.), probably written in the later first century BC or early first century AD.

WESLEY, JOHN (1703–91). English clergyman and founder of Methodism, for which his brother Charles wrote many hymns.

WISDOM LITERATURE. Near-eastern writings about metaphysical problems, of which the best-known are those of the Jews in the Old Testament (see Ecclesiastes, Job, Proverbs) and its Apocrypha (see Ecclesiasticus, Wisdom).

WISDOM (OF SOLOMON, in Greek manuscripts). A Greek book of the Old Testament Apocrypha (q.v.; also see Wisdom Literature above). Written in the first century BC or AD under the influence of Alexandrian philosophical thought.

ZADDIKIM. See Hasidim.

ZADOKITE WORK. See Damascus Document. For Zadok, see Sadducees.

ZECHARIAH. Jewish prophet of the later sixth century BC. The first half of the Old Testament book bearing his name was written by himself, but the second part is much later.

Bibliography†

AMIOT, F., *Les idées maîtresses de Saint Paul*. Paris (translated as *The Key Concepts of St Paul*, Freiburg & Edinburgh, London, 1962).

BARCLAY, W., *The Mind of St Paul*. London, 1958.

BARON, S., *A Social and Religious History of the Jews*. 2nd ed., vol. 2, New York, 1952.

BEARE, F., *St Paul and his Letters*. London, 1962.

BLACK, M. (ed.), *The Scrolls and Christianity*. London, 1969.

BORNKAMM, G., *Paulus*. Stuttgart, 1969 (translated as *Paul*, New York and London, 1971).

BOUTTIER, M., *La condition chrétienne selon Saint Paul*. Geneva, 1964 (translated as *Christianity according to Paul*, 1966).

BRANDON, S. G. F., *Jesus and the Zealots*. Manchester, 1967.

BREZZI, P. (etc.), *Studi Paolini*. Rome, 1969.

BUCK, C. H. and TAYLOR, G. M., *St Paul: a Study in the Development of his Thought*. New York, 1967.

CERFAUX, L., *Le Christ dans la théologie de Saint Paul*. Paris, 1951 (translated as *Christ in the Theology of St Paul*, New York, 1959).

DAVIES, W. D., *Paul and Rabbinic Judaism*. London, 1948 (3rd rev. ed. 1970).

DEISSMAN, G. A., *Paulus*. Tübingen, 1925 (translated as *Paul*, London, 1953).

DODD, C. H., *The Meaning of Paul for Today*. Swarthmore, Pennsylvania, and London, 1920 (rev. ed., 1957).

ELLIS, E. E., *Paul and his Recent Interpreters*. Grand Rapids, Mich., 1971.

FEUILLET, A., *Christologie paulinienne et tradition biblique*. Paris, 1973.

GIBBS, J. G., *Creation and Redemption: a Study in Pauline Theology*. Leiden, 1971.

† Commentaries (often indispensable) on the text of Paul's Letters and of *Acts* are not included here.

Bibliography

GLOVER, T. R., *Paul of Tarsus*. London, 1925.

GRANT, M., *The Jews in the Roman World*. London and New York, 1973.

GRANT, R. M., *A Historical Introduction to the New Testament*. New York and London, 1963.

HANSON, A. T., *Studies in Paul's Technique and Theology*. London, 1974.

HEATHCOTE, A. W., *An Introduction to the Letters of St Paul*. London, 1963.

HUDSON, D. F., *The Life and Letters of St Paul*. Serampore, India, 1962 (London, 1966).

HUNTER, A. M., *Paul and his Predecessors*. Philadelphia, 1961.

JAMES, W., *The Varieties of Religious Experience*, 1902; with introduction by A. D. Nock, London, 1960.

KÄSEMANN, E., *Paulinische Perspektiven*. 1969 (translated as *Perspectives on Paul*, London, 1971).

KNOX, J., *Chapters in a Life of Paul*. London, 1954.

KNOX, W. L., *St Paul*. London, 1932.

KNOX, W. L., *St Paul and the Church of Jerusalem*. Cambridge, 1925.

KNOX, W. L., *St Paul and the Church of the Gentiles*. Cambridge, 1939.

KÜMMEL, W. G., *Introduction to the New Testament*, London, revised ed., 1975.

VON LOEWENICH, W., *Paulus: sein Leben und Werk*. Ruhr, 1949 (translated as *Paul: His Life and Work*, Edinburgh and London, 1968).

MARKUS, R. A., *Christianity and the Roman World*. London, 1975.

MUGGERIDGE, M., and VIDLER, A., *Paul: Envoy Extraordinary*. London, 1972.

MUNCK, J., *Paulus und die Heilsgeschichte* (translated as *Paul and the Salvation of Mankind*, London, 1959).

NEW ENGLISH BIBLE: WITH THE APOCRYPHA. Oxford and Cambridge, 1970.

NOCK, A. D., *Conversion*. Oxford, 1935.

NOCK, A. D., *Early Gentile Christianity and its Hellenistic Background*. London, 1928 (New York, 1964).

OGG, G., *The Chronology of the Life of St Paul*. London, 1968.

PEROWNE, S., *The Journeys of St Paul*. London, 1973.

PFEIFFER, C. F. A., *The Dead Sea Scrolls and the Bible*. Grand Rapids, Mich., 1969.

POWELL, C. N., *Paul through Modern Eyes*. London, 1965.

PRAT, F., *La théologie de S. Paul*. 11th ed. (translated as *The Theology of St Paul*, London, 1926–7).

RAMSAY, W. M., *St Paul the Traveller and the Roman Citizen*. London, 1908.

RENGSTORF, K. H., *Das Paulusbild in der neueren deutschen Forschung*. Darmstadt, 1964, 1969.

RICCIOTTI, G., *Paolo Apostolo*. 4th ed., 1951 (new ed., 1958) (translated as *Paul the Apostle*, Milwaukee, Wisc., 1953).

RUBENSTEIN, R. L., *My Brother Paul*. New York, 1972.

SANDMEL, S., *The Genius of Paul*. New York, 1970.

SCHOEPS, H. J., *Paulus*. Tübingen, 1959 (translated as *Paul*, London and New York, 1961, 1972).

SCHÜRER, E., *Geschichte des jüdischen Volkes im Zeitalter Jesu Christi*. 4th ed., 1901 (translated as *The History of the Jewish People in the Age of Jesus Christ*, rev. ed. of vol. 1 by G. Vermes and F. Millar, Edinburgh, 1973).

SCHWEITZER, A., *Die Mystik des Apostels Paulus*. Tübingen, 1930 (translated as *The Mysticism of Paul the Apostle*, London, 1931 [2nd ed., 1953]).

SCHWEITZER, A., *Geschichte der Paulinischen Forschung*. 1912 (translated as *Paul and his Interpreters*, London, 1912, 1956).

SCOTT, C. A. A., *Christianity according to St Paul*. Cambridge, 1961.

SHERWIN-WHITE, A. N., *Roman Society and Roman Law in the New Testament*. Oxford, 1963, 1969.

SILVER, A. H., *Where Judaism Differed*. New York, 1956.

STACEY, W. D., *The Pauline View of Man*. London, 1956.

STALDER, K., *Das Werk des Geistes in der Heiligung bei Paulus*. Zurich, 1962.

STEWART, J. S., *A Man in Christ: the Vital Elements of St Paul's Religion*. London, 1935 (new ed., London, 1971).

VAN UNNIK, W. C., *Tarsus or Jerusalem*. Trans. from the Dutch, London, 1962.

VERMES, G., *The Dead Sea Scrolls and the Bible*. Harmondsworth, 1962 (rev. ed., 1976).

WHITELEY, D. E. W., *The Theology of St Paul*. Oxford, 1964.

WILES, M. F., *The Divine Apostle*. Cambridge, 1967.

Books on St Paul have continued to appear. The following may be mentioned:

BARCLAY, J., and SWEET, P. (Eds), *Early Christian Thought in its Jewish Context*. Cambridge, 1996.

LUDEMANN, G., *The Great Deception*. London, 1978.

And various books by A. F. SEGAL, including *Paul* (London, 1990). Two books have also been translated from German:

VAN DEN HYER, C. J., *Paul: A Man In Two Worlds*. London, 1999.

MARKSCHIES, C., *Between Two Worlds*. London, 1999.

Index

Index

exorcism, 40, 53, 118, 179
expiation, 70ff., 75, 99
Ezekiel, 114, 229
Ezra, 228f.; *see also* Esdras, II

faith, 78, 86ff., 91–5, 98–101, 120, 122f., 127f., 134, 137, 140, 146, 193f.
Fall of Man, *see* Adam, sin
Farrer, Austin, 33
Fathers of the Church, 23, 88, 92, 116, 123, 126, 229f.
Fayum, 237
Felix, Antonius, 21, 158, 174, 185f.
Festus, Porcius, 21, 158, 185
flesh, 43f.; *see also* Dualism, sex
food, *see* dietetic rules
forgiveness, remission of sins, mercy, 71f., 98f., 101, 123, 135, 148, 174, 214
Franciscans, 212
freedom, *see* liberation

Gaius (Caligula, emperor), 28
Gaius (Christian), 122, 182
Galatia, *Letter to Galatians*, 4f., 25, 69, 87, 99, 101, 140f., 150, 163, 167, 200, 220f., 229, 240
Galilee, 7, 53, 152, 167, 220
Gallio, 16, 156f., 181f.
Gamaliel, 1, 13, 155
Gehenna, 83, 135
Gemara, *see* Talmud
Genesis, 29, 35, 87, 224, 229, 232
Gentiles, 8, 15f., 38, 68, 102, 104, 106f., 140f., 149–57, 159f., 162, 164–7, 169ff., 186, 189f., 192, 220
Germany, 174, 230
Gnostics, 42, 117, 227, 229f., 241; *see also* Dualism
God-fearers, *see* Judaizers
governors, Roman, *see* prefects, proconsuls, procurators
goyyim, *see* Gentiles
grace, 98–101, 120, 122f., 127, 135f., 211
Gregory, St, the Great, 177

Habakkuk Commentary, 87, 229
Haburah Supper, 124
Hadrian, 170
Hanina ben Dosa, 53
Hasidism, 148, 151, 229f.
Hasmonaeans, *see* Maccabees
healings, 40, 53, 58
heathens, *see* paganism

Hebrews, Letter to, 63, 73, 102, 139, 159, 219, 230
Hebron, 170
Hegesippus, 230
Hell, underworld, 40, 135, 139, 209, 228; *see also* Gehenna, Sheol
heresies, 56, 60f., 144f., 159, 166, 192, 218, 223f.
Herod Antipas, 226, 231
Herod the Great, 7, 238f.
Hezekiah, 77
High Priest, 105, 185, 230, 237f.
Hillel, the Great, 147
Hippo Regius, 225
Honi the Circle Drawer, 53f.
hope, 134, 146
Horace, 31, 230
Horeb, 125
Hosea, 77, 134, 230
Houlden, J. L., 62
Hunt, E. W., 111, 149
Huxley, Aldous and Maria, 108
Hymn Scroll, Thanksgivings, Psalms, 66, 91, 136, 230

Ignatius, St, 60, 71, 81, 183, 190, 192, 229f.
illness of Paul, 25, 37, 109, 203
Illyricum, 201
image, 56, 64
imprisonment of Paul, 4, 21, 168f., 179, 222, 226, 228, 236
Inge, W. R., 32, 133
Ionia, 228
Ireland, 33, 235
Irenaeus, 33, 60, 230
Isaac, 72, 235
Isaiah, I & II, 61, 66, 72, 77, 111, 114, 125, 133, 138, 149, 230
Isis, 143, 234
Israel (kingdom), 6f., 65, 96, 232, 235

Jacob, 235, 240
James the Great (apostle, son of Zebedee), 156, 164, 167, 230
James the Less (apostle), 230
James, Letter of, 42, 92
James the Just (brother of Jesus), 15f., 76, 110, 163, 167ff., 189, 219, 230
James, William, 107
Jason, 180f.
Jeremiah, 96, 111, 114, 225, 230
Jerome, St, 139, 231, 241

Jerusalem, 7, 13–16, 21, 53, 62, 104ff., 110, 115, 150, 152f., 155f., 160–8, 170, 176f., 184ff., 230f., 234–9
Jesuits, 211
Jewish Christians, 10, 15, 39, 110, 115, 153, 159–71, 176, 182, 187, 198f., 192, 220, 226, 228, 230f.
Jewish Revolts, *see* Revolts
Job, 41, 231, 241
Johanan bar Nappaha, 75
Johanan ben Nuri, 216
John (apostle, son of Zebedee), 164, 167, 231, 237
John Chrysostom, St, 221, 231
John, Gospel of, 7, 41, 53, 63, 71, 73, 80, 83, 237
John, Letters of, 41f., 60, 118, 120, 147, 231, 237
John Malalas, 3, 231
John the Baptist, 24, 29, 53, 57, 78, 98, 114, 121, 123, 214, 221, 231, 236
Joh the Elder, 231
John XXIII, Pope, 90
Jonah, 77, 231f.
Jordan, R., 114, 169
Joseph, 66
Josephus, 214, 232
Jubilees, Book of, 80, 232
Judaea (province), 7, 12f., 15, 28f., 128, 156, 158, 167, 170, 231, 236, 238
Judaeo-Christians, *see* Jewish Christians
Judah (kingdom), 7, 96, 232
Judaizers, 150, 229, 232
Judas Iscariot, 162, 170, 219, 225
Judgment, Last, 91, 133ff., 138, 148, 174, 228
Jung, K. G., 45, 47, 58, 112
justification, 86ff., 96, 98, 121
Justin Martyr, St, 232

Kenosis, *see* emptying
Kerygma, 200
Kierkegaard, S., 27, 89
Kingdom of God, Heaven, 76, 91, 133f., 136, 146, 173f., 194
Kings, 77, 232
knowledge, 59f., 88ff., 116f., 146, 163; *see also* wisdom

Lalande, A., 112
Langland, W., 92
Last Judgment, *see* Judgment
Last Supper, *see* Supper

Index